Prophesy, Challenge & Blessing

Visions of 2012 & the Shift

By

Jack Allis

Prophesy, Challenge & Blessing
Visions of 2012 & the Shift
Copyright© 2010 by Jack Allis. All rights reserved.

No part of this book may be reproduced or transmitted in any form or by any means, graphic, electronic, or mechanical, including photocopying, recording, taping or by any information storage or retrieval system, without permission in writing from the publisher.

MAYFAIR BOOK PROMOTION, INC.
PROFESSIONAL PUBLISHING SOLUTIONS

For information contact the publisher:

Mayfair Book Promotion, Inc.
P.O. Box 91
Foresthill, CA 95631

www.mayfairbooks.com
prospct1@foothill.net.

ISBN: 978-1-934588-39-0

Printed in the United States of America.
Distributed by Reality Press for Mayfair Book Promotion, Inc.

Table of Contents

Introduction		 IV
Chapter 1	**The Shift Update**	 1
	Don't worry about the date	
	Darkness before the dawn	
	This is totally HUGE!	
Chapter 2	**What is the Shift? – Short Version**	 27
	The source of our protection	
	The source of our power	
	Connecting with the divine spirit	
Chapter 3	**What is the Shift? – Full Version**	 31
	The astrology of the shift	
	The science of the shift	
	How do we know these things?	
Chapter 4	**Transforming Challenges into Blessings**	 49
	The outcome is not yet determined	
	It's up to us to make it happen	
	Challenges are guidance	
Chapter 5	**Understanding the Dark Side**	 59
	The Matrix of Power and Control	
	The trick to rob us of our Spirit	
	Our world has been tampered with	
Chapter 6	**The Process of Ascension**	 77
	Our primary tool to create the new world	
	How do we raise our frequency?	
	What we need to do and how to do it	

Chapter 7	The New World of Light and Spirit 99	
	Visions of the New Paradigm	
	A totally different world	
	We are going to have to change	
Chapter 8	The Last Time 125	
	The last time there was a shift	
	Real versus fake history	
	It's time to get to work!	

Introduction

April 21, 2010

Before you start reading, there are a few things you should probably know about me, and about what's in the pages to come.

I may look like your basic 61 year old white man, but looks can be deceiving. I may have been born into a white man's body, but even since my earliest childhood, I have never felt like I belonged in the white man's world. And as soon as I was old enough to know what this meant, like in my mid-twenties, I have felt very much like a Native American, trapped in this white body. Or perhaps my roots are with some other indigenous tribe, such as the Maya of Mexico and Central America, or the Kogi of South America, or the Baka of Africa.

I have known since my earliest days that there was something hideously wrong with the white man's world. In spite of what this civilization tried to teach me, it never made a speck of sense to me that God (the divine spirit of a living universe) would create a race of beings who were so totally incapable of managing their own existence, and who were making such a total mess of life on this glorious planet, to the point of destroying the very environment they needed to survive as a species.

As a small boy, I recollect rolling in the sensuous grass, and gazing hypnotically at the fluffy, angel clouds in the sky above, and feeling dizzy with the wonder of it all. I remember waking up at my parents' cabin on Lake Michigan, during summer vacation, entranced by the song of hundreds of seagulls, and by the sunlight dancing and twinkling upon the water. I never wanted to go home. I didn't want to go back to school. My hero was Peter Pan. I didn't want to grow up to the lifeless drudgery of the life that was planned for me.

Unlike the vast majority of the people in my world, I could never just accept these things. And as soon as I was old enough to think, at least like an adult, I set out on the quest of my lifetime: to find answers to all these metaphysical questions that just didn't make sense. Why were human beings screwing up so badly here on planet Earth? Are we really ignorant, greedy and vicious savages, like the priests and the nuns told us? Is this really the natural order of things, like they told us at school and on TV?

It's been a long and arduous quest, but after several decades of a search that has taken me far outside the box of mainstream thinking, and many other boxes outside of that, the light finally went on in my head. Once it did, the dominoes started to fall in an avalanche of truth, some of it very ugly and dark. It was all a gigantic jigsaw puzzle, in which every piece fit, and everything made perfect sense. And I had been right all along that the world had to make sense.

One of the purposes of this book is to share this, as it is highly relevant to what we are experiencing in our world with *2012 and the shift*. This is a time when masses of people are opening up, like never before, and looking for answers. This is because they have no choice. The world they have always relied upon for their answers is crumbling, and it is clear they need to look somewhere else.

As it turns out, the Native Americans and their indigenous cousins spanning the globe had it right all along. They provide the answers, as well as the model for how we can get it right this time, should we choose to try to do so. They are also the primary source of much of what's written in this book. We do still have time, but it is running out.

Theirs was a world that made complete sense. They may not have been perfect, but they knew how to do the one thing that truly matters. They knew how to live sustainably in harmony with the forces of nature and with Mother Earth. They also placed the primary emphasis in their world upon their relationship and their connection with the divine spirit and with the spirit world. This was the primary source of their power. They understood that, ultimately, everything important that we manifest if life, including all the blessings of the material world, comes from our connection with spirit.

These are the things our civilized world has lost touch with, and this is why it is falling apart. So, the answers we're looking for aren't as complicated as they first might appear.

I fully realize that hearing these things is probably not why most of you picked up this book. You didn't want to hear about the collapse of our civilization, or saving our species, or anything like that. You too are probably looking for answers, but in our turbulent and topsy-turvy world, you are looking for answers to your own personal dilemmas and catastrophes. After all, we are in the midst of *the great shift of the ages*, and all the structures of our old paradigm world are collapsing. We have all been affected by this. Nobody is immune. In addition to the financial, which all of us are painfully aware of, and which most of us place high in priority, there are also the social, medical, psychological, religious, political, educational, environmental, and any other I may be missing.

This book contains a very simple message. It is the same as the message of the ancient indigenous prophesies. And yes, this message contains guidance regarding how we can get ourselves together as individuals in every possible way, including manifesting absolutely everything that we need in this world, and fulfilling our destiny as spiritual beings.

That may sound good, but when it comes right down to it, this is not a message people want to hear. In this age of monumental transformation and shift, people are afraid. They are afraid because the world they have always known and trusted has been pulled out from underneath them. Many of them are losing it emotionally, or becoming physically sick. Into this vacuum come the so-called experts and pundits, particularly in the *New Age* movement, with their message regarding how we can create prosperity and wealth in terrible times, and how we can heal ourselves with an amazing array of quick-fix, miracle cures. This seems to be what people want to hear. Our old paradigm world will hit rock bottom in the not so distant future. This means that the whole thing is going to be swept away in a wave of cleansing and purification. But please don't see this as some kind of a doomsday message. As you will see in the pages ahead, this is most unimaginable blessing possible.

There is a solution – a way out. This solution is the same as many of us have learned by hitting rock bottom in our personal lives, which means losing everything. When this happens, we learn that we have only one thing left. And it is something nobody can ever take away. This is our connection with spirit. If we're blessed enough to get this far, we learn that this is all we need. When we nurture this connection, and make it strong and vibrant, it will then shower us with everything we need in this world.

And then we learn something else: we don't need that much.

Our connection with spirit will lead us to our connection with our one true mother. This is Mother Earth. Our relationship with Mother Earth is our most important relationship in life, more important than our partner, our children, our material belongings. If it is loving and harmonious, she will take care of us, and provide for all of our needs. If it is abusive, it is only a question of time before our lifeline is cut off.

This is what is happening today. And there is no compromising on this. It is not possible for us to have one foot in each world. Making a few green changes here and there, like recycling our garbage or driving a hybrid car, just isn't enough. The ancient prophesies tell us that this is a time when one world must die so that a totally new one may be born. If we are to survive, and pull this off, we are going to have to totally change our lifestyle. But we are fully capable of this. This is why I wrote this book, and if you're with me so far, I encourage you to read on.

So, if you're looking for a solution to your personal dilemmas or catastrophes, this is it. There is a grand paradox here. Yes, this is about us, as individuals. And at the same time, it's not about us. It's much bigger than us. It's about us giving it up to spirit and to Mother Earth. This monumental time of transformation, called the shift, is forcing us to do exactly what we needed to do all along. The choice is ours. If we refuse to heed this message, then we will be in for a very rough ride.

I began writing this book in February 2009. My original intent, quite simply, was to render an account of everything I had learned about this topic, *2012 and the shift*, since I interviewed Gregg Braden in September 2004, on a Tele-seminar series I was hosting at that time. In the interim, in September 2007, my own novel on this topic was published, *Infinity's Flower – A Tale of 2012 & the Great Shift of the Ages*.

However, *Prophesy, Challenge & Blessing* quickly morphed into just as much of a personal odyssey as a rendering of factual material. This fits perfectly with the shift because this is hardly a purely academic topic. Those authors and scholars who treat it as such are completely missing the boat as far as what it really means. As we already know, the shift is personal. It's not something we just think about. It's not a head game. There is an exceedingly rare and blessed opportunity here to create an entirely new world. In order to do this, we must all play our part. This means taking action, taking action by changing the way we live, and taking action by engaging in our own spiritual ascension.

As I wrote this book, things were shifting in my personal life at an exponential pace. The eyes through which I viewed the world were in a continuous state of transformation. This was wonderful, and completely in tune with what I was writing about. The only problem was everything I wrote always needed to be revised.

So, in midstream, I made an adjustment by beginning to include some of my personal experiences. As with everything else in my life, this too turned out to be a blessing, as it was the perfect way to illustrate the embodiment of the shift, and what many of these things looked like as they played out in real life.

Of particular note was meeting Tata OmeAkaEhekatl Erick Gonzalez in August 2009. That alphabet soup in front of Erick's name is a fancy way of saying he is a Mayan Elder, trained in a long lineage of the ancient Mayan teachings and wisdom. He is also the Founder and spiritual leader of a group called Tinamit Junan Uleu, which is Mayan for Earth Peoples United (EPU – www.earthpeoplesunited.org). One of the many things EPU is doing is starting two sustainable communities, for the purpose of surviving these times, and forming bases for the creation of the new world. One is at Deer Mountain, which is in the mountains of northern California, just north of Mount Shasta, and the other is at Patziapa in Guatemala, on the shores of Lake Atitlan, in the heart of the Mayan world.

I heard Tata Erick in a radio interview, and I instantly knew I had to meet this man. His metaphysics and spirituality seemed totally resonant with mine, which makes sense because they are both derived from the same source – nature and the forces of the natural world. But in addition to that, EPU was doing the one thing that was missing for me, so far. I had known about the need for sustainable communities for a long time, but I didn't know of any yet, and I was still waiting for my own guidance on this. During the interview, Tata Erick announced that EPU was holding a five day ceremonial gathering at Deer Mountain in less than two weeks, which was open to the public. My guidance had arrived. I made my travel arrangements, and I was off to Deer Mountain.

To make a long story short, this was a connection made in the heavens, and my gratitude to Tata Erick and EPU is incalculable. I have found my tribe. Since then, in November 2009, I also visited their sustainable community in the making in Guatemala, and attended a ceremonial gathering there. And I am making another pilgrimage to Deer Mountain this coming August. When the shift hits in full force, and it's time to head for the hills, this very well could be my next home.

But this story hardly stops there. I'll have to start my next book to cover it all because it just keeps on going and going. At the gathering last August, during our sunrise pipe ceremony, while we were gathered around the sacred fire, I was contacted by a spirit guide. They introduced themselves as the Council of the Grandfathers, and they welcomed me as a member.

This experience was not completely unfamiliar to me. I had been receiving messages and guidance from the spirit world for a few years, but previously they had always been anonymous. And sometimes I just picked things up from nature or from the forces around me, like from the whispering of the wind or the spirits of the forest. And I'm certain I've been guided my entire life, even as that small boy I talked about earlier. We all are. It's simply a question of picking it up. I am now blessed to be one of these Grandfathers, and the elders of this council have been guiding me ever since. This is just a smattering of how it is for me right now. So, I think you can probably see how challenging it is to write a book, with things shifting at such an amazing pace. Many of you are probably experiencing similar things, hopefully.

But more importantly, I am also sharing this for the purpose of illustrating how the process of this shift works. One of the things you're going to be learning in the pages ahead is that the shift is occurring because our planet is experiencing a shifting of its vital energy fields. In order to play our part in creating the new world, it is necessary for each of us to shift our energy, so that it resonates and is in harmony with the energy in the fields surrounding us. I, and many others like me, am endeavoring to live my life in such a way that I am doing this. We'll go into what this means, and how to do it, in the chapters ahead. For now, I simply want to illustrate the direction in which things move when somebody does this. And I'm not anybody special. If it works for me, it can for you too.

When we resonate in harmony with the energy in our world, we begin to manifest incredible things in our lives. When enough of us do this, which is referred to as *critical mass*, we will generate the power to create an entirely new world, one that is in harmony with the forces of nature and in harmony with the divine spirit. Contrarily, the vast majority of the people in our world today are resisting the flow of this shifting energy, and pushing against it. They are doing this by clinging to the energy of the old paradigm world, which has lost its connection with spirit, and is in a state of collapse. As a result, they are feeling the angst of a crumbling world.

I must also express my profound gratitude for the guidance of Robert Ghost Wolf, author of *Last Cry – Native American Prophesies & Tales of the End Times*. Ghost Wolf's spirit departed this world several years ago, and I never had an opportunity to meet him, at least not in this incarnation. However, his influence on me and my work is also incalculable. I discovered him quite by accident, when I received an e-mail of the transcript of an interview he did on the Art Bell Radio Program in the late 1990s, when he discussed *the quickening*, among many other things. Every word instantly connected with my spirit, just as it did when I read *Last Cry*, and continues to do so as I reread it, constantly. I know in my heart and in my spirit that he is another of my spirit guides. And yes, we can also be guided by books. Hopefully, you will receive some from *Prophesy, Challenge & Blessing*.

Due to the pace of these events in my personal life, the primary challenge I faced in finishing this book had to do with the order of everything. By the time I got to the end, I was a different person, with a lot of new information and insights, none of which was reflected in the first part of the book. As I explain in Chapter One, I attempted to remedy this by writing a final chapter, and placing it first. I thought that would be the end of it, but wrong again. Things kept popping for me personally, and in order to keep up with this, I had to almost completely rewrite Chapter Three also. Once I did that, I managed to catch up to myself, and the rest of it was OK. The only problem with all this is there is a little choppiness and a few redundancies along the way. I apologize for that. Actually, I think this also turns out to be a good thing because most of these are things it doesn't hurt to hear more than once anyway. It certainly beats the alternative, which is writing a book that never ends.

Chapter One

The Shift Update

> *Don't worry about the date*
> *The darkness before the dawn*
> *This is totally HUGE!*

The Last Chapter First

    If the date is some time after December 21, 2012, as you're reading this, don't be dismayed, and please don't stop reading. If that's the case, my guess is you already know what I'm about to say. It's Winter Solstice 2009, as I write – exactly three years now until that portentous date, at least in the minds of many, when the Mayan Calendar ended, signifying the end of one world, and possibility of the birth of another, and I emphasize the word "possibility." There are a few things we already know about the shift, or *the great shift of the ages*, which are as true as I write this as they will be when you read it, whenever that might be.

    One is that the shift is not a point in time, as in a single date, but rather a window of time of longer duration. All of the ancient prophesies, as well as all of the other evidence, does clearly point to this age of ours as the time of this shifting of worlds from old to new. There is also good reason to believe that Winter Solstice 2012 may be the midpoint, or close to the midpoint, of this window. We don't know how large this window is, but as I write this, we do know that the shift is already well underway, and has been for some time now. Ours is a world in turmoil, where our civilization is in a state of rapid decay and collapse. It is also a world that is experiencing a shifting of its energy, setting the stage for the opportunity of the birth of a new world from the ashes of the old, and I emphasize the word "opportunity."

    As you will read in the pages ahead, the death of the old world, or paradigm, is a certainty because this is a world that is unsustainable. It takes from the world far more than it gives back, so the time must come when its tank runs dry, and that time is upon us. However, contrary to what so many people believe, particularly the starry-eyed Pollyannas in the *New Age* scene, the birth of the new world is not going to happen all by itself. It's up to us, the human beings of the Planet Earth, to make it happen. That's one of the things this book is about – how we can make it happen.

    Another thing we know for certain is this opportunity presents us with a monumental challenge, which demands that we call upon the highest of our higher powers. I know that's not what most people want to hear, but that's the way it is. However, the message in these pages is not a negative one, hardly. The message here is that we are fully capable of reconnecting with our heritage as magical beings, and taking advantage of this monumental opportunity to create the new world. But we have to get to work. If we are not up to the task, then the days ahead will be dark indeed.

Winter Solstice is a perfect time to be writing these opening words because it so perfectly illustrates the essence of *the great shift of the ages*, and what we are currently in the midst of experiencing in our world. With Winter Solstice, these are the days of darkness. And yes, this is the darkness before the dawn, before the dawn of the new light - the ascending light, when the Sun reaches the nadir of its pendulum swing in the sky, and begins to move in the other direction. Both are the eternal cycles of life and death, and with both, our current time is the time of death. By the time you read this, this may have changed. Such is how rapidly things are changing in our world at the current time.

But in a divinely ordered universe, like ours, nothing ever dies. Energy is merely transmuted into other forms of energy. Ours is the time when the old cycle must die, but in which the seeds of the birth of an entirely new cycle lie dormant. It is a time of darkness, but this is the darkness of the womb, in which the light of a new life has germinated. We are perched on the precipice of this exceedingly rare cosmic opportunity to birth an entirely new world – a world without the weights and constraints of our material world – a new world of light and spirit.

Beginning this book is a challenge because things are changing so fast, at least if we allow them to, that the very act of writing a book is nearly impossible. Assuming a book takes six months to a year to write, by the time you get to the end, so much has changed that the whole thing needs to be updated. And in this case, in addition to the changes in our world, as in the world you and I share, these changes include the changes in my world, as in the world I, and many others like me, choose to perceive.

The planet Earth today has entered a vast sea of shifting energy fields. This is one of the primary features of the shift. We'll go into the details of this in Chapter Three. There are many of us who are aware of this, and who are tuned into these shifting energies, resonating in harmony with them with the vibration of our energy. As a result, we are indeed experiencing transmutation in our lives at a warp speed. Those who are resisting these energies, and pushing against them, are experiencing the angst and pain of a crumbling world.

There was only one way for me to keep up with the pace of this. This was to write my last chapter, and place it first. This is what I am doing now. As you read on, I'm certain you'll see these changes in the tenor of my writing, which turns out to be yet another blessing in disguise because it is one of the best ways I can think of to show how the process of the shift works. After all, we're talking about a time where there is an opportunity for monumental transformation, on every possible level. Any author who's walking the walk, and not just talking it, should embody this.

This is not a time to stay the same, or to act like we've got it all figured out. This is at time to be continually transmuting. As you will see, I changed as I wrote this book. I got lighter and lighter, and continue to do so. I also got a bit more tangential than usual. But this is the way things are now. I am learning so much, and there are so many threads to this topic, going off in so many different directions. What a beautiful way of illustrating the essence of the shift - without even trying.

As it turns out, this also was absolutely necessary. I've been working on this for a little over ten months. With all the shifting that's gone on, an entirely different set of priorities has emerged for me as far as what's most important about all this. Starting at the end provides me with the luxury of addressing these things, and saying what really needs to be said about the shift, and saying it now. There are certain vital features of this that people really need to hear about, and they're not. They're not hearing them because most of the so-called experts on the shift aren't saying them. And this is no minor matter. These things are vitally important.

So, this first chapter amounts to a shift update. It is the highlights of the chapters to come, and much more, as far as the new things I am learning every day. It is also a wonderful way for me to weave this material together in different ways, as I see it differently, and make new connections. This does create a few redundancies, but that's OK. These things are so important that it's good to hear them over and over.

One of the things we learn on the spiritual path is that the divine spirit loves to work with paradoxes. One of these is the more things change the more they stay the same. This too is the case here. In spite of all this talk about change, what you are going to hear in this shift update is things that are guaranteed not to change. They are based on spiritual principles that are eternal. These are things I don't have to concern myself with updating again.

This is Monumentally Huge!

The first thing people need to hear is how vitally important this is. This topic, *2012 and the great shift of the ages*, is so monumentally huge that it is difficult to find words to describe it. When all is said and done, all the other topics will be derivatives of this one. No part of our world, animal, vegetable or mineral, will go untouched by this.

For about five years now, I've thought about little else except the shift, and I have changed my lifestyle accordingly, placing a far greater emphasis upon the ongoing process of my spiritual ascension, and taking responsibility, as much as possible, for every aspect of my own life. I have endeavored to learn as much about the shift as possible, from as many different sources as possible. The more I learn the truer it becomes that this is unimaginably huge. And I don't mean huge in the way that most people think – doomsday. I mean huge as in - other-worldly.

When I talk to others about the shift, and when I check out what the other so-called experts have to say, it seems to me that the hugeness of the shift is being watered down in the minds of many – not counting the doomsdayers, of course. In many ways, this topic is suffering, and is becoming diluted, because it has become so popular. This has become the hottest of topics, and is guaranteed to grow progressively hotter as we approach December 21, 2012, the date the Mayan Calendar ended, allegedly. Everyone is jumping on this bandwagon, including Hollywood, as well as most of the biggest names in the *New Age* and self-help scenes, most of whom don't have a clue what the shift really means.

Many of the *New Age* celebrities acknowledge that this is a time of major transformation, but then they endeavor to fit it into the box of all the other self-help techniques they're pitching. And, even worse, they try to squeeze it into the box of mainstream perception, where it definitely does not belong. They seem to be reassuring us that we've been through these things before, and like the others, this too will pass. And the world will go on.

Well, this leads us directly to two of the things that people really need to hear about the shift. It also begins to convey the flavor of why this is so huge. First, we've never been through anything like this before, at least not in 26,000 years. And second, the world, at least the world as we know it, will not go on.

The Collapse of the Old Paradigm is a Blessing

Let's cover the second one first, as this lays the foundation for the rest. The world, as we know it, is collapsing, and its days are numbered. This is not the same as doomsday, at least it doesn't have to be. As you'll hear again and again here, the death of this world provides the opportunity for the birth of a totally new world – more about that shortly.

The world that is collapsing, and about to die, is our old paradigm world. This is the world that Western Civilization has built, over the last 6000 years of our so-called history, which has been orchestrated almost exclusively by the white race. Actually, it is more accurate to say that this has been orchestrated by elitist elements of the white race, operating entirely behind the scenes, and using the governments of the major nations of the world as their hand-picked puppets. Actually, that's not entirely accurate either, but we'll cover all this in detail in Chapter Five. For now, you get the basic idea. The world does not work the way we are told it does.

The collapse of the old paradigm, from its very beginning, has been inevitable. It is also an unimaginable blessing, which I know is extremely difficult for most people to understand. This is because the old paradigm world is unsustainable. It cannot possibly survive because it is built upon a foundation that is in fundamental violation of natural and divine law. What are natural and divine law, you might ask? Natural and divine law are how nature and the universe behave when they are allowed to flow freely, without any outside interference. As spiritual people, our primary responsibility is to live with a vibration that is in harmony with the rhythm and flow of nature and the forces of the natural world. When we succeed at that, it is not arrogant for us to say that we know what natural and divine law are – because we are living it.

The foundation of the old paradigm rests upon two philosophical premises, which doom it from the start. The first is materialism, which means placing a primary emphasis upon matter or material things in life, at the expense of the spiritual. As spiritual people, we know it works just the opposite. Everything important in life manifests from our connection with spirit, including our material goodies, such as our money and our relationships.

The second is control, which refers primarily here to the effort of Western Civilization to control the forces of nature or the environment, for the purpose of achieving a material outcome. The ancient indigenous peoples of the planet, including the many Native American tribes, a precious few of which are still intact, have shown us the model for how to live a sustainable life, in connection with spirit. These people lived in harmony with nature and with the environment. They understood that we are all, ultimately, children of the Earth, and they loved her and treated her like their sacred mother. Their connection with the Earth was the source of everything in their world, including their spirituality.

These ancient indigenous peoples, from cultures spanning the globe, including the Maya and the Hopi, all had the same message for us, which was foretold in their prophesies. They told us that there was no way the white man's civilization could survive because it violated the divine law that was the basis of everything in their world. The white man had lost its connection with the rhythm and flow of life and nature, and lost its connection with spirit. And they told us that the end was due to come during this age of ours. We'll talk more about the dates and time frames of all this later.

These indigenous people, from around the planet, both past and present, are one of our most reliable sources of information – about sustainability, spirituality and lots of other things. They are one of the most important influences on my work, my metaphysics, and what you'll be reading in this book. They are credible because they were in touch with their world. Their survival depended on it. It is not a stretch to say that their world was more real than ours. It was not as distorted. Our old paradigm in the civilized world is an illusion. It is a fabricated reality, perpetrated by our rulers, for the purpose of tricking us into believing we are free, when, in fact, we are their slaves. It is also a self-imposed illusion, due to our disconnection with the rhythm and flow of nature, which scrambles our ability to see the world as it really is.

In addition to being one of our most credible sources on sustainability and spirituality, they are also one of our most credible sources on the Earth's history, and this includes *2012 and the great shift of the ages*. There is a very important reason for this. Once we know this, it's one of those things that totally flips around how we see the world – again. Don't worry – you'll get used to it. And it's good for you.

The reason they are so credible is because there is a very good chance that many of these indigenous peoples, including the Maya and the Hopi, were here the last time the Earth was at this point on this cosmic cycle, and experienced an age of transformation comparable to what we are heading into now. They were here, and they were making observations about what was happening, and when, which they then passed down in their lore, which was mostly verbal, but a lot of which was preserved in artifacts. There is also a very high probability that there were other beings here too, from other worlds, who had come here for the purpose of colonization, and who had formed highly advanced civilizations. We'll get to that later too.

When we take a look at the ancient histories of many of these indigenous peoples, we find a version of history that is totally different from the one we are spoon-fed in the old paradigm. The traditional, mainstream version of history dates back approximately 6000 years to the first civilization in Sumer. According to these indigenous histories, many of these people appear to have roots that date back much farther than that – tens of thousands, possibly even hundreds of thousands of years.

For example, Hopi history tells us that we are currently at the end of the fourth world, on the verge of entering the fifth, with the world already having been destroyed three times. And the Hopi claim to have been here the entire time.

Virtually all of the indigenous prophesies foretold the collapse of our old paradigm world, and foretold that it would happen during this age of ours. As stated earlier, the collapse of the old paradigm is a blessing. The reasons are fairly obvious – because it's morally wrong – because it cannot possibly work – and because it robs us of our most sacred gifts in life – our connection with the Earth and our connection with spirit.

If you too believe the universe is divinely ordered, and perfect in every way, there is a logical question that comes up here. If it doesn't, it should. The question is: how did things get so knocked out of balance? How could the divine spirit have created a race of organic beings, white humans, who are so totally incapable of managing their own existence? This doesn't make one shred of metaphysical sense.

The Christians would like us to believe it was because the serpent tempted Adam and Eve to break their vow with the Creator, resulting in our fatal flaw, original sin. There may be some truth veiled in this metaphor, but once we take our blinders off, the real answer is far simpler. The *New Agers* tell us that this unfortunate state of affairs is simply part of our natural development, implying that we had to get it wrong before we could get it right, or some such thing. Well, this doesn't cut it either. That's not how nature works. The divine spirit only programs for one thing, and nature only programs for one thing. That is success. That's how the universe works, if it is allowed to flow freely. All of the other life forms on the planet, plant and animal, get this right every time, no problem.

No, I'm afraid the answer is quite a bit more nefarious than all this. Humanity has allowed itself to become so disconnected and imbalanced because it has been tampered with, as has the natural order of things on Planet Earth. We will cover all this in Chapter Five, when we cover the part played by *the dark side* in our world. For now, let's just say that an insidious game has been foisted on humanity, the purpose of which is to trick us into giving up our freedom and our spirit. This has been perpetrated by a small group of extremely rich and powerful people, or beings, who operate entirely behind the scenes, through deceit, manipulation, and worse. The sad state of affairs in our world today is all part of this dark design, which appears to be working quite well – much more later.

But the collapse of the old paradigm is a blessing for one more reason. We've gotten to a point in our long history where the old paradigm is getting in our way. Its very existence interferes with our ability to create a new and better world. I think it was Einstein who said it is impossible to solve a problem with the same methods that created the problem to begin with. In our case, this is the same as saying that we cannot create the new paradigm with the methods of the old paradigm – materialism and plundering nature.

There are those, most notably on the liberal end of the political spectrum, who are optimistic because they believe many of these new paradigm methods and ideas are already being implemented by the mainstream system, particularly now that Obama and the Democrats are in control of the government. Their favorite example is the environmental or so-called green revolution, where the consciousness of the masses has been raised to where it recognizes the imperative need for such things as recycling and alternative sources of energy.

I hate to rain on anybody's parade, but this is just more of the same, and part of the same old paradigm illusion. This kind of talk has been going on since the mid-'70s, and absolutely, and I mean absolutely, nothing has changed. A few token ecological scraps, like hybrid cars and a windmill here and there, aren't going to change anything. What needs to change is the lifestyle of an entire population, which lost its connection with how to live in harmony with the rhythm and flow of nature and life, and lost its spiritual bearings. Nothing short of this will work.

So, it's necessary to get rid of the old paradigm in its entirety. We must start from scratch, and begin building the new paradigm with the proper foundation of spirituality. Fortunately, it appears as though *the great shift of the ages* is in the process of taking care of this for us, and it won't be much longer before this is complete. And yes, it is a wondrous blessing.

The inevitability of the collapse of the old paradigm, and the belief that this is a blessing, are two important differences between the message you'll be hearing in this book and many of the other so-called experts on the shift. There are many of these differences now that so many have jumped on this bandwagon. I will be highlighting most of these differences in this first (last) chapter. I believe understanding them is a key to fine-tuning our understanding of the shift. The message here is a new paradigm message, not an old paradigm one. Creating the new paradigm in an old paradigm way is an impossibility, which we will not be spending any time on.

I am fully aware that the collapse of the old paradigm is causing extreme hardship and pain for many, many people. I don't want to sound insensitive to this, or like I have a cavalier attitude. I am actually trying to help in the best way I know how. The reason for their hardship and pain is the fact that they are clinging to the old paradigm, which makes complete sense. This is the world they are familiar and comfortable with. They have been conditioned to believe that this is the world of their hopes and dreams, and now this once safe world is being completely pulled out from underneath them.

It is crucial that these well-intended folks wake up to the truth about their old paradigm world, and about themselves. The energy of the old paradigm is destructive because it is in fundamental violation of natural and divine law. When you cling to destructive energy, bad things eventually will happen. Our conditioning (brainwashing) in the old paradigm reinforces this dependency. The powers that be tell us that the universe is random and cruel, and that we are helpless in the face of this. They tell us that we need the structures of the old paradigm to take care of us from cradle to grave, and to protect us from all the boogie men out there, which, by the way, they have created. As long as we follow the rules of our servitude, it will provide everything we need. If not, we will be squashed like bugs.

The solution for us here is so exceedingly simple that it's almost laughable. Rather than cling to the old paradigm, we simply need to let it go. When we let it go, we also let go of the destructive energy that binds us. Of course, this means a profound shift in how we see ourselves. It means embracing our personal power, and reassuming complete responsibility for our own lives, like our indigenous sisters and brothers. When we let go of the old paradigm, or perhaps I should say when enough of us let go of the old paradigm, it will simply go away. We are what holds it up. Without us, it can no longer be.

We are far more powerful than they would like us to believe. We are fully capable of taking care of ourselves, or at least relearning how to do this, which is our birthright. Of course, if we are to pull this off, we will also need to pull together, as in uniting for the purpose of sustaining ourselves in harmony with the Earth. This too is easily within our grasp. Once we learn (or relearn) to trust our hearts, and to trust our connection with the Earth and with the divine spirit, we learn that that's all we need. With this trust and this connection, the Earth and the divine spirit will shower us with unimaginable blessings.

Taking Responsibility and Sustainability Here on Earth

The opportunity to shift from the old paradigm to the new is also something we've never been through before, at least not you and I, not in our current lifetime. It is part of a 26,000 year cycle that is coming to a close during this age of ours, so that the cycle may renew itself – yet another reason why this is so huge.

This does not mean there have not been other points along this cycle, where the Earth and its inhabitants have experienced times of monumental shift and transformation. For example, in Chapter 8 we're going to discuss how the last time the Earth and its inhabitants experienced a facelift, comparable to what we're on the verge of experiencing now, was approximately 13,000 years ago. At this time, there was a great flood, of global proportions, in which entire land masses were submerged, with others rising to replace them. Most of the evidence points to this as the time when the ancient, highly advanced civilization of Atlantis sank into the Atlantic Ocean – much more about all this later. However, this again only serves to illustrate how monumentally huge this time of ours is. If something this colossal happened at the half-way point of this grand cycle, we can only imagine what is on verge of happening now, at the completion of the cycle.

So, now that we've covered the hugeness of this from the point of view of the end of the old paradigm, let's take a look at it from the point of view of the opportunity to create the new paradigm. When we do, this goes from totally huge to even huger.

When discussing the creation of the new paradigm, there are two distinct features of this: the Earthly and the other-worldly. Here again is another of the differences between this message and most of the others. Virtually all of the other scholars on *2012 and the great shift of the ages* cover one of these – not both, and some of them neither. But both must be included, as both are part of the total picture.

Let's begin with the Earthly, which, in this case, is hardly mundane, and progress to the ethereal. When the old paradigm officially comes to an end, the first thing we are going to have to deal with is whether the human race can survive. This is where those of us who have made a commitment to creating the new world, and who understand the shift and the forces that are involved, are going to have to take charge.

There are many possibilities as far what might topple the old paradigm once and for all. This could be triggered by man-made influences, such as a collapse of the world economy, a collapse of the technological infrastructure, a world war, or many other possibilities. Or, it could be brought about by the colossal Earth changes, which are both part of the ancient histories and prophesies, as well as part of the geophysical reality of what's already happening in the world. There are also numerous possibilities here, including a magnetic pole shift, or a repeat of the great flood of 13,000 years ago, which could be caused by lots of things.

In any event, the challenge facing us is the same. For those of us who are committed to creating the new world, the first step is to begin thinking in terms of sustainability – both individually and collectively.

As individuals, sustainability begins with each of us making an earnest effort to take complete responsibility for as much of our own life as possible. We must learn to have complete confidence in our ability to survive independently in the universe. This amounts to practicing for that day when this will be necessary. This way, when the old paradigm caves in around us, it won't surprise us, and it won't freak us out because we'll be prepared, both practically and emotionally. And we'll be able to take action – to do whatever needs to be done.

Taking complete responsibility for our own lives also happens to be an indispensable feature of our spiritual evolution or ascension, in which we learn to trust our connection with the divine spirit for everything we have in life, and learn to detach ourselves from our dependence on the old paradigm system to take care of our needs. Spirituality is meaningless, unless it is practically applied to how we live our lives.

The Hopi provide us with a beautiful illustration of the primary importance of our spirituality in relationship to our sustainability. The question is often posed why the Hopi chose to live in such a god-forsaken place as the desert of the American Southwest, where it is difficult to grow food, and the hardships of life are great. The answer is very simple, and yet practically incomprehensible to anybody who has lost touch with their spirituality. They chose to live there precisely because of its hardships. The only way to survive in such a place was to rely upon the higher powers of their prayer, their ceremonies and their connection with the creator. It was their way of forcing themselves to be spiritually fine-tuned. They believed that when life was too easy, the temptations were just too great, and we tend to forget our spirituality, and become seduced by the illusion of our control of the material world. And that's when our world falls apart, as it is now.

We're going to go into all the details of sustainability, individually and collectively, in Chapter 7. For now, let's just stress that for each of us, sustainability begins with taking responsibility. One of the best ways to learn how to take responsibility is to make the effort to detach ourselves, as much as possible, from the mainstream system.

For many of you, like those stuck in jobs working for the system, or working from pay check to pay check, this may seem like a stretch. But you can always start with the little things, and build from there, like taking responsibility for eating healthy food, or taking responsibility for going to natural health practitioners, instead of mainstream doctors.

And even for those of you who feel stuck, you can begin to start thinking about this, and thinking about the best possible escape route. Remember – we're dealing with destructive energy here, and there's no compromising with that. And then start to make some plans – get the ball rolling. This is important! Keep reminding yourselves of that.

Another thing we can all do is think about what we would do in the event of a total infrastructure collapse. What would you do if suddenly our money was worthless, and there was no electricity? How would you take care of your food and shelter? Even without forces as monumental as the shift at work, this is something we should all think about anyway. Our monetary system and our technological infrastructure are extraordinarily fragile. Our debt-based, fiat, paper money is already on the brink, and our technological infrastructure could go out any time, dependent as it is on a centrally-controlled, global network of interlocking satellites and computers, which is terribly vulnerable. The possibility of the Y2K computer glitch is a great example of just how vulnerable this system could be. It didn't happen, but the logic of it was sound.

Putting together a homemade survival kit is a very simple and inexpensive matter, as long as you stick with the basics. I have done this, and my own feeling is I want to be able to hold out for at least three months. I believe this is enough time because if long-term survival becomes necessary, the only way we will be able to do that will be by forming, small self-sustaining communities, in which we pool our resources and work cooperatively on this. And we should all be prepared to play our part in helping to get these started.

Here's your easy and cheap survival kit. It's a simple matter to start stockpiling clean, pure water, in five gallon bottles. You can have it delivered to your house. The water I receive is actually spring water, which comes from deep within Mother Earth, about 20 miles from where I live in Wisconsin. Like with everything else, make sure you shop with discernment.

For food, start by getting lots of one quart mason jars (or bigger). I have four cases for myself. Then, go to the nearest health food store, and start stocking up on bulk raw foods, with long shelf life, like grains (brown rice, barley, etc.), beans (garbanzo, black, etc.) and nuts. You should be going to the health food store regularly anyway. So, buy a couple of items per week, until all those jars are full. Then, go to one of those outlets that sell cheap (and reasonably healthy) canned produce, and stock up on canned vegetables and fruit. As far as the food part is concerned, that's it. That's all you'll need. You could live forever on that diet – probably healthier than you are now. Of course, there are many other possibilities regarding how you can do this, but my focus here is the quickest and easiest.

The rest of your survival is very much like camping. And I think it's helpful to think of it in those terms, at least for those of you who are familiar with camping. You'll need a stove to cook your food, and a small camping stove, which burns liquid fuel or butane, is fine, along with enough fuel to last a while. And you'll need flashlights, candles, batteries, matches, a first-aid kit – you get the picture. If you have to deal with winter, like I do, heat can be a major issue. A wood stove of some kind is probably the best way to go here. But as with any item in your survival kit that might be a problem, or any aspect of self-sustainability, the important thing is you think about these things. If you don't have a source of heat, think of friends, neighbors or people in your network who do, and how you might be able to work with them to meet this challenge.

Those are the basics of sustainability as individuals. If you want to build upon this base, and if you're able to, that's great. Once you get started, it's lot s of fun – like everything in life, once you get your head screwed on straight. And we cannot overestimate the importance of this. There's only one way we can create the new world, and that's as self-empowered individuals, who know how to take care of ourselves, and who are up to the challenge of the collapse of the old paradigm and the shift to the new world.

Self-Sustaining Communities

Equally as important is the collective aspect of this, where we band together as self-empowered individuals, and form communities that are self-sustainable. Obviously, in order to do this part, we must be really serious about this. We must not just talk the talk, but walk the walk. But that's the main point I'm hammering you with here. This is serious! And it is up to us, and this amazing opportunity is spread out before us. When the old paradigm finally does collapse, in its entirety, this is the only way we can survive.

The primary task of our self-sustaining communities will be the same as our indigenous sisters and brothers of yesteryear. This will be to sustain ourselves in harmony with the natural world, and in harmony with spirit. If it seems like I'm saying the same thing over and over again, I am. That's how important it is. And it doesn't hurt to hear it again and again. That's usually the most effective way of learning anything.

In Chapter Seven, we will also take a close look at all the details of these sustainable communities. For now, let's just look at a snapshot. They will be small, along the lines of the tribe, from our ancient indigenous cultures. This is both by necessity and design. It is by necessity because, with the collapse of the old paradigm, we will have no other choice. With the high likelihood that our system of money and technological infrastructure will not hold up, our world will be smaller and more immediate. It is by design because this type of small communal system is the most efficient as far as sustainability. They will also be rural, as far away from large cities as possible. When the old paradigm finally collapses, cities will be places of such chaos that they will not be safe. It is also likely that whatever remnants there are of the old paradigm governments and systems will be in the cities, such as military and martial law, whether they are legal, or not.

Our sustainable community must have a source of renewable, clean, fresh water. In today's world, with most of the Earth's surface water contaminated, a natural spring would be optimal here. We must learn to grow our own food, with seeds we have developed ourselves, from strains that have not been genetically contaminated by the deeply corrupt and sinister multi-national corporations that are monopolizing agriculture and food in the old paradigm. Our energy needs will be very simple at first, consisting of the need for heat to cook our food, and to heat our shelters, if necessary, both of which can be provided by burning wood. Our technological needs, at first, will also be very simple and primitive, like how to most effectively use the substances of the natural world to make our tools and build our structures, and how to most effectively irrigate our fields.

The question of how much more of this kind of energy we will actually need in the new paradigm is one we will answer as we move along. Obviously, energy is something the old paradigm got totally wrong, and this is one of the most glaring sources of its destruction. In Chapter Seven, we will discuss in detail this critical issue of energy, and how human beings can get it right this time. For now, let's just consider the one possibility that the new paradigm here on Earth will be more primitive.

The question of how much progress we need, or how much progress is consistent with natural law, is one we'll have to answer. One of my favorite tidbits of wisdom on this comes from Jean Liedloff, author of the book *The Continuum Concept*. In the 1970s, Jean lived with a primitive, indigenous tribe, the Yequana, in the jungles of Venezuela, who had little contact with civilization. She made the radical observation that these people were totally and unconditionally happy, living each and every moment of life for the sheer joy of it. They had nearly perfect physical health, and their family and tribal social systems worked with cooperation and harmony. She also observed that the Yequana had practically no interest in progress. Everything was OK the way it was. Doesn't this beg the question: if we are totally happy, how much progress do we need? What more is there?

Whatever new technology we do invent will be completely different than that of the old paradigm. The vast majority of our old paradigm technology serves the old paradigm agenda: materialism and controlling nature rather than harmonizing with it. And on an even more insidious level, it distracts us, and disconnects us from spirit.

Now, I know many of you are probably totally wired into the modern high-tech world. You love your techno toys, and you probably don't like the sound of this. But please don't be dismayed. This does not mean that we will be less advanced, or that we have regressed. In the ways that truly count, we will be more advanced.

Like everything else in the old paradigm, old paradigm technology is very heavy and dense, with its reliance upon hardware, wires and gadgets – material things. Modern science prides itself on being mechanistic and measurable. But to achieve this, it was necessary to eliminate two of the most important variables, or perhaps I should say the two most important variables. One was the human factor, or the consciousness of the observer or scientist. The other was the spiritual factor. As long as modern scientists included God in their formulations, the world they wanted to measure couldn't be pinned down at all. With these two variables factored out, the old paradigm scientists were dealing with a world that consisted totally of matter, and that they could measure with near 100% certainty, but it was a world that had been so deflated of its vital essence that it no longer had any real meaning. It was just stuff. It was a dead world.

Science and technology in the new paradigm will be wholistic, which means it will include these variables, and as a result, it will be far more advanced. One way of illustrating this is with space travel or inter-dimensional travel. Most people think of this as being done with huge ships, using some form of renewable fuel, and capable of traveling faster than the speed of light. However, most of the experts on this, as well as those with first-hand experience, agree that these notions are actually quite old-fashioned, and even clumsy.

For thousands of years, sorcerers and shamans from indigenous cultures spanning the globe have performed this kind of travel without using any ships at all. This is referred to by a variety of names, such as journeying, dream journeying or light travel. This means that in altered states of consciousness, they are able to travel inter-dimensionally, or to any place in the universe, and they do this on the wings of their perception. They do not use their physical bodies, but rather their energy or spirit bodies. And as far as space travel, whatever material ships we might use will be lighter and more energetic in their form, kind of like traveling on beams of light, or like the transporter in Star Trek. Whatever fuel we might need could be extracted from the free energy that exists everywhere in the universe, even in open space. This is energy that old paradigm science has never learned to tap into.

In addition to self-sustainability, our new paradigm communities will be built upon the foundation of spirituality. Here again we have the model of our indigenous brothers and sisters, for whom spiritual ceremonies were one of their most important methods to keep the focus or the intent of the community (tribe) where it belonged – on spirit. Ceremonies were one of the centerpieces of their lives. Ceremony also will be an essential feature of our new paradigm lifestyle. Ceremony here means any specific activity or ritual, in which the community gathers for the purpose of creating a vibration that allows them to connect with spirit. In indigenous cultures, ceremonies include fire circles, with drumming, chanting and dancing, sunrise ceremonies, pipe ceremonies, purification ceremonies, such as sweat lodges, medicine plant ceremonies, such as peyote, and the list goes on and on.

Our new paradigm communities will be bases from which we can engage in our ceremonies, and do the work necessary to develop the full powers of our spirituality. When all is said and done, this will be the key to creating the new world. Remember – everything important we manifest in life comes from our connection with spirit.

Don't Push – Flow

Obviously, with *the great shift of the ages* and the opportunity to create the new world, we are facing a monumental challenge. I know this probably sounds daunting for many of you. That is not my intent. Every word I write comes from the point of view that this opportunity is a spectacular blessing to fulfill our destiny as spiritual beings. We simply need to understand this, and what to do with it. Along the way, we are probably going to be looking at some things that make many people uncomfortable. I'm fully aware of that. But we can no longer tiptoe around these things, and worry about peoples' feelings. Time is too short, and it's supremely important that people look at these things.

And it's my job to point them out. My guidance has made this abundantly clear to me. This is another of the many differences between the message you'll be hearing here, and the others. If this frightens you, you don't have to run away. You can learn to manage your fear. So then, you can focus on what really matters.

I know the thought of beginning to start sustainable communities is a leap for many of you. It was for me too. Being well-versed on this subject, I have known about the need for sustainable communities for a long time. At the conclusion of my novel, *Infinity's Flower,* published in 2007, the old paradigm has collapsed, and my two heroes, David and Kelly, have been guided to a group of people who, like them, understand the true meaning of the shift, and who understand that the universe is forcing them to band together to start to build the new world. However, none of this had played out in my own life. I didn't know of any such communities, and I didn't know yet how this fit for me. My own guidance told me to wait, and that the answer would come.

Then, in August 2009, I was guided to listen to a radio program, where I heard Erick Gonzalez, a Mayan Elder, talking about the two sustainable communities that the group he founded, Earth Peoples United (EPU - www.earthpeoplesunited.org) was starting - one in California and one in Guatemala. The one in California was at Deer Mountain, in the mountains of Northern California, just north of Mount Shasta, one of the most sacred power points on the planet, and a place that has always had a powerful attraction for me. I had actually been considering moving there for years. One of the many reasons was the water. Mount Shasta's public water is pumped directly from a natural spring that comes from beneath the mountain – no kidding! The metaphysics and spirituality I heard from Erick also seemed to resonate perfectly with mine, which, trust me, doesn't happen very often. He announced that in two weeks he and his group were conducting a five-day gathering at Deer Mountain, in which he would be leading the attendees in many traditional Mayan ceremonies.

Well – I didn't even have to think about it. My guidance had arrived. I just went. This was *Infinity's Flower* come to life. To make a long story short, the event and the people were perfect. It was a magical experience that resonated perfectly with my spirit. It also had a profound influence on how I practice my spirituality – with more ceremony. As did the place, far away from the madness of civilization, and with its own natural spring bubbling up from Mother Earth – the absolute cornerstone of any sustainable community. Then, in November 2009, I attended another of EPU's ceremonial gatherings at their sustainable community in the making at Patziapa in Guatemala, on the shores of Lake Atitlan, in the heart of the Mayan world. That too was a life-changing experience.

As I write this, January 2010, what part Erick and EPU play in my life, or what part I play with them, has yet to be determined. I know I am not finished with them, and I sense that this is just the beginning. But I don't know for sure yet. All of this is still unfolding. And I continue to wait for guidance as to what the next step is. Perhaps it will come to me before I finish this chapter, and hence, this book.

Yet here again is another beautiful little illustration of how things are working in these fast shifting times. Things are changing so rapidly in my life, and in the world outside me, that I am not able to write, and finish, this book from a fixed point of view. Everything now always seems to be in process. Nothing is ever finished. And it looks like this is the way it's going to be for some time. Perhaps this is the way it's going to be from now on. Nobody ever said it would be easy to build the new world of light and spirit from the ashes of the old. Well, actually, lots of people have, but you get what I mean.

And there is another very important lesson here, which I thank my guidance for. On the spiritual path, sometimes the best possible thing we can do is wait. Sometimes too, it's the only thing, which makes it the best thing in a divinely ordered universe. This too might appear to be a challenge in these fast-changing times.

Didn't we just say time is short? It is. Here is one of those divine paradoxes. It never serves our purpose to rush, even when time seems the shortest, like now. It never serves our purpose to push against the flow of the universe. The new paradigm will be a world where we no longer have to push and drive ourselves to do everything, like in the old. We will learn to live in the flow of the energy we embrace. Once we do, we can simply allow things to come to us. This takes no effort – just trust. We simply allow things to happen, and when they do, we trust it – because we're in the flow.

Sometimes it's best to wait, even when it seems like time is running out. Once we learn to trust our guidance, time is no longer an issue. We know that our guidance will deliver, when the time is right. And when it does, we'll know. This is a particularly important lesson in these times of shift and prophesy. We are much better off trusting our guidance than we are a clock.

Look at the World Through New Paradigm Eyes

And yes, with everything we're talking about here, with the shift, with the collapse of the old paradigm, and with this opportunity to create the new world, we are facing a monumental challenge. But this is not a bad thing. Actually, it is a most wondrous blessing, even though it may be dressed up to look like something else. In a divinely ordered universe, everything happens for a reason – including hardships. All challenges, invariably, present us with the opportunity to learn whatever we need to learn next, and to take it to the next level in our lives. In this way, challenges are blessings. They are guidance.

Like the Hopi in the desert, when life is too easy, we become soft and stagnant. We are not at our best. And very often it's the most severe challenges, the ones that force us to hit rock-bottom in life, when we lose everything, that also force us to recognize that our greatest power in life comes from the only thing that's left – our connection with spirit.

For most people, this all just seems too impossible. It just seems way too big for us little human beings. It seems like there's no way we could survive some of the colossal Earth changes that people hear forecasted, like the shifting of the magnetic poles. When they hear about the possibility of another great flood, they simply say no way – we'd all drown – just like last time. And when you couple this with the imminent collapse of our civilization, which most can see is painfully obvious, it all just seems too impossible. There's no way we could survive.

Well, even though that might seem logical, this is definitely not the message here. And, if we get this right, this is not the way it's going to work. In order to understand the reason why, it's necessary to understand one very important thing. The reason it all seems so hopeless is because we are looking at it through our old paradigm eyes. And when we look at it in this way, it is hopeless. Remember – the old paradigm is a dying world. If we look to Obama to lead us to the new world, we could be in for a long wait.

There's only one way to look at the shift and this opportunity to create the new world, and that is with new paradigm eyes. The new paradigm is a world where we place our connection with the divine spirit first, and everything else manifests from that. The new paradigm is a world, in which we are reconnected with life's vital energy and with the rhythm and flow of the natural world. When we plug ourselves into these kinds of forces, we become more powerful. It's just that simple.

We have the power to attract everything we want and need in life, even if it's less. We have the power to live our lives with feelings of peacefulness, joy, reverence, gratitude and trust. When we learn to live with this vibration, our entire world changes. We become capable of far more, with less effort. We become capable of things that previously we never could have imagined. Our connection with nature gives us the power to have physical health and vitality, and to live to be a hundred years old, at least. Our spirituality gives us powers that can only be described as supernatural or inter-dimensional. We'll be talking a lot more about this in the chapters ahead.

In the new paradigm, we will be different. We'll have to be, or we won't be able to get there. This cannot be emphasized enough. We will not be weighed down by all the limitations we learn to place upon ourselves in the higher densities of the old paradigm world. We will be more like the sorcerers of the ancient indigenous world, with powers that can only be described as magical.

We will be different, and our new paradigm world will be different. It will work by an entirely different set of rules. The rules of the old paradigm material world are linear, in which strict cause and effect applies, like billiard balls striking each other on the table, all behaving according to mathematical formulas. Our new world will be more like the world that the quantum physicists discovered at the beginning of the 20th Century. They discovered a world in which everything, in its most basic form, consisted of energy that pulsated at lightning-fast speeds. It was a world in which all the particles/waves of this energy were interconnected, a vast and dynamic spider web of luminosity. It was a world in which none of the customary rules of the 3rd dimensional material world applied. This world did not obey the laws of cause and effect. These particles/waves of energy could even be in two different places at precisely the same time. The quantum physicists were so dazzled and awe-inspired by this world that they agreed, without any scientific proof, that it had to be governed by an unseen intelligence of some kind. It was a world in which anything was possible.

This is how we must think when we think about the world of the new paradigm. This is what it means to see with new paradigm eyes. This also explains not only how we will survive the colossal challenges ahead, but also how we will flourish, and live to create the new world of light and spirit. In order to pull this off, we will have to be different. This is the turf upon which we must confront this great challenge. Or perhaps, I should flip that metaphor into a new paradigm one. These are the energy fields where we must confront this great challenge. If we confront this challenge on the battleground of the old paradigm, we have no chance.

Is this the same as saying we must rely upon the powers of the supernatural, the magical and the apparently miraculous? Yes, it is. But we are fully capable of these things. This is our heritage as spiritual beings. This also happens to be the only way we can pull this off. But this will take total commitment, and lots of hard work. But what better way do we have to spend our time?

The Only Date that Matters is NOW!

When it comes to the dates and the particulars of the shift, I'd like to be more definite about all this, but I don't believe that's possible. In the infinite sea of possibilities, we don't know what's going to happen, or when, or how. Nobody does. I know a lot of people think they do, and say they do. There are lots of folks making lots of predictions, with certain things happening on certain dates, and maps of the geography of the future world, after the Earth changes – those sorts of things. People do seem to have a lurid fascination for these kinds of particulars, particularly if they're catastrophic – like watching train wrecks on TV.

All of the predictions and particulars regarding the shift end up being more of a distraction than anything else, kind of an intellectual game that provides entertainment – particularly since most of the people who pay so much attention to these kind of things never seem to actually do anything about them. It is a distraction from the one thing that really matters most, and that is getting to work on our spirituality. This is the source of our protection, and the source of our power, in the face of these possible Earth changes and paradigm shifts.

We know that the shift has already started. We've already entered this field of shifting energy, and this period of monumental transformation has already begun, Once we know this, none of these dates, predictions and particulars matter anymore. There's no point in waiting for something that's going to happen in the future. The only date that matters is now. And the only thing that matters is us getting to work on aligning our energy, both individually and collectively, with the shifting energy in our world, as opposed to clinging to the destructive energy of a dying world.

The Hopi, again, give us wisdom on how all this works. They believe that the Creator has already destroyed the world three times, with us currently on the brink of the fourth. This is because human beings always fall into the same trap, and make the same mistake. Eventually this harms the Creation, to the point of almost destroying it. The mistake is straying from the spiritual path, as put forward by the Creator, and becoming preoccupied with mastery and dominion over the material world. On each of the three previous occasions, only a tiny minority remained true to the spiritual path, and each time the Creator chose to spare these, and allowed them entry into the next world, along with the opportunity to endeavor to get it right this time. If history repeats itself, I intend to be one of the select few, and I would be honored if you joined me.

The New Paradigm and the Other-Worldly

In the last few pages, we've been covering the Earthly aspect of the shift, as in what we can do here on Earth, and what this will be like. Now, let's take a look at the other-worldly part of this. This is where this gets as huge as it can get.

I refer over and over to the fact that the shift presents us with a tremendously rare and blessed opportunity to create an entirely new world. To be more specific, this new world is a world of pure energy, light and spirit. And this is not a metaphor. It is to be taken literally. This new world is very much like the quantum world that we discussed a moment ago. The quantum world is not a world of matter. It is a world of energy, governed by an unseen intelligence, which exists behind the illusion (or our perception) of the world of matter. In this way, the quantum world beautifully illustrates the two primary forces of which this new world would consist – energy and intelligence or consciousness.

The best model to explain this is the concept of dimensions. This too we are going to be covering in depth in the chapters ahead. For now, let's just say that a dimension is simply another world. Another one of the lies we are conditioned to believe in the old paradigm is that there is only one world – the material world we perceive with our five tangible senses. However, in the cosmos as whole, there are an infinite number of other dimensions or worlds. The quantum world is another such dimension.

The old paradigm, material world is most commonly referred to as the 3rd dimension. In most of the material I've looked at, the new paradigm, or this new world of light and spirit, is understood to be the 5th dimension. There are those who believe it is the 4th. There are others who believe we recently reached the 4th, which explains what we've been feeling for the last several years, and why things have gone so haywire. But it really doesn't make any difference. A higher dimension is a higher dimension, and all the same principles apply. For our purposes here, we will refer to the new paradigm world of light and spirit as the 5th dimension.

We know that everything in the universe, including matter, consists of energy. The primary difference between dimensions is the frequency at which its energy vibrates. As we rise in dimension, we also rise in frequency. The frequency of the energy in the 3rd dimension is very low, so low that it actually coagulates into the forms of matter that this world consists of. This is indeed a very heavy and dense world. As energy rises in frequency, it moves beyond physical form and into realms where it takes energetic forms. The 5th dimension, then, is a world of higher frequency energy, which is beyond physical form.

As human beings, we too are energy. As such, we have the capability to move to higher dimensions. Like all other energy, we do this by raising the frequency of our vibration. This may sound very profound or esoteric to many of you, but when you break it down to its basics, it's really quite simple, at least as far as the concepts. The actual doing of it is another matter.

This is also something about which every spiritual tradition on Earth, at least the viable ones, past and present, have agreed. As energetic beings, we raise our frequency by learning to experience our lives with certain feelings. Specifically, these feelings are feelings of relaxation, joy, reverence, gratitude and trust. As spiritual beings, it is our job to endeavor to live as much of our life as possible with these feelings. For the vast majority of us, this takes considerable commitment and work because in the old paradigm we have been conditioned since our earliest days to experience life with feelings that are the antithesis of these.

When we learn to live our lives in this state of being, we are connected with the divine spirit of a living universe with the power of the vibration of our energy. This is the frequency of creation. Needless to say, when we do this, we change, and our world changes. We acquire many new powers, one of which is the power to experience other worlds or dimensions. This is similar to the journeying or dream journeying, referred to earlier, in which we actually visit other worlds, or are visited by them. This spiritually transcendent state of being, or the ability to move to higher dimensions by raising our frequency, is known as ascension.

One of my favorite ways of illustrating the process of ascension is from the Mexican Indian sorcerer, don Juan, from the books by Carlos Castaneda, which, despite all the controversy surrounding them, continues to be a major influence on me and my metaphysics. I don't care if don Juan was real or fictional. All I care about is his teachings touched my spirit like none other. For me, that's all that matters.

One of the hallmark characteristics of don Juan and the sorcerers of his lineage, which he referred to as the sorcerers of ancient Mexico, was the ability to *see*. *Seeing* meant that in altered states of consciousness, these sorcerers were able to *see* the world of energy directly as it flowed in the universe. In addition, they were also able to enter this world, and act in it. This was the source of their stupendous and supernatural feats, such as flying and moving through physical matter, which could only be described as magical. They were able to do this by what don Juan referred to as acquiescence, which is the same as ascension. Acquiescence basically meant they were able to merge or blend with the energy of this world by harmonizing the frequency of their own energy with it.

This too is the purpose of our spiritual ceremonies, in which we intend to connect with the divine spirit, or the spirit world, both individually and collectively, by raising the frequency of our vibration. This can be facilitated in many ways, such as reaching trance states through drumming, chanting and dancing, such as purification, as in sweat lodges or fasting, or such as the use of medicine plants. At their most adept, sorcerers are able to reach these altered states the good old fashioned way, by intending them. It was the goal of every sorcerer to be able to do this volitionally, with the simple act of their will.

Ascending from 3rd Dimension to 5th

What does all this have to do with *2012 and the shift,* and the other-worldly aspect of this, you might ask? All of the ancient indigenous prophesies were telling us one major thing. And this is another thing about which they all agreed. We also hear this from other sources as well, which we will go into in the pages ahead. This is the hugest and juiciest part of this whole thing.

We are hearing from all these sources that the true meaning of the shift is not the collapse of the old paradigm world, nor is it the opportunity to build a new world here on Earth. They are all telling us that the shift is a once in every 26,000 year opportunity for our entire world, and all of its people, to ascend from the 3rd dimension, which is dying anyway, to the 5th dimension.

Once again, the reason for this is all about energy. The Earth and our entire solar system take a cyclical journey through the universe, which lasts 26,000 years. Located at an area on this cycle, there is a vast cosmic energy field, called the Photon Belt. This is the field that the Earth has entered, which is responsible for the shifting of its vital energy fields. The energy of the Photon Belt is of a significantly higher frequency. This is one of the many things we are feeling on Earth at the current time. We have no way to measure these things at this time, but it appears as though we are still moving into the heart of this field, and as we do so, the frequency of this energy will continue to rise.

The energy of the Photon Belt, as well as the higher frequency energy of the 5th dimension, is a different kind of energy, unknown to established, old paradigm science. We referred to it a few pages ago when we discussed the energy that advanced forms of space travel would use. Alternative and new paradigm sciences often refer to it as "new" energy. New energy is far vaster than the energy of the visible electromagnetic spectrum, such as the electricity that runs through the wires of our electrical devices, or the light from the Sun that lights up our world.

This new energy is holographic. This means that in addition to energy, it also includes the other fundamental force of everything in the universe, and that is intelligence or consciousness. Remember – everything in our spiritual model of the universe is alive, and this conceptualization of energy takes this into account. Mystics, sorcerers and ancient healing traditions from everywhere on the planet have been telling us about holographic energy for a long time. Ancient Chinese healing refers to it as Chi, and eastern traditions call it Prana. Wilhelm Reich, a visionary energy healer from the US in the 1940s and '50s, called it Orgone. Holographic energy is energy that exists everywhere in the universe, including in apparently empty space. And it is vital that human beings learn how to tap into this energy, both for practical and spiritual reasons. This energy appears to be infinitely renewable. This is the kind of energy our technology in the new paradigm would utilize.

As individuals, we all have the capability to ascend to the 5th dimension, regardless of what age we live in. Many of us actually do this quite frequently, but we must come back, because it's not our time yet. As we already know, this does require that we do the necessary spiritual work, which is quite a task for most of us. What's so different about this age of ours is the fact that the process of this ascension is far easier. We are already closer to other dimensions simply by being in the higher frequency energy of the Photon Belt. Entering the Photon Belt is the equivalent of entering a space in the universe, where a doorway or portal is opening to higher dimensions. As we continue to move into this field, and as the frequency continues to rise, this portal is opening wider and wider. This is what is meant by the veils thinning between the worlds. And they are.

What's so extraordinary about this age of ours is the fact that our entire world, including our entire solar system, shares this incredibly rare opportunity to ascend to this higher dimension. When the prophesies and the ancient wisdom talk about this being an age when one world must die, so that a new world may be born, this is the new world they're talking about. It is not a continuation of life here on Earth, only in a slightly different form, as so many think. It is the creation of an entirely new world – a new world of light and spirit. The 5th dimension, simply put, is not of this world. And it is within our grasp to make this happen.

This is another major difference between the message you're going to be hearing here and so many of the others. It is something that many of the so-called experts either don't understand, or that they water down on purpose because they don't want people to know the truth. And yes, there is a very important reason why some of them do this, which we'll go into later. Be patient. There's a lot to cover here.

The shift presents us with this monumentally huge opportunity to create this new world. This is nothing short of the next step in our spiritual destiny. It also appears as though this is a step that the people/beings of Planet Earth have faced before, more than once quite possibly, and failed. The 3rd dimensional world is dense and heavy, and the temptations of matter usually prove to be too much for humans/beings to resist. When we are in the 3rd dimension, there is a strong tendency to forget our heritage as spiritual beings, and why we are here. The shift presents us with this wondrously blessed opportunity to "get out," and to move our spiritual residence to a world of pure light. It is an opportunity to transcend this world of limitation, and move our spirit essence to a world where there are no boundaries. This too is the objective of every viable spiritual tradition on Earth, past and present, indigenous and non-indigenous, alike – is it not? - To connect with the spirit, and to be transported to that world.

Transmutation from Caterpillar into Butterfly

We already made the point that this is not only an opportunity for us as individuals, but also for us as a collective, as well as our entire world, including our entire solar system, to ascend to a higher dimension. This is a hard one to grasp for many people primarily because, again, they are stuck in looking at it through old paradigm eyes. A common question I get is, "What's going to happen to the Earth? Does it just go away, or what?" We must remember, as indigenous people know so clearly, that the Earth is a living, breathing organism, with a soul, as are all of her creatures. In our model of a divinely ordered universe, everything is alive. Everything is alive with energy, intelligence and spirit. This is also true for the Sun, the Moon, all the other planets, and every other particle, or wave, of our solar system, and any other beings or entities not known to us, yet.

We are all traveling through this shifting energy field together. We are all experiencing the same higher frequency energy, and we all share this energetic and spiritual opportunity. Like sorcerers and shamans, when we move to the 5th dimension, we don't do this with our physical bodies. Our physical bodies are not invited to this party. We move to the 5th dimension with our energy and spirit bodies, and with our consciousness. We'll be covering all the details of this in Chapter 6.

The same applies for every other particle/wave of our solar system. The energy, consciousness and spirit of Grandmother Earth, and all of her creatures, will join us in our ascension to the 5th dimension, along with that of the Sun, the Moon and the other planets. All of the beings and entities in our solar system are experiencing this same opportunity to transform from an aspect of themselves that is old and dying to one that is being reborn. Like with Winter Solstice, this is the true essence of the shift.

This 5th dimensional world is not limited to humans, nor is it limited in terms of location, as in the Earth or this solar system. As I understand it, it is open to anything in the universe that vibrates at the proper 5th dimensional energy. It is a true intergalactic sisterhood and brotherhood. As far as location, it is true that we currently have an advantage over our sisters and brothers from other places in the universe, due to our position in relation to the Photon Belt, just as some of them will when their time comes to move into this field. Here we have yet another thing that makes this age of ours so remarkable.

Our sustainable communities, then, would be bases where we could survive, and begin to build a new world here on Earth. But, far more importantly, they would also be bases where we could participate in our spiritual ceremonies, and work to develop our spirituality to its highest. This way we would be ready to make our ascension to the 5th dimensional world when the time and the energy are right. So, in its truest sense, the shift is not about this world. It's about moving, or ascending, to the next.

The essence of the shift is transformation, but it is really more accurate to call it a transmutation – a change from one thing into another – a metamorphosis from caterpillar to butterfly. We've already discussed our ascension process as human beings, and we'll go a lot more deeply into this later. All the same principles of this transmutation apply for Grandmother Earth and everything else in our solar system. It is both a cleansing and a purification through fire. In order to become ascendant beings, we must cleanse ourselves of the poison of our old paradigm conditioning, and we must recreate ourselves in harmony with higher frequency energy and consciousness. Like a phoenix, we must be reborn not only from the ashes of the old paradigm world, but of our old paradigm selves. In order to become ascendant beings, we must first die.

This is one of the best ways to understand the Earth changes that are prophesized for this age of ours, which have already begun. Like us, Grandmother Earth is in need of a cleansing. She has been terribly abused for a very long time now – 6000 years by our civilization, and far longer when you consider prior civilizations, of extraterrestrial origin, which abused her too. Grandmother Earth is a world out of balance, and the only way to regain it is to transmute into something else. We can see and feel this in global warming, the full impact of which is not yet upon us. We can see and feel this in radically changing weather patterns, everywhere on the planet, and in extremes of weather, of all possible kinds, the magnitude of which we haven't seen in a long time. We can see and feel it in dramatically increasing earthquake and volcano activity, again everywhere, triggering tsunamis, which are of a magnitude, again, not seen in a long time. I recently returned from Guatemala, a land of active volcanoes, and I could hear Grandmother Earth rumbling.

Grandmother Earth is feeling it. The fires of purification are burning deep within her belly. The time for her cleansing has come. Perhaps the time has come for her to reverse the polarity of her electromagnetic fields, totally changing her face, and that of the life on it. Perhaps it is time for her to get back in balance by correcting the tilt of her axis. Or, maybe she'd feel better if she changed the direction of her rotation.

It is definitely time for her to fight back. Like all of the universe's organisms, it is time for her self-healing systems to kick in, and for her to purify herself of the toxins and pests that have disturbed her sacred balance. And we all know what this means. If the human race doesn't get its act together, quickly, we could be part of this detox process. And she is fully capable of it. She's done it before.

It Always Comes Back to Us

No matter how you cut it, it always comes back to us. And by us I am referring to you and me, as individuals. And this is another one of those things that makes this so monumentally huge. But this is where it starts – always. People often ask me, "What should we do?" After talking a little bit, it's clear that what they mean by this is, "Where can we go where it's safe? And how can we protect ourselves from all the ravages that are about to come?" My answer is always the same: "Get yourself together spiritually." Most people seem to get that. Most of us know, in the deepest parts of ourselves, that when we get our act together spiritually, we never have anything to fear – ever!

It always comes back to us, and it always will. It's all about us, as individuals, getting ourselves together spiritually, and embarking upon our own ascension process. It's not about politics, or structures, or systems, or society, or any other old paradigm concept. It's all about us, as individuals, raising the frequency of our energy, taking complete responsibility for our lives, and harmonizing it with the energy of the new paradigm world. When enough of us do this, the world will change, regardless of the scenario – Earthly or other-worldly.

I don't know about you, but for me, and many others like me, this is a tremendous relief. Knowing this, and fully embracing it as true, lifts such a tremendous weight from us – at least it should. It's in our hands – nobody else's. If we don't trust that, we need to learn to. Our old paradigm methods and systems have been hopelessly corrupted and contaminated by the forces of *the dark side*. We can't trust them with something like this. We'll go into all this in Chapter Five. It is an indispensable part of this story. This is why creating a new world seems so totally impossible to most people. But we don't need to rely upon these old paradigm methods and systems. They are all part of a dying world anyway. They have no usefulness.

So, what can I do to play my part in the shift, and create the new world of light and spirit, you might ask? The answer is simple. Look in the mirror. Get to work on yourself spiritually. Become a spiritual warrior in this great cause. If you do, and if you are sincere, and if you make a genuine effort, the rest will flow all by itself. Creating the new paradigm has nothing to do with old paradigm methods or systems. It has to do with energy. And when we reach a certain level of energy with our spirituality, which is known as *critical mass*, the rest will take care of itself. We will also be covering *critical mass* in detail in the pages ahead. Changing the world begins within the heart and spirit of each and every one of us.

And the real beauty here is this is precisely what we all need to be doing anyway. Even if most of what I'm saying here is absolute rubbish, there are certain truths here that are irrefutable, and eternal. They can be found in every viable spiritual tradition on Earth, past and present. Everything important we manifest in this world springs from our connection with spirit. The old paradigm world is collapsing because it has lost its connection with spirit. If we too have fallen into this trap, then the only way we can get our life back on track is by reestablishing this connection. This means placing our spirituality where it belongs – first. This also means making the ongoing commitment to working at this each and every moment of our lives. Nobody said it would be easy, at least nobody you'd want to listen to. Not only will this allow you to get your life back on track, but you will also be playing your part in creating the new world. What could be better than this? And this is only scratching the surface of the other amazing things that will flow from this.

We Can Only Help Those Who are Willing to Help Themselves

There is one other question and concern about all this that always comes up that we need to address. It goes something like this. What about all the human pain, suffering and death that will come with the shift? If these things occur, the collapse of the old paradigm, or any of the colossal Earth changes that are predicted, the vast majority of humanity will have a difficult time surviving. What can we do about this? More specifically, what are you, with your three months supply of food and water, or you in your sustainable community in the mountains, or you in the 5th dimension, going to do about this?

I agree – the way things are going right now there is a high probability of chaos, misfortune and death. What am I going to do? The quick and snappy answer is I'm going to do what I'm doing right now. This means expending every bit of my energy on a few things. The first is the process of my own spiritual ascension. If you're not tired of hearing me say that yet, you probably will be soon. This is where it starts for all of us. Second, I will continue writing books, creating DVD's, and traveling the country giving talks and workshops on this, in an effort to reach as many people as I can, and do as much as I reasonably can to prevent these catastrophic scenarios from coming about. They don't necessarily have to. That's not etched in stone either – nothing is. I want all of this to go as smoothly as possible too, you know.

So much of this, again, depends upon us. If humanity wakes up to the truth about all this, and takes the proper steps to prepare, both practically and spiritually, then anything is possible. That's what I am working for. And if we were to make significant strides in this direction, then we begin to enter the sphere where *critical mass* kicks in, and miracles are possible. If we are to survive this time, and create the new world, it does appear as though we are going to have to call upon the highest of our higher powers.

And thirdly, I will follow my own personal guidance, as always, as far as when the time has come to head for the hills. I will not expend one ounce of my precious energy trying to save the old paradigm. It must go. There is also nothing I can do to help those people who choose to cling to it. Expending my energy on either of these could only end in one thing – failure and destruction for all involved, including me. I may go down, but it will not be on the sinking ship of the old paradigm. I have too much to do in playing my part in building the new paradigm. The only hope for those who are clinging is to let go, and I have made the choice to endeavor to help them with that. Yes, this is one of those tragic instances where we can only help those who choose to help themselves.

It is not possible to straddle these two worlds, with one foot in each. They are mutually exclusive. We must choose one or the other. And as energy fields and paradigms continue to shift, and as Grandmother Earth continues her purification, the time will come for all of us, in the not so distant future, when we will be forced to make this choice. We will forced to choose which world is ours – old paradigm or new. And with every shred of my energy, and with love in my heart, I invite all of you who are still clinging to the old paradigm to let go, and join us in our flight into the new.

Chapter Two

What is the Shift? Short Version

> *The source of our protection*
> *The source of our power*
> *Connecting with the divine spirit*

The Only Thing We Need to Know

We are currently in the midst of the shift or *the great shift of the ages*. Regardless of when you're reading this, this is what's happening. I am not going to waste one second of your precious time here, or mine. Let's get right to the point by sharing a mantra, which encapsulates everything we need to know about what we can do in these times of monumental transformation. If you remember nothing else that you read in these pages, remember this:

> *The primary source of our protection in these times of monumental Earth changes and paradigm shifts, and the primary source of our power to create the new world of light and spirit, is our higher consciousness and spirituality.*

On the topic of *2012 and the shift*, this is really all people need to hear. With a topic this vast, and potentially complex, it is vitally important to keep things as simple and uncomplicated as possible. This is the essence of all true spirituality anyway – simplicity – so simple that little children understand it without even trying. It is also the essence of virtually all the ancient prophesies, from indigenous cultures spanning the globe, dating back tens of thousands of years, and sometimes far longer. This includes the Maya, the Inca, the Kogi, numerous other tribes in South America and Africa, and the Hopi, and virtually every other Native American tribe.

These are sources that are far more trustworthy than mainstream, civilized sources because they have retained their connection with the one true source of higher consciousness and spiritual knowledge, and that is their intimate relationship and love affair with the natural world. The old paradigm is unsustainable, and is collapsing, as it must, because this is precisely the connection the Western, civilized world has lost. It has lost the connection with life's vital energy, and with the rhythm and flow of life, and fallen into the fatal trap of placing its primary emphasis on the material world, at the expense of the spiritual.

These ancient indigenous cultures, at least the ones that weren't contaminated or destroyed totally by Western Civilization, never lost their intimate connection with the natural world. Their keen observations of natural cycles allowed them to become expert astronomers, scientists and cosmologists, as well as sorcerers and magicians, who were capable of stupendous feats that apparently violated the rules of ordinary, linear, cause and effect reality.

The Message of the Prophesies – All of Them

And as far as the shift is concerned, and this extraordinary time we are now living in, these prophesies all had the same basic message for us. Here it is, in my words.

> *This is a time of colossal Earth changes and paradigm shifts. It is the completion of a 26,000 year inter-galactic cycle, in which the old world, one of materiality and the attempt to control the forces of nature, will collapse, and there will be an opportunity to create an entirely new world, one that is governed by the spirit. Winter Solstice 2012 is a key date in virtually all of these prophesies. This also is the date the Mayan Calendar ended. However, beware of placing excessive importance on this, or any other, specific date, as most of the prophesies point to this time in general, and portray the shift as more of a gradual process, taking place in a window of time around 12/21/12, as opposed to one dramatic point. We have no definitive way of knowing how large this window of time is, but at the time I am writing this (February 2009), it is clearly obvious that the shift has already started. The shift is happening, and it's happening NOW!*

> *However, the shift is not going to just happen by itself. It's up to the human beings of the planet Earth to make it happen. And there's only one way to do this, and that is with the power of our higher consciousness and spirituality. This process of potential transformation is one of ascension – ascension from heavy to light - from higher density to lower density – from lower frequency to higher frequency. And these Earth changes and these paradigm shifts will be a monumental challenge for us, the inhabitants of the planet. This has happened before, and these changes were colossal in nature, and probably will be again. These Earth changes include the possibility of the reversal of the Earth's magnetic poles and its rotation, several days of total darkness (or light), great floods, intense winds, greatly increased earthquake and volcano activity, and the disappearance of land masses and emergence of others – the equivalent of a massive face lift or cleansing. Please take special note of the use of the term "possibility" in relationship to these Earth changes, as none of this*

> is etched in stone. We are clearly in uncharted territory here.
>
> The prophesies also agree that those human beings who are not prepared, and who don't have their act together energetically and spiritually, could be in for a very rough ride, possibly ending in the extinction of the entire species. But again, it's up to us. The fate of the planet rests in our hands, and it is clear what we are called upon to do.

To call this story the most important of our time in a silly understatement. And simplicity here, again, is so vitally important because few topics have been as needlessly complicated and confused as the shift, invariably resulting in stimulating fear of hysterical levels, and catastrophic visions of doomsday scenarios, which was not the intent of the prophecies. As glorious as the Internet revolution has been in giving masses of people exposure to this vast frontier of unfiltered information, it also has its flipside. Sometimes too much can be too much, when any zealot or nut case has equal access to this medium, and can use it to get their message out there.

The same principle applies for what are known as disinformants. As we will discuss in Chapter Five, there are those among us, usually in positions of power, whose true agenda is not the spiritual fulfillment and liberation of the human race, but rather its suppression and enslavement. I will be referring to them as *the dark side*. The Internet is a perfect medium for *the dark side* to disseminate false information (disinformation, propaganda, brainwashing), the purpose of which is to confuse the issues, and knock people off the track of truth, with the objective of enhancing their power over them. Not everybody is who they say they are, and disinformants are rampant throughout our world, and sadly, this is painfully true in such ostensibly benevolent movements as the *New Age* and the greens.

All of which means it is incumbent on each of us to be aware of this, to filter through this vast sea of information with due diligence, and to decide what is right and wrong for us. Things are never as complicated, or terrifying, as they are usually made out to be. A good standard rule is: if it's too complicated, or if it doesn't feel good, look somewhere else.

How Do We Create this Vibration?

> Connecting with the divine spirit of a living universe with our vibration - this is the primary source of our protection and our power.

It sounds nice and sweet and simple to me, but perhaps to some, this might sound vague or esoteric. And it really isn't.

We are not just our physical bodies. We are our totality – body, mind and spirit. As the Mexican Indian sorcerer, don Juan, from the writings of Carlos Castaneda, says: we are luminous beings. In altered states of consciousness, the sorcerers of don Juan's lineage saw humans as egg-shaped clusters of luminous fibers, which had awareness, and which were connected to all the energy surrounding them in the entire universe, like a gigantic spider web of luminosity. This energetic view of the world was confirmed by quantum science, which discovered a world, where everything, in its essence, was interconnected energy, which was governed by an unseen intelligence of some kind. This, of course, is the essence of true spirituality.

Like all energy, we have a vibration, a frequency. And there is a direct relationship between our energetic vibration and our emotions and thoughts. Emotions and thoughts are, actually, energy flowing along the pathways of our physical body, and beyond. And there is unanimous agreement among every spiritual tradition worth its salt, from everywhere on the planet, past and present, that human beings are at their spiritual peak when they experience life with certain feelings and thoughts. Specifically, these feelings are feelings of relaxation, joy, reverence, gratitude and trust. And these thoughts are reflections of these feelings, springing from a mind that is quiet and still, and that sees the brilliance of the world.

When we experience life in this peak spiritual state, this puts us in alignment or resonance with the divine spirit of a living universe, the source of all creation. This is what it means to be in the rhythm and flow of life, and in harmony with the forces of the natural world, which is the same as being in resonance with divine law. This is when our spiritual power is at its maximum. And this vibrational connection is the one true source of manifesting what we want in life. Everything, ultimately, springs from our connection with spirit.

In order to create the new world, it is necessary for us to make this energetic and spiritual connection both as individuals, and in mass, which is referred to as *critical mass*. *Critical mass* is the energetic point, at which a sufficient number of human beings have retained this connection, where amazing and unprecedented things will start to happen. Like *the 100th monkey*, once enough of us reconnect with our spiritual power, we become a force that cannot be stopped, and we won't need crumbling political, economic, religious and social structures to help. No thank you – we can handle it on our own. As David Rhodes, one of the heroes of my novel, *Infinity's Flower*, says: "If we are in tune with the Earth, and if we are in tune with the divine spirit, then the Earth and the divine spirit will shower us with unimaginable blessings." This is the source of our protection and power in the face of this challenge, or any other, and that's all we need.

Chapter Three

What is the Shift? Full Version

> *The astrology of the shift*
> *The science of the shift*
> *How do we know these things?*

Guidance to a New Message

I lied.

In Chapter One, we talked about how the only way I could capture the essence of these rapidly shifting times, and my rapidly shifting self, was to write the last chapter, and place it first. Of course, I was assuming that the rest of the book would be pretty much OK the way it was. Well, good luck with that.

The purpose of this chapter was to provide all the particulars about the shift, from as many different perspectives as possible, and filling in any details we haven't covered yet. We are still going to do this, but once again, it's necessary to make a few comments about other changes that have occurred since this chapter was first written. This book keeps morphing into something different than what was originally intended – another display of the shift in action.

During my final edit, it only took a glance to see that I was going to have to rewrite much of this chapter too. The content was fine. But there was something odd about the way it all fit together. And the tone wasn't right. As I read, it felt like I was trying too hard. It felt too heavy, rather than just letting the message flow.

By tone here, I mean this quite literally. It is now February 25, 2010. I was recently guided to the awareness that it was time for this message to move away from words and intellectual concepts, and move more into the realm of pure vibration. And I mean this too quite literally. By vibration here, I am referring to the vibration that connects us with the divine spirit. As we've already mentioned, and certainly will again, we create this vibration by experiencing life with feelings of relaxation, joy, reverence, gratitude and trust. One of our most effective methods to create this vibration is our use of ceremony.

This fits perfectly with the message of the shift. This message has a natural progression, which begins with our thoughts in our minds, and progresses to our spirit, our soul. First, we must learn what we're dealing with here, and gain an understanding of this grand cycle, with all the forces and possibilities that are involved, and most importantly, the part that we play in making this happen. Once we gain this perspective, it becomes clear, if we understand it properly, that we're helpless to do anything about any of this, without calling upon the higher powers of our higher consciousness and spirituality. This was the primary message of all the indigenous prophesies. So, this message is primarily one of taking spiritual action.

This is also a perfect fit for me because this is one of the dramatic new things I have recently learned. It's been seven months now since my first five-day ceremony with Mayan Elder Erick Gonzalez and Earth Peoples United at Deer Mountain in California. That was a major breakthrough for me. The Mayan ceremonies that Erick led resonated perfectly with my spirit, and I could clearly see how essential they were in connecting us with spirit. Since then, ceremony has become a centerpiece of my lifestyle.

What do I mean by ceremony, you might ask? A ceremony is anything we do with the purpose of focusing our intent upon spirit.

Since I don't have a tribe where I live in Wisconsin, I do most of my ceremonies by myself, and I make most of them up myself. What I do comes directly from my heart and spirit, and from my relationship with the forces in the world around me. But this doesn't make any difference anyway. All ceremony is the same. It's all about the vibration. I am able to resonate perfectly with the Mayan ceremonies, even though I understand none of the words, and little of the symbolism. And yet, I have no problem shaking my sacred shakers, humming and chanting along, dancing, and looking into the fire – and feeling the joy, reverence and gratitude – and the connection with spirit.

I learned about my new message quite naturally as function of the flow of my life. After a hiatus of eleven months, I was scheduled to hit the road again in a few weeks with expos, conferences, presentations and book signings, for the purpose of promoting my new book and DVD. Well, as you can see, I obviously missed the deadline, but no matter. I no longer have a set script for the talks I give. This message is so imbedded into my soul that I no longer need one. But it did begin to occur to me that I probably needed to start thinking about what I was going to talk about. As you know, this message has transmuted quite significantly in these eleven months.

So, I put this out to the spirit world for guidance, as I always do. Then, one morning, during my sunrise pipe ceremony, it came to me. It came from my primary spirit guide – The Council of the Grandfathers. This is a spirit entity that introduced itself, and welcomed me as one of them, last August at Deer Mountain. You see how fast things are changing. They have been guiding me ever since. They only talk to me in words infrequently, but this kind of communication doesn't really seem to be necessary. The guidance is still very clear. I can feel it in my body, and I can sense it in the forces in the world around me.

On that morning, as I was praying, and singing to the heavens, while shaking my shakers, I was feeling the presence of the Grandfathers very powerfully. It feels like an energy possessing me, like a beam passing through my body. And then, the words popped into my head, the way they always do when the Grandfathers speak to me, so simple and so pure. "This is your new message."

I understood perfectly what this meant, even though it was not necessarily what I wanted to hear. I have always thought of myself as a writer, not a musician, and certainly not a priest or a spiritual elder. Words have always been one of the primary ways I reached out to people, and connected with them. Obviously, I was being guided to rethink all that.

Here too was yet another leap into the unknown, and trust me, I've been challenged with many of these in my life, particularly in the last few years. I have also been on the spiritual path long enough to know that when our guidance says leap, we must leap. The more we leap the better it is. This means we are doing our spiritual work. As we travel the spiritual path, life becomes a continuous leap into the unknown. Such is the nature of life when we relinquish our control to the divine spirit. We also learn not to fear these leaps, but to celebrate them. As long as we are connected with spirit, spirit will protect and guide us with everything we need in this or any other world.

So, I am being guided to talk less about this opportunity to shift to the new world, and to do more to show, with ceremony, how to create the proper vibration to do this. Once again, this is totally consistent with this message and with the prophesies. This message is about taking spiritual action. And people really need to be hammered with this. This is serious business. This isn't idle banter or some kind of head game for entertainment purposes.

In addition to ceremony, I can also teach people about this vibration, and how to create it, by using the example of my personal experience, and those others in my circle, or this circle, who understand the true meaning of these times, and who are doing the necessary spiritual work. This is yet another reason why this new message is such a perfect fit for me. This is also why I've shifted gears in mid-stream here, and started disclosing more about my personal life. This is because I am living this message. I am its embodiment. I hope that doesn't sound pompous. It's simply a statement of fact. All of the things I am writing about are happening in my life. Plus, I can see all of the amazing things that are happening in the lives of so many of my sisters and brothers in this great cause. What better way to illustrate the true meaning of the shift than by showing it in action in the lives of real people. These things are happening, and here's what they look like. The most effective way any teacher can ever teach is with the example they set. If they don't embody their message, then there is no message.

This new message is a good fit for one more reason. The more I learn about the shift, and the more intimate I become with its message, mostly from the prophesies, the simpler all this becomes. There really isn't a lot to say. I know you've heard me say this again and again, but the list of things people really need to know about the shift keeps getting shorter and shorter. I answer these questions all the time. I used to agonize over what I perceived to be the complexity of this topic. Now I can sum up everything people need to hear about the shift in a few sentences. And nothing is left out.

The question goes something like this: "So, what's going to happen in 2012?" Here's the answer:

The shift is not about 2012. It's about now. It refers to these times, not a specific date. All of the indigenous prophesies agreed on this, including the Maya. And this is a source we can trust because these were people who didn't lose their connection to the original wisdom and their connection to the divine spirit. This is the time on the grand 26,000 year cycle, where one world will come to an end, and there will be an opportunity to create an entirely new one. Throughout these cycles, humans continue to make the same mistake. They allow themselves to become enticed by the temptations of the material world, and they lose their connection with spirit. This is why this world cannot possibly sustain itself. There's only one way to correct this imbalance, and that's regain this connection with spirit. These times provide the opportunity to do this. If enough humans regain this spiritual connection, then two amazing possibilities will open up to them. One is the opportunity to build a new and sustainable world here on Earth, this time in harmony with Mother Nature. And the other is to transcend the 3rd dimensional material world all together, and create an entirely new world of light and spirit, which is beyond matter. This is what's known as our ascension to the 5th dimension. At this time on the 26,000 year cycle, and in the immediate time to come, our opportunity to do this is exponentially greater than at any other time since the last time we were at this point. The window is open, and it is opening wider by leaps and bounds.

The Astrology of the Shift

So, there it is – the new shift update – everything you really need to know. Please keep this in mind, as we move forward with the original purpose of this chapter – to fill in all of the details about the shift that we haven't covered yet. If all of this starts to seem too complex or overwhelming, just remind yourself that this always comes back to you, and us, getting ourselves together spiritually. Come to think of it, that's always good advice, about anything.

One of the most commonly discussed aspects of the shift is the alignment of the Earth, at this critical time, in relation to our galaxy and the rest of the universe. There are two distinctly different ways to look at this. And as far as I can tell, they don't seem to have that much in common, though they do reach the same conclusion - that we are dealing with a 26,000 year cycle, and that the window of time around Winter Solstice 2012 is the turn-over point in this cycle. One is from the perspective of astrology. Astrology is what we see with our human eyes from our perspective here on Earth, as we look at the movements of the Sun, the Moon, the planets, the stars and the constellations in the visible sky above us, and track these movements over time.

The other is from the perspective we discussed earlier when we talked about the Earth entering the Photon Belt, a vast cosmic energy field, as a function of the cyclical 26,000 year journey our solar system takes as it travels through the universe. As far as I can tell, based upon all my sources to date, this perspective is far more esoteric and, for lack of a better word, mysterious. You might say it's less Earthy. It's more like a great cosmic eye in the sky, which sees the bigger picture of things from the perspective of outer space, and even from other worlds.

This doesn't make it any less credible. As we've already pointed out, our old paradigm methods of thinking have lost touch with reality because they have factored out consciousness and spirit. So, in order to find the truth, it's necessary for us to stretch the parameters of our thinking, and search in new and unexplored realms.

Much of what we know about the Photon Belt, such as the holographic nature of this energy field, is totally outside the scope of old paradigm science. Plus, many of our sources here are not of this world, coming as they do from various entities in the spirit world, and channeled through human mediums.

Let's begin with the astrological alignments of the shift. This clearly is the perspective that is referenced most often in the literature. After all, astrology is very popular, reaching as it does even mainstream audiences. Very many people in our world speak the language of astrology, and see the world through these eyes.

I must start by saying that I am not an expert on astrology. I did study it for several years, about thirty years ago, and I went as far as learning how to do birth charts, and interpret them. So, I'm certain I have more knowledge in this area than the average person, even the average astrology buff. However, I am blessed to have among my friends many astrology experts, most notably Cayelin Castell, Co-Founder of the Shamanic Astrology Mystery School (www.shamanicastrology.com). Much of what's forthcoming is based on discussions I've had with Cayelin, as well as a few of her articles, though it's quite possible she would take issue with some of the spins I give it.

An astrological chart is a picture of the celestial bodies in the sky at any given moment. This picture is a circle, with us, the viewer, in the middle. The circle shows the positions of the Sun, the Moon, the planets, and all the constellations at that moment. When we track this over time, we see the movements and cycles of these celestial bodies, which is the equivalent of a huge cosmic clock.

One of the most significant of these cycles, and most relevant to *2012 and the shift*, is the Precession of the Solstices and Equinoxes. On a chart, the line connecting the winter and summer solstices forms a 90% cross with the line connecting the spring and fall equinoxes. The Precession of the Solstices and Equinoxes is the time it takes for this cross to turn through all the constellations and return to a starting point. This is known as *The Great Wheel of Time*. And this cycle is approximately 26,000 years. The reason for the Precession is the tilt of the Earth's axis at 23½ degrees. This is the reason we have seasons, and this is why the celestial bodies we see in the sky are always changing.

But since all points on a circle are the same, what is it that distinguishes this time of ours? Why are these times the end of the old cycle and the beginning of the new? According to Shamanic Astrology, the starting point of our cosmic clock is Galactic Center. Galactic Center is the intersection of the plane of our galaxy, the Milky Way, with the plane of the Ecliptic, which is the path the Sun, the Moon and the planets take as they travel through the sky over time. Since both the Milky Way and the Ecliptic appear as planes or bands, not straight lines, Galactic Center is not a single point, but rather an area roughly the shape of a rectangle.

At the current time, Winter Solstice is aligned with Galactic Center, which means that the sun is rising within this area at the intersection where these two planes form a cross. Just as sunrise is the beginning of each day, sunrise at galactic center is the beginning of our cosmic clock. And yes, it would be remiss if we didn't stop here to note the symbolism of the Sun (son) on the cross.

However, this basic alignment with Galactic Center is in place for several other winter solstices on either side of Winter Solstice 2012. Specifically, the Sun touches this area on the cross for 36 years, from about 1980 until 2016 at Winter Solstice. Once again, from yet another point of view, we have confirmation that the shift, which is this turn-over point on our cycle or clock, is not a single point or date, but rather a window of time in the neighborhood of this date. In this particular case, the window would be 36 years, and 12/21/12 isn't even the midpoint of this window, which is Winter Solstice 1998.

We can look at this slightly differently, and our window gets even bigger. Winter Solstice remains within one degree of this alignment with Galactic Center for approximately 144 years, having entered this range in 1926. As I write, it is 2010, which means we are just past the midpoint of this longer window, which, again, was in 1998. So, this basic alignment has been in place a long time, and we still have quite a ways to go. And certainly the time since 1926 has seen a rate of change in our world that has been constantly accelerating, and accelerating at an exponential rate into the present day.

All of which supports the one thing we really need to know here. This too just happens to be the primary message of the indigenous prophesies. We are in the window of time of the shift, and we are very close to this turn-over point.

All of the rest is speculation, speculation in an infinite sea of possibilities, and speculation that serves no real purpose, other than sensationalism, head games, and, far too often, fear. And it doesn't make any difference anyway. This is why getting hung up on predictions, dates and the particulars of the shift can be such a distraction, and why I harp on this so much. Once we know that we are extremely close to this turn-over point, and once we realize that this means the time has come for us to get ourselves together spiritually, the only time that matters is now, the present moment. From a purely spiritual perspective, this is always the case.

Nobody knows for sure. If there's a big-bang event involved, like an infrastructure collapse or a pole shift, it could happen tomorrow, or next year, or in five years, or ten. And it simply doesn't matter. The only thing we know for certain is that all of these are possibilities. And the only thing that matters is we prepare ourselves – practically and spiritually.

Another thing that matters is we continue to follow our guidance, as always. These are very challenging times that test our spirit. On the one hand, we know we don't have much time. As I write, there is a little over two and half years until Winter Solstice 2012. Even if this date isn't significant, we know we're in the window, and we know we're close. And yet, most of us have not yet built the sustainable communities we will need in the years ahead. In my case, with Tata Erick and Deer Mountain, many of the pieces are in place, but there's a lot of work to do.

So, does this mean we need to hurry up, and push the pace of our efforts? Does this mean I need to sell what's left of my worldly belongings, and move to Deer Mountain immediately, to avoid being too late? No, it does not, and here is where we have another of our paradoxes, which our divinely ordered universe seems to so love to throw our way. Even though time is running out, it's not necessary for us to do anything any differently than we ever do. Just like always, the most important thing we can ever do is to flow with the forces that present themselves to us. We must never rush, ever. We must never push against the flow.

My own personal guidance, the Council of the Grandfathers, has been very clear on this. Be patient, the Grandfather Elders tell me again and again. Wait for your guidance. When the time is right, you will receive it. And when you do, you'll know. Then, and only then, should you take action, whatever that action might be – whether that means going to Deer Mountain, or whether it means doing something else, somewhere else. And always remember – the divine spirit works in mysterious ways. We're dealing with the ways of the new paradigm here, not the old. In the new paradigm, what works according to our reason or logic is not necessarily the path to follow. Our new path will be the path of the spirit and the supernatural.

That's all I'm going to say about the shift from the specific perspective of astrology. That doesn't mean there's not a lot more to say. There is. But that's all the deeper I choose to delve into it. All of my astrologer friends assure me that there are other significant alignments coinciding with Winter Solstice 2012 and with these times in general. But what interests me more than these alignments, many of which I don't understand anyway, is the interpretations and the meanings that the astrologers are giving them. Here there seems to be total agreement with what we know about the shift from all our other sources. Astrology confirms that these are the times, on the 26,000 year wheel, where the old world will come to an end, and there will be an opportunity for a totally new world to be born from its ashes. And astrology confirms that the window of time in the neighborhood of Winter Solstice 2012 is the time when the potential to take advantage of this momentous opportunity will be the greatest.

The Science of the Shift

In addition to astrology, our other perspective of the shift is the cosmic eye in outer space, which sees our entire solar system entering a vast holographic energy field, known as the Photon Belt. I'm not going to say much more about this because we've already covered what we really need to know. Plus, as we already know, there's a lot about this perspective and the Photon Belt that we don't know. This does not have the mathematical precision of astrology. This is new paradigm knowledge that we are in the process of learning, and that we are creating as we move along the path.

One thing we do know for certain is we've already entered the Photon Belt. In this chapter, we will be going over all the reasons why we know this. We don't know when exactly because we know so little about the nature of this field. This kind of energy is so new to us we don't even know how to measure it yet. But we certainly can feel many of its effects. And much of this we can measure, even with our old paradigm science.

So, let's take some time here to cover this aspect of the shift. Let's examine how we know the shift has already started on the basis of what we can conclusively measure with the methodology of old paradigm science. Some of this is glaringly obvious, such as the dramatic Earth changes we've been experiencing in recent years. These are not only increasing in intensity, but they appear to be doing so at an accelerating rate. Grandmother Earth is feeling it, and she is expressing herself with extreme weather, earthquake and volcano activity, and tsunamis, with intensities we haven't seen in a long time, and getting worse.

When we look at the literature on the science of the shift, there are three things that always seem to be referenced. They are the changing of the Earth's electromagnetic field, the changing of the Earth's temperature, and the changing of the Earth's Base Resonant Frequency.

Let's begin with the Earth's electromagnetic field. The intensity of the Earth's electromagnetic field is decreasing, and this is also happening at an accelerating rate. As we examine all the forces of the shift, these rates of change become a recurrent theme. We are not only experiencing dramatic changes, but the rates of these changes are increasing at an accelerating rate. In other words, as we move deeper into the Photon Belt, everything is speeding up fantastically. Robert Ghost Wolf, in his classic book, *Last Cry – Native American Prophesies & Tales of the End-times*, refers to this as *the quickening*.

There is nothing new about the Earth's decreasing electromagnetic field, as this has been happening for about the last 2000 years. What is unique about our age is the fact that the Earth's electromagnetism is becoming very weak, and is heading toward zero. There are those in the scientific community who believe that this *zero point*, as Gregg Braden called it, is the point at which the Earth's north and south electromagnetic poles will shift. Again, as I understand it, this is how electromagnetism works. For any physical mass, the electromagnetic field tends to wiggle around, and at periodic intervals, it shifts polarities. Again, there are many scientists who believe that the current behavior of the Earth's electromagnetism supports the notion that the Earth is due for such a pole shift. I believe this is actually where the term the shift originated.

Ghost Wolf tells us that there is a direct relationship between the Earth's diminishing electromagnetic field and the ascension process, which is a feature of this momentous opportunity to create the new world. He points out that electromagnetism is the fundamental force, or glue, that holds matter together. Since this glue is weakening, matter itself is separating and coming apart. It's becoming more spacious. And this, of course, includes our physical bodies. If the nature of matter is changing, then it follows that all of reality is changing.

Since everything in a divinely ordered universe happens for a reason, there must be a reason for this. In the context of spiritual ascension, the reason there is more space between the particles of matter is to accommodate the influx of light, or energy. Ascension is all about moving from lower to higher frequencies of energy, and from denser to lighter bodies. And that's exactly what we see happening here. And this is exactly the energetic opportunity that exists for all of us in our world today, and which will be enhancing at an enhancing rate.

The temperature of the Earth is also significantly changing as a result of its entry into the Photon Belt. The Earth is unquestionably warming up. There can be no debating this. The only debate is to what extent these rising temperatures are caused by humans burning fossil fuels, and to what extent they are part of a natural cycle. The politicians, media and other puppets of the global elite, those behind-the-scenes powers who own and control the world, would like us to believe that we are responsible for global warming. This will be an important ploy for them, in the critical years ahead, to increase their regulation and control of us, in their march toward one-world fascist government, or the *New World Order*. We'll be covering all the hideous details of this in a later chapter. Unfortunately, this is something we need to be aware of, in order to protect ourselves from it.

However, though human beings may be responsible for a fraction of global warming, the vast bulk of it is due to other forces. Global warming is part of a natural cycle, and this cycle is the same 26,000 year cycle that we've been talking about. And we know this for an absolute certainty. This is because the Earth is not the only place warming up. The Sun is warming up. All the other planets are warming up, as is our entire solar system. Certainly humans aren't polluting the entire solar system. The reason for this is the same thing we've been talking about – our position on the 26,000 year cycle, where we are in the higher frequency energy field of the Photon Belt.

The Base Resonant Frequency (or Schuman Cavity Resonance) of the Earth is another commonly cited scientific principle, showing that the Earth's vital energy fields are shifting. Here again, I must emphasize that I'm no scientist, at least not in the traditional sense, and I admit that I have struggled with my understanding of this one. There is significant disagreement about what I'm about to say, and, as I see it, a good deal of the confusion stems from the radically different views of the world that are held by old and new paradigm science. After all, old science sees the universe as basically consisting of particles or stuff that are impersonal, and which are governed by fixed scientific laws. And new science sees the universe as a vast energy field, which is alive, and which is far more mysterious and unpredictable, due to the inclusion of the variables of consciousness and spirit.

Base Resonant Frequency is a concept that has its roots in old paradigm science. It is basically the average measurement of the frequency of the charge of electromagnetic energy that exists in the area between the Earth's surface and the outer edge of the Earth's atmosphere, known as the ionosphere. Since its discovery in the 1950s, this frequency has been relatively constant, at around 7.8 Hertz. In recent years, many scientists, most notably Gregg Braden, have observed that the Base Resonant Frequency has been increasing significantly, to levels at high as 11, with some projections that it could go as high as 13 by the year 2012. However, things are quite murky on this point, as there are many other scientists who question these findings, and many others who deny them completely. There is also the implication in this debate that the old paradigm scientists have a vested interest in covering up what's really happening.

Here again too, we have such a vivid illustration of the differences between old and new science, particularly as concerns the effects of this kind of a phenomenon. Old science sees this charge as existing solely in between the Earth's crust and the ionosphere. And that's the end of it. New science sees the changes in this frequency as much more far reaching, as it affects all the other energy in this field, including all the biological systems of planet Earth, including us. Certainly, it makes logical sense that since the Earth has entered the Photon Belt, then not only would the Base Resonant Frequency of the atmosphere increase, but so would the frequency of this entire living system.

Ghost Wolf, again, helps to make sense of this with his concept of *the quickening*. When he discusses the affects of the Photon Belt upon the living system of the Earth, he suggests we think in terms of the Earth's metabolic rate. With her entry into the Photon Belt, the metabolism of the Earth and all her living creatures is increasing in proportion to the increasing frequency of the energy of the Photon Belt. If we look at this through the eyes of old paradigm science, which basically sees the Earth as a lump of inanimate matter, then this doesn't make much sense. With our new paradigm eyes, we see the Earth as part of a field of quivering energy, behind the façade of matter. With the increase in its Base Resonant Frequency, this energy is quivering faster, as is ours.

We Can Feel These Things

In addition to science, how else do we know these things? How do we know that the shift has already started? How do we know we've already entered the Photon Belt? When I read about the science of the shift, the first question that pops into my head is that we can feel all these things, can't we? We can feel these things in our bodies. We can feel the diminishing electromagnetic energy. We can feel the increasing Base Resonant Frequency of the matter surrounding us, including our physical bodies.

And the answer is yes, we can. The quantum model is such a simple one, and yet it answers so many of the questions that go unanswered with our old paradigm thinking. We consist of the same basic quantum energy and consciousness as the world surrounding us, as well as the force fields in which we are enveloped. All of this energy and consciousness is interconnected. We are all one field. If one part of it ripples, the whole field feels it. Even the tiniest stone causes the entire lake to ripple.

We are this energy. So yes, we have the capability to feel it when it shifts, as well as the full spectrum of these shifting energies, including the extremely high frequency, holographic energy of the Photon Belt. We are all feeling *the quickening*, on some level or another. There is a huge difference in how we feel it, depending on our own frequency. For those who are tuned into it, it feels sublime, like the smoke from our pipes drifting up and vanishing into the heavens. For those who aren't, it can feel pretty scrambled, like static on a radio, or like things spinning totally out of control. This is one of the primary reasons why there is so much unhappiness and sickness in today's world. Peoples' frequencies are scrambled.

Contrary to traditional wisdom in the old paradigm, our direct experience of our world, both individually and collectively, and the awareness we derive from this, are always a primary source of our knowledge, about anything, ever. Traditional wisdom tells us this is too subjective, and not credible because it lacks proof. But remember - traditional wisdom has factored our consciousness and our spirit out of its formulations because it doesn't trust these things. This is the equivalent of sucking the life and the truth out of this world.

In the new paradigm, where we trust our consciousness and our spirituality, our subjective experience of our world, and yes, how it feels to us, are our most important sources of what we know about this world, or any other. And here again, we have the invaluable lesson of our indigenous sisters and brothers of yesteryear, whose entire systems of knowledge, including the metaphysical, were based upon their direct experience of the natural world, and all of its forces, including the other-worldly, or spiritual. And one more time, this is the connection that Western Civilization has lost, which is primarily responsible for its demise.

This is the essence of the true source of our spiritual knowledge anyway, is it not? We simply know things because we do. We know there is an unseen intelligence at work in life, and in the universe, because we can see it, and feel it. We can see it in the seasons and in the miracle of the cycle of birth, life, death and regeneration. Little children understand these things, without even thinking about it. Once, when doing an interview, I was totally thrown for a loop by the question of what I meant by spirituality. The only way I could think of to answer that was to say you either see it, or you don't. And that's not too far from the truth.

As spiritual people, one of our first lessons is to learn to trust ourselves. We are the final judge of what we choose to believe, and what we don't. The divine spirit resides within the mind, heart and spirit of each of us. And the ultimate source of our awareness is our connection with the divine within us. It doesn't come from outside. It doesn't come from books, or workshops, or laboratory experiments. It comes from within – from how we see and feel things.

Don Juan, again, sheds invaluable light on how this works. Everything don Juan taught Carlos basically made him nuts. Carlos was a typical neurotic Westerner, whose mind worked in a very linear fashion, and for whom anything outside the bounds of his rational logic was unacceptable. To be honest, it's never made sense to me what don Juan saw in him, and why he put up with him. With his continuous attitude of protest, even condescension, Carlos continuously asked, "How do you know these things? This is totally crazy."

Don Juan always gave him the same answer: "I know these things, and the sorcerers of my lineage know these things, because we *see* them" – which, of course, freaked out Carlos even more. This is the essence of what we're talking about. Their system of knowledge was a direct result of their experience of the forces of the natural world and the spirit world. In altered states of consciousness, don Juan was able to *see* the energy of the quantum world directly as it moved in the universe. He was also able to act in this world, which explained his incredible feats of sorcery that defied rational logic. So, his knowledge came from his experience of the world.

So yes, we can feel the shifting energy. Everybody's feeling something, even though they may not be consciously aware of it. And yes, quite often, this experience is totally subjective. This means that what you and I are feeling might be completely different than anybody else. Everybody, for that matter, might be feeling something different. This doesn't invalidate any of it. We're in completely uncharted territory here. There are no laws in place to explain any of this, and we are making it up as we go along. What's so unprecedented about what we're experiencing now is that most of us are feeling things that are completely outside the realm of anything we've ever experienced before.

This is all so new and different that consensus reality hasn't even kicked in yet. Consensus reality is the reality we perceive to exist because it has been dictated by our culture for generations, and everybody agrees on it. Consensus reality is the norm in brainwashed cultures, where people have lost touch with their inner wisdom. Without a consensus reality, there's no way to label any of this, and fit it into our customary boxes. It just all seems crazy. And our old paradigm system compounds this craziness by telling us that nothing unusual is happening, and that everything will return to normal. On one level, people may want to believe that. And yet on another, they don't – because they can feel it.

What are people feeling? Again, we don't know for sure, but this is my sense of it, based upon my own experience of it, and based upon what I've heard from many others, both new and old paradigm types. People are feeling an intensification of the experience of living on Planet Earth. Much of this is being caused by the collapse of the old paradigm, which is clearly well underway, as well as the dramatic Earth changes, which have also begun, such as extreme weather and earthquake activity on a scale we haven't seen in a long time. There are few whose lives haven't been touched by these things in some way.

The collapse of the old paradigm, particularly in the financial arena, is causing severe hardship and distress for many, many people. After all, this was a world that they were told was safe and secure, and which they built their dreams upon. Now, it is being ripped out from underneath them. Once again, there is a hidden blessing here, as this is the spark that is helping many of these people awaken to the truth that this world was a lie and an illusion. Truth may be painful, but in the long run, it's always the best thing.

We not only feel this shifting of worlds because we can see it happening, but we can also feel it because we can feel the energy of it, as in the higher frequency energy of the Photon Belt. Most people agree this feels like a *quickening*, even though they may not be sure what they mean by that. We are just beginning to develop the framework to talk about it.

Common themes to this *quickening* seem to be pace and change. The pace of our lives seems to be speeding up all the time, as is the change we are experiencing, both as individuals and as a society. The influences of the amazing advances in our technology are partly responsible for this, but not entirely. There are other forces at work, such as the shifting energy fields. And how we feel all this pace and change can be both positive and negative. To some, it feels absolutely insane, like things are spinning totally out of control. To others, it feels sublime, like reconnecting with our heritage as magical beings.

Most people seem to feel like their perception of time is changing, and what I hear most is people saying that time seems like it's speeding up, with life just flying by. They report that more and more experience seems to be crammed into smaller and smaller units of time. I go both ways on this one. Most of the time, it seems to me like time is slowing down. As I write this, there are still two years and nine months until Winter Solstice 2012, and that seems like an eternity. This probably has to do with how I experience my life. I am endeavoring to value every moment of my life more. As I do, I slow down, and my life slows down – even though I get a lot more done, which I've never understood. There is agreement from virtually every viable spiritual tradition that as we evolve on our path of spiritual ascension, we will reach a point where time will stop, and everything will just be – in timelessness.

Another thing that we are obviously feeling is our emotions. As we move into these shifting energy fields, our emotions are becoming more highly charged, both positively and negatively. One of the primary determinants of how we feel these things, and perceive them, is our frame of reference. A tiny fraction of us, but growing by leaps and bounds, understand the shift and the forces at work. So, we understand what's happening, and we have a frame of reference. So even though our world is topsy-turvy too, at least it makes sense. So, we tend to be able to handle it all with more calmness. We are always able to deal with things better, and with less fear, when we are prepared, and when we know what we're dealing with, and in this case, when we are in resonance with it.

For the vast majority of people, they have no frame of reference. They have no idea why all this is happening. They too can feel something in their bodies, but they don't know what it is, or what's causing it. They too can see that the world, as we know it, is going down the tubes. They can feel the same frantic pace of things, and the same manic rate of change. But without a frame of reference, it's nearly impossible to get an emotional handle on the whole thing. Their bodies feel anger because things are so out of control. And they feel stress, fear and anxiety over all the unknowns that come with such massive change. Many of them feel like they're going crazy. And many of them are. It's usually a great relief to them, when they learn about the shift, and begin to get a frame reference. It helps to lift the burden that they believe something's wrong with them, or that they're doing something to cause how they feel.

On the other end of the spectrum, for those who do have a frame of reference, and who are in resonance with these forces, we can see amazing things happening. As these people move along the path of their spiritual ascension, they literally become lighter, and yes, you can see and feel it in their presence. They have a definite glow, and their physical bodies appear less impeded by gravity and the other densities of the material world. They are totally relaxed and mellow, and yet their metabolism is higher. Having more energy does not mean you have to be in a hurry or hyperactive. This is the energy of a happy turtle. These people are lean physically, which is effortless, and a natural offshoot of the ascension lifestyle, which we'll discuss in Chapter Six.

People tend to be drawn to these ascended folks, as their personalities are highly charged magnetically with the vibration of love. And the divine spirit always seems to shower them with the blessing of everything they need in this world, which is the true meaning of manifestation. It's difficult to see these ascended beings staying in this high density much longer. Many believe the time is coming very soon, when these ascended spirits will start popping out, and moving to higher dimensions. This is just no longer their world, which precisely follows the script the shift has written.

The Prophesies and Guidance from the Spirit World

Of course, our two other sources of how we know about the shift, and how it has already started, are ones we've already talked about. One is the prophesies and the ancient wisdom from indigenous cultures spanning the globe. And the other is the messages and guidance we receive from the spirit world. And when we take a look at these sources, we quickly learn that they overlap in many ways. They are also more mysterious than the other sources, often requiring that we use our own intuition and wisdom to understand them. Most of the prophesies are vague, and express themselves in symbolism that is open to interpretation. Rarely do the prophesies predict specific dates, preferring instead to tell us what will happen, often cryptically, and implying that this is how we will know the time has come. So, they actually do it in reverse order.

It's vital for us white folks to remember that the world the indigenous people saw was totally different from the world we see in the old paradigm. This is because their world overlapped the spirit world. And they actually saw this, with their eyes. This is not some kind of metaphor. The world they perceived was actually different. When they looked at their world, they not only saw the trees, the birds and the sky, but they also saw the spirit essences of those things. Ghost Wolf, again, sheds valuable light on this, as it pertains to the prophesies. He said that we should not make the mistake of seeing the prophesies as immutable reality or etched in stone. This is too much of a left-brain way of seeing our world, which was not the way of the indigenous people. We should see them, instead, as possibilities or potential outcomes, and that this was the spirit in which they were given.

And let's clear up a possible source of confusion about what we mean by "the prophesies." I am fully aware that I often use this term generically, and in so doing, I am taking the liberty of lumping together thousands of different prophesies, from hundreds of different tribes and locations, not to mention eras. It is reasonable for somebody to object to this on the basis that different prophesies say different things, and I'm certain there is truth to this.

I also have to make a personal confession here. I've been using the term "prophesies" generically for several years now, ever since I started learning and writing about the shift. And I always felt like I was on very solid ground here, even though I hadn't done that much research. Ghost Wolf's *Last Cry* was my primary source, and an excellent one. Ghost Wolf was of mixed blood, referring to himself as a mongrel, which included several Native American tribes and some European. He was also an emissary to numerous indigenous tribes, mostly Native American, and his teachings came from these traditions.

He was the true "Rainbow Man," about which he wrote so much. Ghost Wolf was in agreement with so many of the indigenous elders that the only way to heal Mother Earth from her current malaise was through a broad coalition of people, both indigenous and non-indigenous alike, from everywhere on the planet – hence, the rainbow. This is the primary reason why so many of the elders, from so many traditions, are coming out of hiding at this momentous time in our history, and reaching out to the white people, and other non-indigenous people, with the ancient teachings from these traditions. Not only is the timing right, with the shift at hand, but the elders also believe that many of us are finally ready.

In *Last Cry*, Ghost Wolf constantly refers to "the prophesies" in general, and with good reason – because so many of them were saying the same thing. Besides,

I've been hearing these kinds of references in so much of what I've read and heard since the late 1960s, when the alternative culture discovered the virtues of Native American and indigenous cultures and spirituality, much of which was reflected in the *New Age* movement that followed, which, in many ways, had good intentions. All these prophesies and all this ancient wisdom always seemed to have the same message. And this message resonates perfectly with the message of this book. It is a message about these times of ours, and the death of our world because it refuses to live in harmony with nature. It is a message telling us that the only way to survive these times, and build the new world, is with the power of our higher consciousness and our connection with the divine spirit.

But in spite of all this, I still had a nagging voice in the back of my head that said I needed to do more research on these prophesies, so that I could make sure I could back up what I was talking about. I had scarcely begun to do this, when, once again, all kinds of forces popped into place, providing me with a totally new and totally different lesson about one of the most important sources of our information – about anything. This is yet one other thing I have learned about very recently, and am writing about for the first time, as I rewrite much of this chapter. Are you following all this? What you're reading now is newer than what you're going to be reading when you get to the end of the book. I finished the book. Then, I wrote a new first chapter, and am now rewriting most of the third. And I've read ahead, and the final five chapters are going to stay pretty much as is. So, in real time, the end of this chapter will be the end of the book – for me.

The first thing I did was begin to reread Ghost Wolf's *Last Cry*, and pay special attention to the actual sources of the prophesies he talked about. I also decided to check out any literature Ghost Wolf cited, of which there was practically none, due to the fact that most of his information was from firsthand experience, as in directly from the mouths of elders, directly from his own contact with the spirit world, or directly from the verbal lore of these tribes. However, there were two, both of which turned out to be hugely influential, and both of which perfectly fit the overall picture I had been painting here. One was *Book of the Hopi* by Frank Waters, and the other was *Return of the Bird Tribes* by Ken Carey. And, as divine destiny would have it, it was precisely at this time that I met Mayan Elder Erick Gonzalez, and got a huge dose of the ancient Mayan teachings, when I attended ceremonial events at Deer Mountain and Guatemala.

So, there was quite a stew brewing here, and from the very start they all told me the same thing. This information, and the sources from which it came, such as the prophesies, was very personal. After all, it came from ancient traditions where there were no books or computers, and it had to be communicated in different ways. And ultimately, this information came from two basic sources. One was the elders, who are the spiritual leaders for each tribe or tradition. Wisdom Keepers is another name for them, and preserving the ancient wisdom was one of their primary responsibilities. They did this by carefully passing it down from generation to generation, through their hand-picked apprentices, who became the next generation of elders. And they also did it through their use of ceremony, which was essential to the fabric of life of indigenous people. Ceremony was not only one of the most important ways of communicating and sharing the ancient wisdom, it was also the primary way of preserving it.

However, as spiritual elders, these men and women didn't merely pass information along. They also channeled it, which means they received information directly from the spirit world in the form of messages and guidance. Here we have yet another source, and ultimately, the most important one. And often, ceremony is used as the means of channeling this guidance from the spirit world.

And when we trace this ancient wisdom back as far as it can go, and when we question where it all originates, the answer is always the same. As spiritual beings, our most important wisdom comes from our connection with the divine spirit of a living universe. It comes from our connection with the forces of nature and with the world around us. It comes from our connection with the Earth, with the Sun, with the rain that comes from the heavens, and with the plants that grow from the Earth. And it comes from the spirit essences of all these things. Everything we learn from the traditions of these elders we also have the capability to learn from within ourselves. Nobody has a monopoly on this wisdom. It's just out there, for all of us to grab. The only difference between us and the elders of hundreds of thousands of years ago is they didn't stray as far from their connection with spirit. They didn't have to work as hard to talk to the spirit world. They could see its essence in everything.

So yes, the sources of these prophesies and ancient wisdom are personal. They are intimate. The elders didn't just teach this stuff to anybody. And not everybody was invited to their ceremonies – at least not until recently, with so many of the indigenous elders, from so many traditions, coming out of hiding, and opening up their wisdom and their ceremonies to the outside world. Heck, they found me.

My new stew of sources was all telling me exactly the same thing. Ghost Wolf continuously referred to elders, from numerous tribes. Some he named, such as a Tuscaroran Elder, named Mad Bear Anderson, and others were anonymous. Much of this wisdom and these prophesies was channeled directly from the spirit world through these elders during ceremony. Ghost Wolf himself was guided by his own contacts in the spirit world. He also makes continuous references to prophesies from tribes and cultures spanning the globe. Just this morning, to test this, I randomly opened *Last Cry,* and started reading. On the page where I turned (pages 180 & 181) he mentions the prophesies of the Hopi, which were painted and carved in stone, the prophesies of the Peacemaker of the Iroquois, the prophesies of the Mayan Calendar, the prophesies found deep within the Pyramids of Egypt, and the prophesies of the Tibetans, the Aztecs, the Cherokee, the Osage, and the Lakota. How's that for a stew?

And this is pretty much the formula for this all important source of our information regarding the ancient wisdom and the prophesies. It comes from the elders, past and present, from tribes and cultures spanning the globe. And it comes from the spirit world. Perhaps this too tells us something about how our new paradigm world is going to work.

Book of the Hopi, by Frank Waters, tells exactly the same story. This book, as it turns out, is the definitive guide on the history, the culture, the ceremonies and the spirituality of the Hopi, and 100% authentic, seeing this world through the eye of the Hopi, not the white man. Where does this information come from? Well, it comes from a batch of Hopi Elders, who decided, in the early 1960s, that the time had come to share their story and the wisdom from their tradition with the outside world, and they chose author Frank Waters as their mouthpiece.

Here again we have the theme of the indigenous elders connecting with the outside world, for the purpose of sharing their ancient wisdom. Why? Here again we have the theme of this book, and the message of the prophesies. Because now is the time, and as we already know, the 1960s wasn't too early. It is the time of the ending of one world, so that another can be born from its ashes. It is the time to share the ancient wisdom because we can only create the new world through a broad, rainbow coalition of people, indigenous and non-indigenous alike, from all around the globe. And it is the time because in these times of monumental shift, many of these non-indigenous people, like you and me, have made the necessary shift in consciousness, and they are ready. We are ready.

And now into this stew we add my new soul-brother, Mayan Elder, Tata Erick Gonzalez. Here too we have the same story. Tata Erick is taught and trained in the ways of the ancient Mayan wisdom by a long lineage of Mayan Elders. I have spent many days and nights basking in the glow of the ancient teachings as they flowed through Erick's words, and many hours (days) experiencing them in the ceremonies he leads. His message resonates almost perfectly with the message of this book.

I hear him constantly saying that the elders are our most important guides and teachers. And he is not only talking about the Mayan Elders, of whom he has a vast and rich network. He is talking about all of our living elders, from every indigenous tribe and culture on the planet. He is also talking about the elders from non-indigenous groups, like me, and possibly you, who have managed to tune into the ancient wisdom in other ways. I am honored to say that Erick refers to me as one of the white-corn elders, adding that there are not that many. Like Ghost Wolf, Erick is a true Rainbow Man. One of the missions of his group, Earth Peoples United, is to unite all these elders, from everywhere on the planet, and the two sustainable communities, at Deer Mountain and Patziapa in Guatemala, will be bases where this can be done.

I hear Erick refer again and again to the prophesies. And here again, the message is the same as everywhere else in our stew. And he doesn't limit himself to the Mayan prophesies. He refers as well to the Hopi, the Kogi, the Tibetan, and countless others. After all, they all basically say the same thing. And this makes sense, does it not? It makes sense because they all come from the same source. It comes from the elders, or spiritual leaders, who receive their wisdom and guidance from the same source. Ultimately, this is their harmonious relationship with the forces of nature and the spirit world. And this is the most important source of our information, about anything.

We are All Guided

So, ours is not a standard research project, with footnotes to lots of books and periodicals in the professional literature. Our sources are more personal. And in order to cover the entire picture here, we need to add one final source. And that is me. After all, all of this information is being funneled through me, is it not? I am the final judge of what goes into this book, and the final judge of what I believe, in general. If what you're reading here resonates with you, it's because you trust me, as your source.

And I too am guided. Since August 2009, the Council of the Grandfathers has been my spirit guide. Prior to then, I received messages of an anonymous nature. And even when there weren't specific messages, as in a voice in my head, there was still guidance. All of the events in my life have served to guide me to where I am now. This is true for all of us. The guidance is simply there, always, in the divine quantum space of which we are a part. It's up to us to reach out, and grab a hold of it.

The primary difference between us is our purpose in life. If our purpose is shallow and materialistic, then so will be our guidance. I have known since I was a small boy that the message of the established mainstream system was a crock. It was a message of fear, unhappiness and limitation. Even as a child, I was smart enough to know that god wouldn't create a world like that. My purpose has always been to find the truth, no matter where I needed to look, and to endeavor to play my part to fix an apparently hopelessly screwed up world. This was my path, and as long as I stayed true to it, this is precisely where I have always received my guidance. I have been guided every step of the way, even though most of the time I wasn't even aware of it. I was guided to don Juan in the 1970s, and again thirty years later. I was guided to Ghost Wolf, who himself was guided by the spirit world. As I illustrated a couple of pages ago, every time I open up *Last Cry* and start reading, I receive guidance directly from the spirit world, through him. I know because of how perfectly it resonates with my spirit. Guidance works in many different ways. And yes indeed, the divine spirit does its work in mysterious ways.

We are all reflections of the divine spirit of a living universe. Once we become aware of this, and once we put it into practice by living our life with the proper vibration, we quickly learn that we are our most important source of information – about anything. Everything we need to know is etched into the rhythm and flow of the natural world, of which we are an integral part. It is our connection to this rhythm with the power of our vibration that is the source of everything important in our lives. It is the wisdom of our hearts, and the wisdom of our spirits, which provide us with our guidance on this path. Once we learn to trust that wisdom, we learn that's all we need.

Chapter Four

Transforming Challenges into Blessings

The outcome is not yet determined
It's up to us to make it happen
Challenges are guidance

There are Limitless Possibilities

What about the outcome of all this? What's our world going to be like after this paradigm shift?

The answer to that too is a simple one: we don't know. The outcome has yet to be determined. It could go in any one of several directions, and, like with anything, the possibilities are limitless. We've already mentioned the two extremes. On one end, there is this exceedingly rare and blessed opportunity to create the new world of light and spirit. As we go along here, we will be taking a closer and closer look at this world might be like.

On the other end, there are those who believe this is doomsday, the end of the world. There are also many different scenarios, in which they say this might play out, both religious and non-religious. But since this is not the point of view taken here, I'm not going to spend any time going into this – not to mention the fact that talking about it just for the sake of talking about it does tend to give it energy, which I would never do.

And along this spectrum of possibilities, there are many others. On the negative end of the spectrum, one such possibility is the *New World Order*. For those who don't know, the *New World Order* is the term used for the fascist, world government that is currently taking shape around us, and the conspiracy to make this happen. Like all the energies referred to earlier, the pace of this too is increasing at an accelerating rate. And this too is connected to the phenomena of *2012 and the shift*. The hidden powers that own and control the world are well aware of 12/21/12 and the shift, and of the possible threat this poses to their solidly entrenched power structure, and their agenda for world government. And they understand that the clock is ticking, and if they don't get their *New World Order* in place quickly enough, the extent of these massive changes and paradigm shifts might be too huge even for them to handle. Their whole house of cards might come toppling down, and there won't be anything even they can do about it.

Either that, or the forces of light might just beat them to the punch, and create the new world of light and spirit. As unenlightened as it sounds, this is a battle.

However, we, the forces of light, have chosen as our primary weapon the awesome power of our spirit energy. We're not going to be attacking or killing anybody, nor are we going to try to deceive or manipulate anybody. We're going to be right out there in the open, in the light, for everybody to see.

The financial crisis of 2008/09 is the just the most recent in a long string of fabricated crises, engineered by the global elite, for the purpose of increasing their power and control, at the expense of the freedom of the people of the world. I'll be going into the details of how all this works in the next chapter. 9/11 was another such event, and at the time I am writing this (May 1, 2009), there is an apparent outbreak of Swine Flu in Mexico and the US, with the potential to become a pandemic. In the alternative culture, at least that part of it with knowledge of the global conspiracy, it is commonly believed this hybrid, mutated virus was created in the labs of the Pharmaceutical Cartel, and has been foisted on the people of the world through vaccines, or some other means, which amounts to act of bio-warfare. Or, this could be a hoax, or a false flag, much like the Swine Flu scare of 1976.

But even these false flags serve a definite purpose, which is creating fear, and planting seeds in the minds of the people for the next fabricated crisis, not to mention making a lot of money off vaccines. And bio-terrorism fits the overall agenda of global government, power, and control perfectly, as this is a crisis beyond borders, and it provides a wonderful excuse for such things as quarantines and martial law. And we can see in all these fabricated crises and manipulations the truly sinister nature of the forces of *the dark side*. It is indeed satanic.

By the time you read this, you will probably know whether this was an epidemic or a false flag. Circumstances may require that I write about this in the pages ahead. Or maybe it will just go away. Or maybe I will be forced to flee this world because I will never consent to a forced vaccination or some kind of quarantine. But if not this, it will be something else, most definitely. This is how this game works. *The dark side* has been operating this way for thousands of years, and they are not about to stop now. And this provides us with a perfect illustration of the forces at work in our world today. There will come a time, in the not so distant future, when all of us will be forced to make a choice regarding which world we choose to live in – old paradigm or new. Yes indeed, the stakes are very high here.

I am going to go into the global conspiracy in more depth in the next chapter. But what needs to be said here is the movement toward the *New World Order* must be included in our discussion. I am painting a huge picture here of everything that's relevant to the shift and creating the new world. The *New World Order* is way too large a piece of this total picture to leave out. If we did, when we got to the end, the total picture wouldn't be clear. It wouldn't make sense. And as we already know, in a divinely ordered universe, everything must make sense. And it is incumbent upon us to make as much sense of it all as we possibly can.

It is essential that we have an awareness of the *New World Order* for many reasons. A very insidious game is being played here, the purpose of which is to trick us into giving up our freedom and our spirit. Without an awareness of this game, there is a much greater chance we will fall for the trick, and get stuck in the game. Which amounts to just another version of the age-old pact with the devil, in which we get seduced into bartering away our soul, in return for the promise of riches and security in this world.

There are many in the *New Age* scene, who say we shouldn't discuss *the dark side*, or even think about it, because this empowers it. To them, I say cut the crap. Whenever I hear this, I can't help but think that the disinformants have truly succeeded in getting into the heads of these people. What could be better for the hidden powers than to sell people on the idea that they shouldn't talk about them, or even think about them? I feel almost silly saying something this self-evident, but you can be aware of something without empowering it. I am aware of the war in Iraq and the other crimes of the Bush Administration, and yet I am capable of attaining this awareness without giving this one speck of power. And not being aware of something this obvious, like the proverbial purple elephant in the living room, amounts to an act of ignorance, not to mention stripping you of your power to do anything about it. You have to tip your cap to the incredible brainwashing that these folks/beings have managed to pull off, as wicked as it is – more in a bit.

There are an Infinite Number of Other Worlds

One thing we know for certain: this is an age of monumental transformation, regardless of which way it goes. This world will not be the same after the shift plays out. We also know for certain that the fate of the planet rests in our hands. Or perhaps it would be more accurate to say that the fate of the human race rests in our hands. The planet's been through this before, and came through it just fine. The Planet Earth is an organic being, with a soul, and a miraculous capability to regenerate.

It is also clear what we must do. If we are to create the new world of light and spirit, a *critical mass* of humanity must connect with the divine spirit of a living universe with their vibration of peacefulness, joy, reverence, gratitude and trust. This is the only way through the energetic portal, which is opening at this monumental time, to a dimension of higher frequency. This is another critically important area, where virtually all the ancient prophecies agreed.

And this vital spiritual principle is timeless. Changing the world always begins in hearts and spirits of the people of planet Earth. This applies equally for any time or era – not just the one surrounding Solstice 2012. The primary difference between our time and all the others is these energetic and spiritual opportunities and possibilities are not only enhanced, but exponentially enhanced.

But let's get more specific about what we're talking about here. When we talk about creating the new world of light and spirit or moving to a higher dimension, what exactly are we talking about?

First of all, what do we mean by a dimension? This is another one of those concepts that we often make much more complicated and confusing than we need to. If we just trust the childlike gifts of our intuition, so many of these things just pop into place, and make perfect sense.

The old paradigm world that we perceive with our five senses, and which we are conditioned to believe is real, is only one of innumerable worlds that are available to our perception. And as we've already discussed, the old paradigm world is an illusion. The only reason people see it as real is because they are brainwashed to believe, and very importantly, to agree, that it is real. This is what's known as consensus reality. It exists because everybody agrees it exists. And once we are 100% sold that this is the only reality, we pass this on to our children, who pass it on to theirs, and on and on. With time, the box gets smaller and smaller, and pretty soon the box is all we can see.

Here again we can learn much from shamans and sorcerers, like don Juan. Don Juan's system of metaphysics was based on the concept that in altered states of consciousness we have the capability to shift our perception, and to perceive, or to *see*, entirely new and different worlds. These altered states of consciousness could be achieved in several different ways. The use of psychotropic and medicinal plants was one way, and sorcerers often had to use these with their apprentices to help them break through the barriers that they were unable to break through in other ways. Extreme physical illness was another, when, in delirium-like states, people often took trips to completely different worlds, which seem just as real as this one, and, in fact, are.

Sleep is another such state, where our perception shifts when we dream. An essential technique for don Juan and the sorcerers of ancient Mexico to achieve these altered, perceptual states was actually called dreaming or journeying. However, they were very careful to distinguish between this kind of dreaming and the ordinary dreaming most of us are familiar with. Ordinary dreams are the kind we learn about in Psychology 101, the Freudian variety. An ordinary dream is the equivalent of watching a movie of what's going on in our subconscious mind. It is a projection of our innermost subconscious material into a symbolic or visual form. Ordinary dreaming is a totally valid concept and real phenomenon, and it can be a very valuable tool of self-understanding. These kinds of dreams can play a very important part in changing the entire course of our lives.

However, the dreaming or journeying of don Juan and his fellow sorcerers was very different from this. Sleep was only one of many states in which this could be done. It could also be achieved in other states of altered consciousness, such as meditation, or other trance-like states, which could be induced through various forms of hypnosis, music or other sound vibrations, chanting, and many other ways. When sorcerers become proficient at journeying, they are able to reach this state of consciousness at will.

So, a dream journey is when we volitionally shift our perception, and perceive one of the multitude of other worlds that are available to our perception. These other worlds are what we mean by dimensions. A dimension, simply, is any world other than our old paradigm, consensus reality. A dream journey is actually a departure from the physical body, and an actual journey to a completely different world. Journeying is not an act of our imagination. These worlds are as real as any other. They are worlds we can live and die in, and if we lose our way, they are worlds we might not return from. It is not our physical body that takes this trip. It is our perception. It is our energy body, or our spirit. It is a journey on the wings of our consciousness. And it can take us anywhere in the universe, in the blink of an eye.

There are a few other critically important differences between this kind of dream journeying and ordinary dreaming. In ordinary dreaming, the person usually doesn't have awareness of the dream until after they've awakened, and often it is forgotten all together. In journeying, the sorcerer is fully aware of the dream, as it is happening. They know they are dreaming, and they also have complete volitional control over their actions in the dream. And very importantly, when a sorcerer travels to other dimensions, they often are not bound by the physical laws that govern old paradigm, consensus reality, such as gravity and cause and effect. They, or rather their energy bodies, are able to do amazing things that defy rational explanation, such as flying, moving through matter, and much more. Sorcerers, in these other dimensions, are without the limitations of the old paradigm. If ordinary, consensus reality is a box, then in dreaming the walls of the box vanish, and the dreamer has access to infinity.

In this sense, this is more like the quantum world of Quantum Physics, in which so many of the rules of old paradigm science no longer apply, such as a particle being in two places at the same time. The quantum world, clearly, is another dimension. And it is a heck of a lot more reasonable to say that the quantum world is the real world, rather than the illusion of the old paradigm.

Once we understand the sorcerer's ability to move dimensionally, we begin to understand the source of their incredible, apparently magical, powers. It's not hocus pocus. This is exceedingly important in the context of understanding how human beings have the capability of overcoming the apparently insurmountable odds of overcoming the colossal paradigm shifts and Earth changes of the shift, and defeating the sinister and hugely powerful Goliath of the established power structure. In order to do this we must learn how to access many of these other-dimensional powers. When we do, there's nothing that can be done in the old paradigm to stop us. And these are powers we can only access with our higher consciousness and spirituality.

And whenever we are talking about moving to other dimensions by shifting our perception, there is another aspect of the part consciousness plays here that we must understand, and the extraordinary power it has. This has to do with the relationship between the consciousness of the observer and whatever is observed. Let me illustrate what I want to say here with another example from don Juan. Whenever don Juan was performing his stupendous feats of magic for Carlos, like flying, Carlos was only able to perceive this when he was in an altered state of consciousness. If somebody in an ordinary state of consciousness had been watching the same thing, they probably would have seen nothing, or at least not an old man flying. This is one of the reasons why some people have lots of UFO sightings, and others have none. It's a function of a difference in their consciousness. And extraterrestrials, who are seeking human contacts, almost always select people with altered consciousness because their door is more open.

This too was one of the most revolutionary lessons for the quantum physicists. They learned that their consciousness, as scientific measurers and observers, had a direct relationship on the behavior and activity of the energy they were observing. For example, the way the experiment was set up, or how it was measured, had a direct result on the outcome.

So, our consciousness is an essential variable in the world we perceive or create. It is essentially important in shifting our perception, and moving to other dimensions. And moving dimensionally is something we must learn how to do if a *critical mass* of us are to move through the energetic gateways of *2012 and the shift*, and create the new world of light and spirit.

Ascension

So, a dimension is nothing more than a different world. Now let's get more specific about the process of ascension, which is necessary to create the new world of light and spirit. From a dimensional point of view, in virtually all the literature on this topic, the old paradigm, consensus reality we've been discussing is referred to as the 3rd dimension.

As we've discussed, the 3rd dimension is an illusion. It is an illusion in a couple of extremely important ways. We've already touched upon the first, and we will cover this more in depth in the next chapter. 3rd dimensional reality is an illusion as a result of deceit, manipulation and fabrication. This illusion is perpetrated by the behind-the-scenes powers that own and control the world, *the dark side,* for the purpose of forcing of us into a box, in which we are cut off from the higher powers of our freedom and our multi-dimensional spirituality. This makes us easy fodder to control, and keep under their thumb. Yes folks, this is *The Matrix*.

However, the illusory nature of the 3rd dimension goes far deeper than this. Above and beyond this manipulation, this illusion is an inherent feature of the 3rd dimension. Even without the chicanery of *the dark side,* the 3rd dimensional world of matter is still an illusion. This is an essential feature of many spiritual traditions, such as Hinduism and Buddhism, which maintain that this is simply the way the 3rd dimension is.

3rd dimensional material reality is, by its nature, very dense and heavy. It doesn't get much denser than this. The matter and all the material goodies of the 3rd dimension are very seductive to the humans, or any other being, who occupy this dimension. The material temptations of 3-D are so great that when we yield to them, we can develop a form of amnesia, in which we forget our multi-dimensional spiritual potential. There is the inherent tendency to get stuck in this material density, and forget where we came from. It is the equivalent of being in a spell or a trance, in which we are blinded to everything except matter and the material world. We forget that in order to access higher frequency dimensions, the primary emphasis must always be on our higher consciousness and spirituality, not on matter – as opposed to the other way around.

When we break the spell, and raise our energetic frequency with feelings of peacefulness, joy, reverence, gratitude and trust, we begin the ascension process. When we raise it high enough, we move to the 4th dimension. There is considerable disagreement about this, but as I understand it, the 4th dimension is ephemeral. In other words, we don't stay there very long. The 4th dimension is kind of like purgatory in traditional Catholicism. After we've served our time there, we either go up, or we go back down. Many people believe we, collectively, have already ascended to the 4th dimension, and that this is the reason for all the accelerated change, Earth changes and paradigm shifting we are currently experiencing.

When we are finished with the 4th dimension (if we continue upward), we continue our ascension into the 5th dimension. The 5th dimension is the world of pure light and spirit that we've been referring to. This is the dimension that is opening up to us during this monumental time of shifting energy. In other words, this is our goal. We will be taking a much closer look at this 5th dimensional world of light and spirit in Chapters Six and Seven. For now, let's just get our terminology straight.

Many reputable folks don't understand it this way. They don't see the 4th dimension as this temporary, purgatory-like, stop-over point. They believe the 4th dimension is the world of pure light and spirit, and that there is no intermediary dimension after we have left the 3rd. I really don't think it makes any difference, and that this is little like splitting hairs. Ascension is ascension, and the only thing that matters is getting it right, regardless of what we call the various steps along the way. The only thing that really matters is going in the right direction – up, and not down. And I will be saying a lot more about the specifics of how we can get this ascension process right in Chapter Six.

Even though the 5th dimension is all the higher we're going to go in this discussion, that doesn't mean there aren't any other dimensions higher than, or parallel to, this. There are – innumerable. But let's save that discussion for another day.

The Lucifer Rebellion

A wonderful story, which beautifully illustrates these other-dimensional principles, as well as how these dimensions work in relationship to each other, and how *the dark side* fits into all this, is the story of the Lucifer Rebellion. I have borrowed this version of the story, once again, from Robert Ghost Wolf's *Last Cry*. Different versions of this story (same story – different names and places) pop up in many different spiritual traditions, and I'm sure there is undoubtedly an element of truth to it on some level.

It goes something like this. Lucifer and his band of angels were actually light workers, who descended into 3rd dimensional reality from higher dimensions. However, when they arrived, they experienced an unanticipated, but common, 3rd dimensional problem. The 3rd dimensional densities were too heavy for them. They got stuck here, and couldn't figure out how to get out. Many of them experienced the 3rd dimensional amnesia discussed a moment ago, and couldn't remember where they came from. These became known as *the wanderers*, or lost souls.

Having lost their spiritual moorings, Lucifer led a band of these "fallen" angels in a quest to discover a way, in which they could manipulate the rules of the 3rd dimensional material world, to get out. As discussed earlier, one of the inherent features of the non-sustainable, old paradigm is the emphasis placed on controlling the forces of nature. Perhaps the Lucifer Rebellion is where this originated, a long, long time ago, and we are the inheritors of this fallacy. This does amount to a rebellion because it was an attempt to circumvent divine law, which clearly maintains that there is only one way to ascend dimensionally. This is through the use of spiritual means, not material, and by harmonizing with natural and spiritual forces, not dominating them. So, Lucifer and his band were destined to failure, but in the process they left an old paradigm legacy, which exists to this day.

Lucifer and his rebellion are often equated with the devil and with the origins of Satanism. I think this version of the story also beautifully illustrates one of the meanings of Satanism, and what constitutes true evil. We're going to go into this in more depth in the next chapter too, but for now, let's just point out that the devil, Satan and evil all have to do with the attempt to circumvent the harmony of divine law through the manipulation of the material world.

If Lucifer had remembered his origins, and not lost his spiritual moorings, he would have known this, and endeavored to get out properly, through spiritual ascension. He also would have remembered that the optimal opportunity to do this was once every 26,000 years, during the window of time around Winter Solstice, when the veils between the dimensions were thinner, and the energetic portals more open, than at any other time. Perhaps Lucifer's greatest sins were his impatience, and forgetting that the end never justifies the means to that end – also two hallmark characteristics of the crumbling old paradigm.

The Shift is Not Going to Just Happen

Another thing we know for certain is that the shift will present the human race with a monumental challenge. This is yet another area where virtually all the prophecies agree, from every ancient, indigenous culture spanning the globe.

This is another area where there is considerable disagreement within the community of folks who study and write about the shift. Many well-intended folks believe that the shift to the new world of light and spirit is just going to happen, all by itself. They give the impression that we're all going to wake up some day, perhaps on December 22, 2012, and everything's just going to be different, without us actually doing anything. Everything's just going to be rosy, as if by magic.

Many of these folks are the same ones, referred to earlier, who believe we shouldn't talk about, or even think about, the role *the dark side* is playing in all this. Obviously, there are those in the *New Age* scene, who have a difficult time with anything that might be perceived as negative. They believe that when you talk and think about these things, you give them energy, and thereby create them. It follows that such folks would struggle with such things as the collapse of the old paradigm because this can sound pretty negative, depending on how it's interpreted, and which paradigm you've chosen to embrace. I don't like saying this, but the collapse of the old paradigm will assuredly involve hardship and adversity for those who choose to cling to its destructive energies. Many people will be in for a very rough ride. This is already happening. Unfortunately, this is their choice, and there's nothing we can do to help them, unless they are willing to help themselves. We're going to cover all this in depth in Chapter 7.

However, for now, we need to make the point that these well-intended folks, who struggle so much with what they perceive as negative, invariably end up trying to save the old paradigm, rather than just letting it go. They endeavor to try to change the system from within, and they tend to look to old paradigm methods, such as traditional liberal politics, to accomplish this. And it seems like they believe that if the shift's going occur, it will be within these parameters. They have not yet learned that there's only one way to create the new paradigm, and that's with new paradigm methods – higher consciousness and spirituality. The old paradigm methods simply don't work in this world.

All of which amounts to little more than being stuck in the old paradigm. And the prophesies all agree this is not the way it's going to work. It is clear that they are talking about a transformation that is far more profound in nature – a shifting from one world to a completely different one. This is practically inherent in the concept of the shift, as it is put forth in the prophesies, and missing this is the equivalent of missing the entire thing.

Besides, as we've already discussed, the old paradigm is built on the unsustainable foundation of materialism and control. In order to change it, it is necessary to change the foundation. And when you change the foundation, you change the whole thing, as in switching dimensions. This process of transformation, or shift, is the equivalent of starting over, starting from scratch. This means getting back to the basics, as in returning to the power of our higher consciousness and spirituality. It means building the new world on the proper foundation – the foundation of light and spirit.

The prophesies all agree that in order to create the new world, human beings must assume the primary responsibility for this, and must make it happen through their actions. Contrary to what many *New Age* folks believe, it's not just going to happen, all by itself. Yes indeed, the fate of the planet rests in our hands.

Challenges are Blessings

And these Earth changes and paradigm shifts will present a monumental challenge. Though that may sound negative in the minds of some, it's not. In a divinely ordered universe, everything happens for a reason, and this includes the challenges that are woven into the very fabric of life. There's nothing wrong with challenges. As a matter of fact, without challenges, life in 3rd dimensional reality becomes stagnant. Challenges are always one of our primary means of learning new things, and evolving our higher consciousness and spirituality. Even though they may be painful, challenges are always blessings in disguise.

And invariably, the more extreme the challenge, the more monumental will be the potential blessing it holds. Life is replete with stories of those who lost everything in this world, and hit rock bottom, only to see the light, and rebound from this to manifest their dreams. When you lose everything, and have nothing left, what remains is the only thing that truly matters – your connection with the divine spirit of a living universe. And we all have the freedom to choose whether to trust this connection, or not. Remember – everything that truly matters, ultimately, springs from our connection with spirit. Once we learn this, the lesson of all lessons, everything falls into place, as if by magic.

It is essential for us as spiritual beings to learn how to see challenges in this way. And the challenge of the shift is potentially the greatest blessing of them all.

Don Juan, once again, states this more beautifully than I ever could. He told Carlos that the universe was inherently predatorial. At first glance, this may sound severe, and, dare I say, negative. But remember – don Juan was an Indian, from a different generation. He had an intimate relationship with the natural world, and was fully capable of living totally off the land. This kind of lifestyle is inherently tougher than what we are accustomed to in the civilized world, and he could be very rough around the edges. There was not much of what I call *New Age* correctness in his system of metaphysics, or in the way he communicated it.

What don Juan meant by predatorial here was not what was commonly meant. This did not mean to hunt and to kill for the purpose of eating and survival, nor did it mean to plunder or destroy for the sake of personal gain. What don Juan meant here was that the universe was constantly challenging the beings it created, including us. Everything happens for a reason, and the reason here was to test the awareness of these beings, and to give them the opportunity to enhance this awareness. By pressuring them in this manner, the universe forces these beings to either enhance their awareness, or if they don't pass the test, to perish, meaning either to physically die, or at least to die energetically and spiritually, which amounts to the same thing. Obviously, the reason for all the apparent problems in our world, and the demise of the old paradigm, is because a *critical mass* of humanity have taken this test, and failed. This is what must be changed.

Remember – indigenous spiritual teachings and quantum physics tell us that the universe is guided or governed by an unseen intelligence, and that everything is energetically connected to everything else. When the universe forces these beings to enhance their awareness, this allows the universe to enhance its awareness of itself. Consciousness exists on both macroscopic levels, as in the mind of the universe, and microscopic levels, as in the minds of its component parts, including us as individuals. And on the highest spiritual level, all these minds have the capability to blend, and to work as one.

So, when we, as individuals, accept the universe's constant challenge, and enhance our awareness, we are contributing to enhancing the awareness of the whole. We are playing our part, if you will, in enhancing the awareness of the universe, or the divine spirit. So, this entire miraculous process becomes one of infinite expansion, where there are no limits to this awareness, both on a universal, as well as an individual, basis. The universe is not only expanding physically. The consciousness of the universe is also expanding, and if we get it right, we contribute to that, as co-creators.

So, all challenges are blessings. And a life that is without challenges is no life at all. And yes, the challenges that we, the human race, are facing with the Earth changes and paradigm shifts that are coming with *the great shift of the ages* are indeed colossal. But the greater the challenge, the greater the potential blessing it holds – in this case, the creation of the new world of light and spirit.

And our challenge is compounded even further by the fact that we must deal with the part played by *dark side* in all this – those hidden powers that own and control the world, whose agenda for us is one of bondage – not liberation and spiritual ascension. And, after teasing you for four chapters, let's turn to that now.

Chapter Five

Understanding the Dark Side

> *The matrix of power and control*
> *The trick to rob us of our spirit*
> *Our world has been tampered with*

The Most Positive News Imaginable

Many of the *New Agers* often accuse me of being negative because of my insistence on including *the dark side* in our discussion of the shift and the 3rd dimensional world in general. They say that to discuss such things, or even think about them, means to give them energy, which empowers them, implying that if we just ignore them, they will go away. There is also the strong implication here that these negative forces don't exist to begin with, and that we are responsible for creating them with our perception.

As you will see, nothing could be further from the truth. Quite contrarily, understanding the role *the dark side* plays in our world is the most positive thing imaginable. This is because it gets us, the human beings of the planet Earth, off the hook.

Bear with me here, and follow my thread. The situation of the planet Earth at the current time is grave, with wars, poverty and famine, environmental destruction, epidemic levels of physical and mental sickness, and on and on. Why humans are botching it so badly on this beautiful planet is one of the most challenging questions of them all. There don't seem to be any logical answers, so we are stuck with just one possibility: it's our fault. We, human beings, have created a total mess on Earth, through our ignorance, greed, savagery and depravity. And this is precisely the message that is reinforced through virtually all the established religions, as well as by many in the *New Age*. We are just another beast, like all the other animals, and bad will always defeat the good, as long as we are running the show.

Not a very rosy picture, is it? Well, it's also a bunch of poppycock. When we open our eyes, and take a look at the part *the dark side* plays in our world, one of the first things we learn is that the world is not the way it is, nor are its people, as a function of a process of natural development. We, the people of the planet, have been deceived and manipulated. We have been tampered with. And the world is as messed up as it is as part of an agenda. This is precisely how it was all designed to unfold.

So yes, this is the most positive news of all. Once we know this, we can step back, and we can begin to look at ourselves differently. It's no longer necessary to see ourselves as the victims of some kind of cosmic insanity, or original sin. We can begin to look at ourselves as we truly are – as reflections of the divine, and potential co-creators of a world that is all good – not all bad.

What is "the Dark Side?"

OK - let's begin with an extremely blunt statement, which accurately reflects the current situation in our world. I do this on purpose, to get your attention. Sometimes there's no substitute for shock.

Here goes: *the dark side* is currently in control of the planet Earth. This has been the case since the beginning of our civilization, 6000 years approximately, and as we borough farther and farther down the rabbit hole of truth, we can see that this time frame is far, far longer.

And let's be very careful to say exactly what we mean here. The best way to do this is by making another very blunt statement – very short and simple, and totally accurate.

Here goes again: the world is owned and controlled by a very small group of people/beings, who operate entirely behind the scenes. They operate entirely through deceit and manipulation, the purpose of which is to trick the people of the planet into giving up their freedom and their spirit. They accomplish this by creating a vast illusion, in which the institutions of the mainstream system are perceived by the people as existing to serve and benefit them, when in fact their purpose is bondage, and disconnecting people from the true sources of their multi-dimensional power. This includes virtually every institution of the established system, including the major religions, government, banking and financial institutions, science, medicine, and education. These people/beings and this agenda are what I mean by *the dark side*.

Quite a trick, I agree, and the closer we look at this diabolical scheme, the more ingenious it becomes. But only ingenious if the people of planet Earth fall for the trick, which they have to a staggering degree. It is indeed remarkable how people have so totally allowed the wool to be pulled over their eyes. This is sleepwalking through life of the first order. And Americans are more guilty of this than any other. Even our first cousins, the Europeans, see the Americans as totally oblivious zombies.

I call this *the dark side* because it is indeed dark. The people, or beings (explanation upcoming, if you haven't figured it out already), are dark. And their agenda is dark. And yes, by dark I do mean evil. And before all the *New Agers* go totally nuts over my use of that term, let me define what I mean. That usually clears everything right up, and we don't get caught in any semantic traps.

The definition of evil is any human act that violates divine or natural law – simple and very straightforward. I am using the terms divine law and natural law synonymously because they are the same thing. These are laws that are an inherent feature of the rhythm and flow of the natural world of the universe. Evil, then, is anything that attempts to interfere with or impede this natural flow.

In this case, what *the dark side* is doing is clearly evil because they're breaking just about every divine law in the books. Their agenda is one of dominance and control, not harmony and balance, and they are attempting to achieve this through deceit, manipulation, and worse. They are definitely pushing against the grain of the flow of the universe. It doesn't get much more wicked than that.

Another facet of the *New Age* movement that irks me is the position that so many of them take on the moral issue of good and evil. They claim that evil doesn't exist, and any evil that we see in the world is the result of our perception, or to be more specific, it is some sort of a projection that we make of *the dark side* within ourselves. In other words, it's our fault – which sounds suspiciously like the running of a very old tape - called original sin. As we've already alluded to a few times, this is a function of their obsession with seeing everything as positive, when in reality, everything isn't – yet another case where it appears that *the dark side* has succeeded in getting into the heads of these people, and having it their way.

To quote one of my heroes, George Carlin, "Excuse me, while I puke in my soup." To begin with, evil does exist in the universe, and it does exist independently of us and our perception. In other words, it exists – period. And in this case, the evil perpetrated by *the dark side* on human beings and upon the planet Earth exists, and, again, it exists independently of us and our perception.

Yes, it's true that human beings feed this dark energy in a host of ways. Humans feed this through their blindness to it, which amounts to ignorance. And they feed it by allowing themselves to play the game that *the dark side* is foisting upon them. When humans see *the dark side* for what it is, and refuse to play the game, *the dark side* is stripped of its power, and it will be forced to simply go away. It is just that simple. For the most part, *the dark side* can't do any of the nasty things they do without our permission – that is, short of murder, which, as we all can readily see, is also part of their game.

I agree that the moral question of the existence of good and evil is one of the most perplexing metaphysical questions of them all. After all, so the reasoning goes, if the divine spirit, the source of all creation, is all good, why would the divine spirit include evil in its creation? This doesn't appear to make any sense, and as we've already made clear, everything in a divinely ordered universe must make sense.

The answer to this dilemma is not as complicated as it might appear. All we need to do is recognize an essential variable in the creation, and a sacred one. This is *free will*. When the divine spirit created the universe, this included the creation of a multitude of different beings, who were blessed with awareness or consciousness. In other words, these beings were aware of themselves, and they could think. They were free to make decisions, which played an important part in determining their path or destiny.

An inherent feature of *free will* is the freedom to make incorrect decisions or mistakes. These beings are even free to decide to act in ways that are contrary to, or not in harmony with, the divine laws of the universe. This is what Lucifer and his band of fallen angels decided to do. This is what *the dark side* has been attempting to do, with great success, on planet Earth for a long, long time.

And this *free will*, this choice to follow good or to follow evil, permeates the cosmos, on every level, in every dimension. In the spirit world, there are good spirits and bad spirits. In the world of extraterrestrials, there are benevolent ET's and malevolent ET's. And in the case of planet Earth, the bad spirits have been in control for a very long time.

The Illumined Ones

So, let's borough deeper down the rabbit hole of truth, and take a look at the particulars of who *the dark side* is, and how their insidious game works.

As far as who they are, this is a very difficult question to answer. This is a very carefully guarded secret, and they're doing an exceedingly good job of it. These are folks/beings who do not mess around. In addition to *the dark side*, a few of the terms commonly used to refer to them are the Illuminati, the elite, or the global elite, the shadow government, and a host of others. I often refer to them as the *hidden powers that own and control the world* because this is quite vivid, not leaving a lot of room for misinterpretation due to semantics.

When I give my Powerpoint presentation, and when I get to this part, I show the *seeing eye pyramid* on the screen. For those of you who don't know, the *seeing eye pyramid* is one of the symbols *the dark side* uses to depict themselves and how they work. Even if you're not aware of it, you've seen this version of it countless times, and would recognize it immediately, as it is prominently displayed on the US dollar bill or Federal Reserve Note. So, if you have one handy, pull it out of your wallet, and take a look at it, and use it for reference as we move along.

As you can see, the *seeing eye* is perched at the very top of the pyramid. It is also encircled by the rays of a glowing light, like the Sun. And it is suspended above the rest of the pyramid, with a space in between them. This pyramid is symbolic of how the world is structured, with *the dark side* occupying their place of power at the top, and with the rest of the world below, and subservient, to them.

The glowing *seeing eye* is symbolic of how *the dark side* sees themselves. They see themselves as the illumined ones. The eye further symbolizes the fact that *the dark side* are able to see, which means they have access to knowledge that is concealed from all of those below them on the pyramid.

These illumined ones see themselves as divinely ordained to rule the people of the planet Earth, much like the kings and queens from several centuries ago. In fact, these illumined ones were these kings and queens from previous eras. The only difference between now and then is the fact that in the modern world, the illumined ones have found it expedient to wield their power surreptitiously, using as fronts or puppets the governments, financial institutions, religions, schools, and all the other institutions of the established system.

The space in between the *seeing eye* and the rest of the pyramid has several meanings. Most obviously, this symbolizes their lofty and separate image of themselves, kind of like gods on Mount Olympus. And quite possibly, as we will be seeing more and more, this symbolizes that *the dark side* has its origins in worlds other than this one.

And the kicker to all this is the inscription that surrounds all of this. It reads: "Annuit Coeptis Novus Ordo Seclorum." I'm no Latin scholar, but as I understand it, this means, "Announcing the Birth of the New World Order." And even the fact that it's in Latin, tells us that this whole agenda goes back a ways.

We've already touched upon the *New World Order*, and we're going to be going into it more in a second. But for now, don't you agree that placing this symbol, together with this inscription, on the US dollar bill, which, after all, is still the world's reserve currency, is sticking it right in the face of the American people and the people of the world. How utterly audacious! It's one thing to do the horrendous things they do, but it's quite another to flaunt it in this manner. These folks sure do enjoy their games, and they do seem confident, to the point of cockiness, that a *critical mass* of the people of the world just won't ever "get it," and even if they do, they're so caught in this web that's been spun that there's no way they can get out.

Well, *the dark side* may have miscalculated all this just a bit, though there is still so much to this drama to be played out. We are currently in the midst of a great awakening, as people around the world are breaking their shackles, and waking up to the truth about how they've been deceived and manipulated, and how this game is played.

I too, personally, am in a perfect position to be a good judge of the extent and the pace of this awakening process. I have been aware of this *New World Order* agenda, and the part *the dark side* plays in it, for a pretty long time, over ten years. As I write this, it is June 2009. As recently as about six years ago, this topic was total heresy, even with non-mainstream audiences, not to mention the mainstream. You could get lynched for talking openly about this in public. When 9/11 occurred, there was practically nobody who was open to alternative explanations of what happened that day.

When I was writing *Infinity's Flower – A Tale of 2012 & the Great Shift of the Ages*, from 2005 to 2007, most people still thought I was pretty weird, but I detected a definite shift. More and more people were getting it. I could actually talk about this with people, even total strangers. They may not have agreed, but there was more of an openness, and people didn't want to burn me at the stake anymore.

When *Infinity's Flower* was published, and I hit the road with my Powerpoint presentation at the beginning of 2008, I admit I was very apprehensive about the part dealing with *the dark side* and the *New World Order*. My wounds were still fresh from all those years when people threw stones at me. I knew it was only a question of time before I had my first heckler, who wanted my head.

Instead, what I witnessed was totally shocking. Invariably, my audiences were totally plugged into what I was talking about. There was none of the typical yawning, going to the bathroom, walking out, and those sorts of things. People stayed in their seats, their eyes fixed on mine, took copious notes, and they did something I'd never observed before, at least not on a mass scale. They nodded. That's right. Entire rooms full of people nodding. I couldn't believe my eyes. Things were definitely shifting - shifting from people throwing stones, to people nodding. I knew I was on the crest of something really big.

In those early days, I did a very thorough explanation of how the global elite and the *New World Order* agenda worked, with written information filling three entire panels of my Powerpoint, covering all these details. I wanted to make sure people got it. But I quickly learned that this wasn't necessary. People were already getting it. So, I was able to reduce my explication of *the dark side* significantly, down to a thumbnail sketch. It simply wasn't necessary to go into all the details. It was a waste of precious time and energy.

Plus, for the entire fifteen months I was touring and speaking, not once did one person take issue with any aspect of my presentation of *the dark side*. This truly was a different world.

How Can They Possibly Pull this Off?

To complete our thumbnail sketch, we need to understand how the global elite wield their tremendous power in the modern world. They do this through a vast network of secret societies. Some of these are more visible than others, such as the Council on Foreign Relations in the US, which is by invitation only, and which poses as a public policy think tank. Others are almost totally secretive, such as the Royal Institute of International Affairs in Great Britain and the Bilderberg Group, which meets at various places in Europe. One thing we know for certain: it is organizations such as these, which the global elite use to wield their tremendous power. These meetings are attended by the world's wealthiest people, or their representatives, as well as those they hand pick from the worlds of banking, finance, business, corporations, religion, media, entertainment, and, yes, politics, the lowest profession of them all.

The aristocracy and royal families from Europe and around the world are also well represented. It is a total misconception, part of the manipulation, that these royal families have been stripped of their power in the modern world, and that they have become mere figureheads. The masses have been duped into believing that these royal families have been displaced by the elected, representative governments, which were the result of the revolutions of the 19th and 20th centuries. Nothing could be further from the truth, and it's all part of the ruse. In Great Britain, for example, Parliament is the figurehead, and the Windsors continue to be one of the most powerful forces in the world, due to their incredible international wealth and holdings.

In Chapter 8, we are going to discuss the real history of planet Earth, as opposed to the hoax that has been foisted upon us, as well as the crucial part played by extraterrestrials in this. At this time, let's simply make the point that ancient, highly advanced civilizations existed on Earth for far longer than the six-thousand years that passes as our official history. ET's arrived here during these ancient time frames, and played a primary role in the development of these civilizations. In these ancient times, the ET's often operated in full view of the indigenous humans of the planet, who often saw them as gods. Ancient texts and lore from cultures spanning the globe are literally loaded with references that strongly suggest this, many quite literally. As recently as ancient Egypt, the pharaohs showed many of these god-like qualities, and were looked upon as gods by the common people. The myth of the gods of Mount Olympus is probably also based on fact, with these beings frequently coming down to Earth, and tinkering in human affairs.

Like the gods of Mount Olympus, the ET's also interbred with the indigenous humans, creating a race of genetic hybrids, part ET and part human. Due to their links to the ET's, and their vastly superior intelligence and technology, these hybrids were able to assume positions of power throughout the world. They ruled as kings and queens, as well as the inventors of the modern systems of money and banking and energy, which are nothing more than systems that keep the people of the world in a state of dependency and slavery.

Many believe that the global elite come from this hybrid genetic stock. Many too believe that the Caucasian, or white, race is one such genetic hybrid, which would explain why they have had such an unfair advantage over the rest of the people of the world, and have used this for the purpose of domination.

It also provides an answer to the age-old question, "How can humans be capable of perpetrating such horrors on each other?" Well, now we have our answer: because they're not fully human.

The global elite are able to wield such tremendous power because they own everything. Most importantly, they own the major international banking institutions, which are totally responsible for the creation of our money. It is another manipulated misconception that the major governments of the major nations of the world create their systems of money. They don't. The national banks of each nation, which are privately owned, and basically by the same people, are responsible for creating these systems of money.

And without going into all the details of how these systems work, which are nothing short of diabolical, these national banks are also primarily responsible for loaning these governments the exorbitant amounts of money they use to operate. It doesn't come from taxes, which any idiot could see just by looking at the numbers. This is the reason why the worst culprit, the US Government, is always able to come up with any amount of money it needs, as if out of thin air, and can go trillions of dollars in debt, with no consequences. The relationship between these national banks and the governments is one of creditor to debtor, which as we all know, is the equivalent of master to slave. Put in its simplest terms, the national banks own the governments of their respective nations.

The global elite own everything else too, including all the huge multi-national corporations, which means they own and control the vast bulk of the goods and services available to the people of planet Earth. Of particular significance here, as far as their ability to control the people of the planet, is their monopoly of the world's system of energy, based on oil. Like our systems of paper money, the world's energy grid, which is centrally controlled by the elite, is yet another system of dependency, in which the people are helpless pawns. They are forced to pay whatever is charged, and the big boys can throw the switch whenever they want, knocking out the entire system, and causing grave misfortune to vast numbers of people. Add to this the addiction to the automobile in the US and many western nations, and this stranglehold over the people is strengthened.

The global elite also own and control all the major media outlets, the entertainment industries, the systems of public (and private) education, and all the mainstream systems of information distribution. Their control of our information on such a vast scale gives them probably their most powerful tool of deceit, manipulation and brainwashing. And specifically, the most powerful single tool, in this regard, is television, with the Internet gaining fast. The herd mentality is so bad in the US and much of the rest of the West that people tend to believe whatever they hear on TV, without questioning it – even if it defies logic and common sense – a mind controller's dream.

However, all of this power and control amounts to nothing, unless the people play their part in this dynamic. Once the people accept their role of dependency, and being helpless victims, then the cycle is complete. This happens when people cease to trust themselves as the primary source of what they know, and what they are capable of achieving or manifesting in life. Once people give themselves up, and trust the virtual reality of their TV more than that of their own body, mind and spirit, then they are dead ducks.

With all of the above, the global elite are able to use their immense ownership and control to create a vast world of illusion – an illusion that accomplishes everything they want. This illusion is, literally, a virtual reality, in which they dictate the rules of a totally different game. It is an illusion that covers up the part the global elite plays. It portrays all of the institutions of the mainstream system, which are puppets of the elite, as the helpers and caretakers of the helpless people, instead of the primary vehicles of their servitude.

And it cements all this by selling people on a philosophy of life that is totally contrary to our metaphysics of universal spirituality, derived from nature, discussed earlier. It is a philosophy in which the universe is seen as inherently random and dangerous, and in which bad things will happen unless people get protection from outside of themselves. And it is a philosophy, in which people are seen as too ignorant and incompetent to understand their world, and take care of themselves.

Obviously, this is a far cry from the metaphysics of our indigenous people, spanning the globe, who believed that when you connected with the divine spirit with your vibration, and harmonized with the forces of the natural world, that these connections and forces would provide everything you need in this world - in other words, a metaphysics in which we belong in the universe, and are safe, and in which we are empowered to create (or co-create) our destiny.

The Objective of "the Dark Side"

The ultimate objective, the crown jewel, of *the dark side* is called the New World Order. The New World Order is a fascist world government, controlled from the top of the pyramid, by the global elite. This would consist of a world government, along the lines of the United Nations, which is a stepping-stone toward this end. It would also consist of a world army, and again the UN Security Force, as well as multi-national armies, such as NATO, are stepping stones for this.

The *New World Order* would consist of a world central bank and a world system of money, ultimately of the non-paper variety. As is usually the case, the international banking establishment is way ahead of the game in this area, with self-appointed, non-elected world banking entities already in place, such as the World Bank and the International Monetary Fund. These are the play toys of the global elite. The

European Central Bank and the Euro are also models for this, as is the way these were imposed on the democratic (so-called) governments and the people of Europe.

At the conclusion of World War II, the people of Europe were sold (brainwashed) on the idea that they needed a European Union and a Common Market to protect against the Hitlers of the future. These organizations were basically put in place (appointed) by the global elite, with practically no input from the governments of these nations or their people. And the European Central Bank, privately owned by the richest bankers in Europe, exactly like the Federal Reserve in the US, imposed the Euro in the same manner. The people of Europe, and their representative (on paper) governments, had little say in any of these decisions.

Cash and hard currency, ultimately, will be eliminated from the world system of money, probably gradually. Hard money, in the form of cash and currency, are the friends of freedom-loving people, and has no place in a system of monetary slavery. Cash and currency actually allow us to take physical possession of our money, and to do with it what we choose, such as hide it from a fascist government entity, which endeavors to illegally seize or steal it.

Hard money will be replaced by some form of digital money, involving some form of scanning technology. This will probably begin with bar codes on some form of debit card or national ID card. Ultimately, the people of the world will be forced, in all likelihood, to accept some form of microchip implant, in order to participate in the world system of digital money. Those who refuse the chip, or the card before it, will be left out of the system, with no access to this money. In the last chapter, we talked about the possibility of mandatory vaccines. Here we have the possibility of mandatory microchips, and another possible scenario where we will be forced to choose between worlds.

Which leads us to the ultimate prize of the *New World Order* – a world data base, in which all the people of the world, at least those who are deemed important enough, will be forced to participate, or left to fend for themselves outside the system. In addition to financial information for the purpose of transactions, all information, once deemed to be personal and private, will be collected in this data base, and will be available to anyone with the means to scan for it. Medical doctors will be able to scan for complete medical records. Police will scan for criminal records. Airport personal will scan for people deemed to be dangerous (terrorists). The system will be able to track our behavior, in everything we do, even to the point of tracking our physical whereabouts by satellite once the microchip is in common use.

This entire *New World Order* scheme is sold to the people of the world with the rationale that they absolutely and unconditionally need it for protection and security in a dangerous and out of control world. And if all of this wasn't nasty enough, here's where it really gets satanic. One of the primary techniques of *the dark side* to accomplish their dark agenda is to create all the catastrophes that make the world so dangerous to begin with. Because they own and control virtually everything, they do have the power to do this, and it's been working like a charm for thousands of years.

For example, the switch from hard money to digital will certainly occur as a result of a severe financial collapse, in which the current paper money has become worthless. People will be told that the system of hard money is antiquated, and primarily responsible for the problem. And the only way to get the system up and running again is through the implementation of a new system of mandatory digital money.

However, the truth of the matter is that the ups and downs of the financial markets, including collapses, are not the result of market forces, as we are told. These markets are rigidly controlled and manipulated by the central banks, which are owned by the global elite. This is done through the way they create money, and when they either pump it into the economy, or drain it out. The global elite have the power to crash the economy any time they want simply by turning off the spigot of the flow of money. And the global elite always benefit from such collapses because the central governments, which they own and control, are seen as the only means to solve the problem, which invariably increases their power, at the expense of the liberty of the people.

The history of Western Civilization is replete with examples of these fabricated catastrophes. As a matter of fact, that's what our history is – a long series of fabrications (see Chapter 8), making history itself a fabrication. The formula is tried and true. Create the disaster. Scare the crap out of people, to the point where they demand something be done. Then ride into the fray on your white horse with the only possible solution, which always involves increasing the power of the central government, and subsequently the global elite, at the expense of the liberty of the people. And please note - none of this would work without brainwashing the people into the helpless victim mentality, which prompts them to look for solutions outside themselves.

Let's go back to the World War II years for a couple examples of how all this works. Soon after Hitler came into power in Nazi Germany, in the early 1930s, the Reichstag, the German Parliament, was burned to the ground in a spectacular fire. In the eyes of Hitler's propaganda, the Communists were the boogie men of that time, responsible for all the bad in the world, similar to the terrorists of today in US propaganda. Hitler and his media apparatus immediately blamed the Communists for the fire, with no real evidence to support this, other than the fact they were such bad guys, who did do bad things. This provided Hitler with the justification to pass a package of oppressive legislation, with the purpose of getting the Communists by increasing the police powers of the state, and again at the expense of restricting the civil liberties of the German people. Years later, after the truth about Hitler became known, it came to light that it was agents of Hitler's regime that started the fire, all part of carefully designed plot.

The parallels between this and the events of 9/11 in the US, and the subsequent passing of the oppressive Patriot Acts, are eerily obvious. I'm not saying that George Bush is guilty of masterminding the plot to blow up those buildings. Certainly, the use of the term "mastermind" in the same sentence as George Bush is comical, indeed. What we know for sure is the official version of what happened that day is a lie. And the track record of history tells us it was agents of *the dark side* who blew up those buildings, concocted a cover story, and blamed it on bin Laden and al-Qaeda, and again, with no real evidence, other than he was a bad guy, who has done bad things. The rest is history.

That's how it works, and there are precious few exceptions. Even World War II, so commonly cited as the good war to rid the world of evil, was part of the hoax. World War II was one in a long series of dramatic steps by *the dark side* to impose the *New World Order,* sacrificing millions of lives to that end. And they accomplished exactly what they sought out to. They took fear to deep new levels with the atomic bomb and the thought of instant world annihilation. They sold the people of the world on the idea that individual nations were no longer powerful enough to deal with the problems of the modern world. They imposed the first world government body on the world, in the form of the United Nations. And the consolidation of Europe, in the form of the Common Market, was the first giant step toward world government. Mission accomplished – job well done.

Many of you may think this is far-fetched. But for proof, we need look no further than one fundamental, and indisputable, fact. Both sides, during the war to end all wars, were funded and supplied by precisely the same people – the global elite. We've already established that the global elite own everything, with their power base beginning with the world's largest international banks in Europe and the US, and trickling down to the huge multi-national corporations from there. It was these folks, or their subsidiaries, in the form of a vast interlocking global spider web, who brought both Roosevelt and Hitler to power in the same year, and supplied them once the war stated. The most glaringly obvious example is IG Farben, which was the huge chemical cartel that was the foundation of Hitler's war machine. IG Farben was a subsidiary of Standard Oil in the US.

The deeper you dig into the real history of World War II the dirtier it gets. There is definitive proof that Roosevelt knew for days, and probably far longer, about the attack on Pearl Harbor, and did nothing to prevent it. It was all part of the plan, as was the US's entry into the war, and entry into the world community. Roosevelt told more lies about the US's entry into World War II than George Bush did with Iraq. This is because he was one of the global elite's hand-picked boys, and he understood the agenda he was to serve.

Litmus Test to Detect the Phonies

OK – there's the *Readers' Digest* version of *the dark side* and the *New World Order.* Yes indeed – this is the most positive information of all. We are not responsible for messing up the Planet Earth so badly. It was all part of this dark design. We can begin to look at ourselves in a completely different light. We're not as bad as we've been told, for as long as we can remember. As a matter of fact, we're not bad at all. We are a reflection of the divine spirit of a living universe, with the capability to recreate the world with power of our vibration.

But ultimately, we are to blame for allowing it. I know there's a lot more to it than that, but that's the truth of it. The first thing we need to do in relationship to *the dark side* is to learn to stop allowing it. It always comes back to that. *The dark side* can do none of this without our permission. We are so much more powerful than we think.

I take that back. I'm wrong. The first thing we need to do in relationship to *the dark side* is become aware of this insidious game, and exactly how it's played. Then, we need to stop playing it. Once enough of us stop playing it, the game will simply dissolve. It will go away. We are the primary players, and without its players, there is no game. And we will have changed the world with this simple act of massive not allowing. See how powerful we are.

Now that we've gone through the maze-like trickiness and intricacy of this dark agenda, I hope everybody can see how desperately and hideously wrong the *New Agers* are, who so passionately believe that we shouldn't talk about this, or even think about it. Once you open your eyes, and think about it, this rationale is pretty darn crazy, and assuredly has its roots with *the dark side* itself.

Again, the *New Agers* claim that we should not talk about, or even think about, the *New World Order*, or any kind of evil in 3rd dimensional reality, because when we do, we empower it. And buried just slightly deeper in this twisted logic is the implication that we actually create these evils. I have heard many *New Agers* state that evil exists in the world because it is a projection that we make, as individuals and as a collective, of our own dark side upon the external world.

What nonsense! Just think about it – if we applied this rationale throughout 3rd dimensional reality, think about all the things we could no longer talk, or think, about. We couldn't talk about, think about, or oppose such things at the war in Iraq, for all the same reasons. It's all really quite silly. The war in Iraq does exist independently of my perception, or anybody's. And in general, we are not guilty of creating all the evil in the world.

And yes, with all we now know about the conspiracy and the *New World Order*, it is totally consistent and reasonable to believe that *the dark side* has succeeded at getting into the heads of these *New Age* folks. This is how this game works. Whenever any movement, such as the *New Age* or environmentalism, becomes mass in scope, as far as reaching the awareness of the masses, they are always contaminated and infiltrated. This is done both through ideas, disseminated through the controlled information system, and through individuals, who are the equivalent of double agents or plants. Pretty soon, the message of these movements becomes diluted and confused, and more establishment, as opposed to non-establishment, in its orientation, which, interestingly enough, makes them even more popular because they are not such a stretch for mainstream thinkers.

So, it then becomes incumbent upon us to use our discernment to distinguish between the authentic messengers and the phonies. As far as the *New Age* and spirituality scene goes, I do have a litmus test I like to apply to distinguish between authentic and fake, or to say this more kindly, between viable and non-viable, trustworthy and non-trustworthy. Here's the litmus test. Whenever a *New Age* thinker or spiritual teacher is unaware of *the dark side,* or at least makes no attempt to account for the role it plays in our world, ask them a simple question. Ask them to explain why they think the world is so messed up, and be very specific by what you mean. If they answer by saying things like, well, the world really isn't messed up – it's all in how we see it – it's all a projection of our own dark side - things like that – I'd start to be suspicious because the world is unquestionably messed up, and we are not primarily responsible for this.

The vast majority of the big names in the *New Age* scene totally ignore *the dark side*, and the part it has played in messing up humans, as well as our planet. Interestingly enough, they also tend to ignore the role played by ET's, and a lot of other things that are outside their rather small box. They all take the point of view, more or less, that we and our planet are so messed up as a function of our natural development, but that it is not too late to change the course of this.

What are we to make of this? Do they really believe that the divine spirit of a living universe tainted the human race with some kind of original sin? If so, this gap in their awareness is unacceptable. I insist that any spiritual teacher of mine have an awareness of the whole picture, not just parts, and that they present me with a metaphysics that is consistent with a divinely ordered universe – not a randomly ordered, chaotic one.

Perhaps some of these *New Age* gurus are actually agents of *the dark side*, and are working the dark agenda. We know for certain this does happen, and some of them are. We can never underestimate the extreme and deeply sinister lengths to which *the dark side* will go, and does go, to implement their dark agenda. This is very serious business to them, of the life and death variety.

And perhaps some of these gurus are actually mind-controlled themselves. This can be accomplished through trauma-based brainwashing. It can also be done with surgical implants, which send the desired electronic messages directly to the brain. We do know for certain that there is a lot of this in our world, particularly in such institutions as the military and other government security agencies, like the FBI and the CIA, in which members voluntarily give up their freedom, and make the choice to serve the dark agenda.

The Universe Does Exist Independent of My Perception

This whole notion that when we talk, or think, about negative or evil things, we empower them comes from a metaphysical concept that is quite in vogue these days. This is the concept that we create our reality, both individually and collectively, with our perception. A couple of the slogans of the adherents of this concept are: perception equals reality, and thinking creates reality. This concept is particularly popular in network marketing circles, where the primary pitch of these sales organizations is that anybody can be a millionaire, depending upon their perception, and holding nothing but positive thoughts about being prosperous in your mind. In other words, if you believe it with one-hundred percent certainty, you will manifest it. This was also the message of the hugely popular DVD, *The Secret*. The secret of *The Secret* was that the key to manifesting success and prosperity in life was the Law of Attraction. This means that we attract what we are, and if we fill our minds with the right kind of thoughts, then this is the reality we will attract, or create.

The concept that thinking creates reality is only partly true. Actually, to be totally accurate, it's half true. The other half, the half that's missing, involves including another essential philosophical axiom in our formulation. An axiom is any concept, which cannot be reduced to simpler terms. This means that there is no definitive way to prove it, regardless of how we might look at it, so it simply must be accepted at face value, based on everything we do know, and based on good old common sense.

In this case, the missing axiom is the fact that the universe, and all the things in it, do exist separately from us. Think about it for a minute. Isn't it just a bit grandiose to think that we humans, pipsqueaks that we are, have created the entire universe with our perception? Just look at all those stars and galaxies, and the subatomic quantum world that we cannot even see with our eyes. Just as we are not responsible for creating all the evil in the world, these are not our creations either. They exist separately from us.

This may seem paradoxical, because both are true, but it really isn't. After all, on the one hand we have that we create our reality with our thinking or perception, and on the other, we have that reality exists independently from us. Any confusion here stems from looking at only part of the picture, as opposed to the whole, and the tendency to look at these things as mutually exclusive. In other words, it's got to be all one, or all the other. This is a very old paradigm or egocentric way of looking at this. As we've established, the old paradigm is all about matter and control, and the perspective of the old paradigm is all about us, human beings, controlling reality. This is one of the old paradigm's tragic flaws.

It is a simple matter to resolve all this by shifting our perspective, and looking at the entire picture through our new paradigm eyes. In the new paradigm, nothing exists independently. In the new paradigm world, everything consists of life's two basic things: consciousness and energy. And all of the consciousness and energy in this world is connected to all of the other consciousness and energy in this world. It is a vast, dynamic spider web of luminosity and intention. The new paradigm is all about interconnection and interaction – not separate existence.

Perception in the new paradigm is always a two way street between the consciousness and energy of the perceiver and the perceived – not a one way street, as *the Secret* tells us, with us the exclusive creators of our reality. Yes, it is true that our perception, which is a function of our consciousness and energy, plays a crucial role in the reality we create. This is confirmed by viable spiritual and esoteric traditions spanning the globe, past and present. Yet, equally important is the signal from the energy and consciousness of whatever we are perceiving. Ultimately, our perception is a function of the interaction between these two signals, between these two energy fields.

The Native Americans, in the '60s and '70s, were aghast at the hippies, with their talk about thinking creating reality, even though these hippies were reaching out to them in many ways, and emulating them. To the Indians, this was actually degrading and disrespectful to the magnificence and sacredness of the universe and the spirit forces, which they perceived as "out there," separate from them. To them, to say I create the universe with my thoughts was arrogant, and ridiculous. They saw it as the other way around, which is more accurate – the universe creates us. Don Juan repeatedly told Carlos: "We are dregs in the hands of these forces."

We Can be Aware of Something Without Empowering It

So now that we know how all this actually works, let's return to where we started. Yes, we can talk about *the dark side*, or think about it, without giving it our energy, or empowering it. And to repeat the primary message here: it is essential to have an awareness of *the dark side*, and the part it plays, in order to disentangle ourselves from this insidious web of illusion that is spun around us, and to help others to do the same.

But let's cut the proponents of this point of view some slack because they are correct about one aspect of this issue. Most of the conspiracy theorists, who study *the dark side*, and who understand the part it plays in our world, are guilty of doing exactly what they say. They are guilty of reporting about the conspiracy in such a way that they do give it their energy, and they do empower it. And this is a tempting trap that we must all be exceedingly careful not to fall prey to.

How do they do this? It always comes back to basically one thing. Conspiracy theorists empower the very conspiracy they are endeavoring to expose by reporting it in ways that are fear-based. The Internet is loaded with conspiracy junkies, who spend way too much time on the Internet, burrowing deeper and deeper down this rabbit hole of deceit and manipulation. For the most part, they are keen in their facts and their knowledge, but their basic message is that we're screwed. Their basic message is that the global elite are holding all the cards, and that the people of the planet are so hopelessly brainwashed that it's only a question of time before the *New World Order* becomes a reality. They maintain that it's all simply a question of what the next fabricated catastrophe will be, and where and when the global elite will instigate it. The agenda is marching steadily forward, and there's nothing any of us can do to stop it.

Not a rosy picture, is it? If this was all there was to it, it would make complete sense to react to this information with fear – intense fear. When people first learn about the *New World Order*, invariably they react with fear, and anger. This makes complete sense. This, after all, is the purpose of these emotions. In spite of what the *New Agers* tell us, once again, we don't want to get rid of our human emotions quite yet. Like everything else, our emotions exist for a reason. They are an essential part of the fabric of life in this physical body, in 3rd dimensional reality. Feeling the full scope of our emotions is an essential feature of living life fully.

We are going to be talking more about how to manage our fear in relationship to *the dark side* and these colossal challenges in the chapters ahead. For now, we simply need to say that once we've felt our fear, then we need to work through it, and take whatever actions are necessary to solve the problem that caused the fear to begin with. If we get stuck in our fear, and are unable to let go of it, then we've got a problem. And the problem here is within us. The problem is that there's something about our psychological makeup that causes us to cling to our fear. This makes complete sense when we remind ourselves that the brainwashing of our insane culture rests on the cornerstone that the world is a terrible place, which we should fear.

What they are missing here is the spiritual perspective. Without the spiritual perspective, the situation would indeed be hopeless, and we would be totally justified in being frightened. If we are to persevere in this great challenge to defeat *the dark side*, and create the new world of light and spirit, we must wage this battle on the proper battleground. If we choose to wage it on the battleground of the old paradigm, we will be squashed like bugs. This is precisely the perspective of the doomsdayers and the conspiracy theorists. There's only one way we can persevere in this great challenge, and that's to wage it on our own turf. And this is the turf of higher consciousness and spirituality. And again, this is something about which all the prophesies agreed.

Yes, it is imperative that we gain an awareness of *the dark side* and their *New World Order* agenda. This awareness is an essential and primary tool to freeing ourselves from this illusion. However, gaining this awareness is only the first step, and if it is taken in isolation, it won't be enough. This is what these conspiracy theorists and doomsdayers do, and look at how far it's gotten them. They are stuck in the web of their own fear.

If we are to get this whole thing right, there are a few other steps we must take. Once we have gained this awareness, it is no longer necessary to research or analyze *the dark side* or the *New World Order* any more. We simply disengage from it. This is what our conspiracy theorists fail to do. They continue to go around and around in the same circle, like a dog chasing its tail, and the farther they go the darker and more hopeless it appears to get. They are stuck in a never-ending web. This is completely unnecessary, and a total waste of energy, because the game *the dark side* plays never changes. It's been the same for thousands, make that hundreds of thousands of years. The particulars may change, as in dates, names and places, but the principles never do.

Once you understand how the game is played, you can simply disengage from it. There's nothing new to learn. It's the same thing, over and over again. Once you understand how the game is played, you don't need to watch the TV news, read the newspaper, read any books, or visit any websites. All you need to do is glance at the headlines, and you see that it's the same old game being played out.

Disengagement means a couple different things. It means you simply don't have to pay any attention to it anymore. It also means disengaging ourselves from the snares of the old paradigm system. It means reassuming complete responsibility for our own lives, and eliminating all the dependency that the system trains us to believe we can't survive without.

This disengagement also frees us to do the one thing we need to do anyway, if we are play our part in the shift, and create the new world of light and spirit. It frees us to work on getting our energy right, and raising our frequency, so we are in resonance with the higher frequency energy of the photon belt and the shifting energy fields of this monumental time. It frees us to focus our energy on the one thing that matters – embarking on our own ascension process. It always comes back to this, and it always will. This is the primary source of our protection and the primary source of our power to transform this monumental challenge into the divine blessing the universe designed it to be.

It's the piece that so many of the others miss.

"The Dark Side" is Aware of the Shift

As you can now see, there are many reasons why it is essential to include *the dark side*, and the role it plays in shaping our world, in our discussion of the shift and creating the new world of light and spirit. But we are leaving one out – a very important one.

We must include *the dark side* because it is one of the primary players both in *2012 and the shift* and the collapse of the old paradigm. Since the global elite is the primary player in virtually everything that happens in our world, does it not follow they would also be a primary player here. Please note I did not say *the primary player* here, because even with its tremendous wealth and power, there are many other very powerful forces here. This includes possible colossal Earth changes, as well as us, as our energy moves toward *critical mass*.

The global elite and *the dark side* are well aware of everything regarding *2012 and the shift*. Remember – these are the illumined ones, the guardians of the secret and esoteric knowledge, and this certainly qualifies. They are also well aware of the tremendous threat we would pose to them if enough of us ever reconnected to our full multi-dimensional, spiritual potential. This is one of the reasons they are stepping up the pace of their *New World Order* agenda at this time. Just like all the other forces we discussed earlier, the *New World Order* is also picking up steam, and doing it at an accelerating rate. This too, then, becomes part of *the quickening*.

They too have their timetables, and this entire push toward the *New World Order* does seem to be moving in unison with all the other forces of the shift. Because they are such saps for this kind of esoteric and spiritual knowledge, it wouldn't surprise me in the least if Winter Solstice 2012 wasn't some kind of target date for the completion of the *New World Order*. The only thing left for them to do is the final collapse of the old paradigm, which, of course, they can do at any time. And then, in their eyes, the completion of the *New World Order* would be the equivalent of the new paradigm or the new world in the prophesies, and all would be perfection. Remember – they do see themselves as the good guys.

Nobody has a clue how much knowledge *the dark side* has about specific geophysical aspects of the shift, such as a reversal of the poles or the reversal of the planet's rotation. If they do have scientific foreknowledge of Earth changes that would threaten the current system, then another possibility is they might want to get their *New World Order* in place before this happens. This would mean a consolidation and strengthening of their power base, which they might see as necessary because once things start shifting, there will be other forces over which they have little or no control. And again, we have no way to know, but perhaps 2012, or thereabouts, is a target date for this.

Chapter Six

The Process of Ascension

Our primary tool to create the new world
How do we raise our frequency?
What we need to do and how to do it

Fine Tuning Our Body, Mind and Spirit

In this tidal wave of Earth changes and paradigm shifts, the one thing that matters above everything else is our spiritual ascension. This is the primary source of our protection, and the primary source of our power, to create the new world of light and spirit.

Getting tired of hearing me say this yet? I hope not. Sometimes there's no substitute for the power of repetition. It is the answer to virtually every question regarding *2012 and the shift*, particularly the fear-based ones. "Yeah, but what about the pole shift? What are we going to do then?" "Yeah, but what about an infrastructure collapse? How could we possibly survive that?" The answer is always the same, and all the prophesies agree on this. As ascended beings, we will be different, with powers far beyond what we have now. And as ascended beings, the world will not be the same to us. A pole shift won't be a pole shift. An infrastructure collapse won't be an infrastructure collapse.

Let's break this down, and get specific here. What is ascension, and how do we do it? How do we get our energy right? How do we raise our vibrational frequency?

We've already established that ascension is an energetic and spiritual process, in which we are able to move to higher dimensions by raising our vibrational frequency. We have also established, in the most simple and basic terms, that we do this by experiencing life with certain feelings, and specifically, these feelings are feelings of peacefulness, joy, reverence, gratitude and trust. When we have evolved to the point where our essence is defined by these feelings, as opposed to the fear and anxiety of the old paradigm, then we are an ascended being, ready to birth the new paradigm.

Attaining this state does take some learning, and some work. This work consists of two basic parts. First, it's necessary for us to disentangle ourselves from our conditioning, or brainwashing, in the old paradigm, which amounts to deprogramming. Then, secondly, once we're deprogrammed, we must reprogram ourselves. This means programming ourselves to feel the way we want to feel, and to think the way we want to think, as opposed to the limitations that the old paradigm crammed down our throat.

So, what does this learning and work consist of? Let's get specific here. Embarking on the process of ascension means fine tuning our body, our mind, and our spirit. This is what is meant by the totality of ourselves. It is with our totality, body, mind and spirit, that we have the capability to ascend to higher dimensions by raising our energetic frequency. To do this, our totality must be as light and lean and fluid as possible. We do not do this with our physical body. Ascension is not a 3rd dimensional, old paradigm process. Doing this with our totality means we do it with our energy body, or light body, or spirit body.

Relaxation – Our Most Powerful Tool

There is a common link between every viable technique for evolving our personal growth and spirituality in the history of the planet Earth. This is where it all starts, as it always should. This is something we all need to learn to do, if we haven't already, particularly in today's crazy world. There are no exceptions.

The first thing we need to learn to do is: relax – plain and simple. Steer clear of any personal growth or spiritual teaching that is not built upon the foundation of relaxation.

The power of relaxation cannot ever be overestimated. Our ability to relax the muscles of our physical body is probably the most powerful tool we have. Relaxation has a positive and healing affect on virtually every part of our body. It starts with our muscles, and spreads from there to our other organs, and to our tiniest cells and DNA. When our physical body is relaxed, this then relaxes our totality, including our mind and spirit. As we will discuss shortly, calming and quieting the mind is also an essential feature of relaxation, and ascension. This means stopping the incessant, negative chatter in our minds, which is the norm in our culture, and making the mind a place of silence and stillness.

In this state of calm body/quiet mind, our physical body is optimally resonant, as far as being able to connect with spiritual forces. The energy of this relaxation extends beyond our physical body, and into our energy field, as well as all the other energy fields in which we are enveloped. Ultimately, this gives us the power to connect with the vibration of the divine spirit of a living universe – the source of creation.

This, of course, is the highest frequency of all – the frequency of creation. And this is the vibration with which we must aspire to resonate on our path of ascension. And if we take a look at some of the words we are using to describe all this, we can get a true feeling of this high frequency vibration – calm, quiet, silence, stillness, joy. Yes, these are just words, but when we clump them together into their aggregate feeling, we get the feeling, the vibration, of creation. And this is what we're after on our path of ascension.

So, the power of simple relaxation is grand indeed. You show me a person who is genuinely relaxed in body, mind and spirit, and I will show you a person who is happy and healthy. And the state of being not relaxed, which means stress and anxiety, is the one primary cause of all the epidemic physical and mental sickness in our world. Chronic anxiety and fear have become defining characteristics of our culture. This makes perfect sense considering the prevailing message of the old paradigm is that we are not safe in this world. The biochemistry and physiology of chronic anxiety and fear devastates the physical body from head to foot. The doctors of the old paradigm system would like us to believe that all this disease is caused by viruses or our genetics, and the message of the old paradigm medical system is that we are helpless victims of these forces. In other words, it just happens to us, and we play no part in it. So, we are stuck with the only two possible cures – pharmaceutical medication or surgery.

Nothing could be further from the truth. The key to optimal health and happiness is not external to us. It lies within the body, mind and spirit of each and every one of us. It is our capability to learn how to relax.

Body Awareness

There are two essential components for learning how to relax. The first is body awareness. And the second is breathing.

Body awareness simply means paying attention to our physical body – paying attention to it from the top of our head to the tips or our toes, and everything in between. The importance of this apparently simple and self-evident step cannot be overstated. And it's not as simple and self-evident as it appears. This is because when our crazy culture gets a hold of us, and runs us through its brainwashing cycle, one of the first things we learn to do is turn ourselves off. The world that the old paradigm creates for us is so frightening and out of control that we need to shut down in order to survive the madness.

Turning ourselves off means we stop paying attention to the world. We stop paying attention to our physical body, and everything else as well. We become benumbed sleepwalkers. We go on auto-pilot, and go through the motions of living according to external scripts, written for us by someone else, as opposed to writing our own, for ourselves. We become the proverbial sheep, following the flock. And we become cut off from our body, almost like it belongs to somebody else, and we need the doctors to tell us what's happening with our body because we've lost touch with it.

The first step in our personal and spiritual growth, and hence our ascension, is to wake up, and start paying attention – to everything. I hope I'm not insulting anybody's intelligence by talking about things that are so obvious, but since the vast majority of us have totally missed the boat on this, at some point in our lives, we must go through it. There is an extremely important principle at work here, which again sounds stupidly obvious. It goes as follows: we are incapable of doing anything about anything, unless we first have an awareness of the thing we want to do something about.

For example, with relaxation, most people who are stressed out and anxious aren't aware that they are. This is because this emotional state has become their norm. This is simply the way they are, and if everybody else in their life is this way too, then the tendency is to see this as OK. It may not feel good, but that's the way life is, or so they're told. This becomes a problem when the anxiety turns into another physical symptom, and they become sick, usually because their body is worn out. This is usually when they seek help, and hopefully they will find a doctor or healer who will correctly diagnose that they are stressed out, and they need to relax. At this point, they have the opportunity to become aware of their anxiety, and they can make the decision to learn how to relax, or not. If we're not aware of something, anything, there's no way we can work on it. If we can't see it, how can we work on it?

To state this differently, and rather crudely: there's no way we can learn to relax, unless we first have the awareness that we are not relaxed, or tense.

Breaking the spell of the old paradigm, and waking up, and paying attention to life, everything in life, is the indispensable first step in our personal and spiritual growth, and our ascension. When we begin to pay attention to our world, it comes to life, and so do we. When we pay attention to our world, we have the opportunity to learn that we are not slaves to an external script, and that we do play a primary part in creating our world, and our life.

With our physical and mental health, paying attention to our physical bodies is vital, and regaining our familiarity with all of its innermost workings. Ultimately, when we get good at this, we are always the best judge of everything that has anything to do with our bodies. When we first begin to pay attention to our bodies, we will discover things we don't like – things that make us uncomfortable, or cause us pain. This is OK – totally part of the process. This is how it works. Just like before, there's no way we can work through pain, and get rid of it, without first becoming aware of it. If we can't see it, there's nothing we can do about it. So, pain, in this case, is just another example of a challenge waiting for us to transform it into a blessing.

Breathing

When we pay attention to our bodies, the most important thing for us to pay attention to is our breathing. Breathing is our most essential tool for relaxing our physical bodies.

Relax and breathe. Relax and breathe. It always comes back to that. My friend, Fredric Lehrman, is a renowned psychologist and maven of prosperity consciousness. This is practically all he ever says: relax and breathe. And you know what? He's never wrong. It's the answer to every question. It perfectly fits any circumstance. If we know only one thing in life, this should be it.

There are many different techniques for learning how to relax and breathe, most of which involve some form of meditation. Here again, it's so important that people don't make this more complicated than necessary. Regardless of which technique you choose, learning how to relax and breathe always rests on the foundation of the same basic and simple steps. Here they are, and when you choose a relaxation or meditation technique, make sure it starts with these:

1 – Stop your normal routines and activities
2 – Sit still, in a comfortable spot – a chair is fine
3 – Straighten your spine

4 – And breathe – slowly and deeply
5 – Focus on nothing but your breath, and relaxing all the muscles of your body, from head to foot
6 – Quiet the mind – stop all thinking

Of course, as you improve and evolve with your relaxation and meditation, you may expand upon and refine these techniques. This is totally OK – just make sure none of these initial steps are skipped.

When graduating to more sophisticated techniques, keep a few things in mind. There are many relaxation and meditation techniques that involve non-stressful movement, such as yoga and Tai Chi. These are wonderful, particularly for those who prefer activity and movement, over stillness. This also allows us to topple two Goliaths with one stone – relaxation, as well as movement or exercise, which we will talk about in a bit.

If you pick one of these techniques, just make sure you aren't using it as a defense against sitting still. There are many people, particularly men, who are more terrified of sitting still than anything else in life. There is only one remedy for this, and that's for these folks to force themselves to sit still, and work through the feelings and thoughts that come up. When we start paying attention, one of the first things we learn is that any feeling this big is telling us something important about ourselves, and needs to be looked at, and dealt with. That's why we pay attention – to see these things, and fix them if needed.

There are also lots of supplemental aids for these techniques, which use sound, music, drumming, singing, chanting and dancing. These are wonderful too. They can be used to help us relax, and reach a meditative state. They can also be used to kick it up a notch from there, both individually and in group ceremonies, to help us shift our perception, and reach altered states of consciousness and trance, where we are able to move to higher dimensions, and connect with the spirit world. We don't do this with our physical body, but rather to get outside of our physical body, with our energy body or spirit body.

So now, with our relaxed body, and our quiet mind, we are in a place of simply BEING. BEING means being fully in the moment. There is no past. There is no future. There is only the moment NOW. BEING is a state of spiritual balance. BEING is the state of calmness and stillness, in which we are optimally energized to connect with our own spirit, and with the divine spirit of a living universe.

Ultimately, the key to spiritual ascension is living as much of our life as possible in this meditative state of calm body/quiet mind. It's not a matter of turning it on, and turning it off, as in now I'm meditating, and now I'm not - particularly if we return to a routine that is too fast-paced and stressed out. This will not work. Our goal with meditation is to practice being this way all the time, which simply means living life with a relaxed and joyous attitude.

There are those who tell us it's not possible to meditate all the time. They infer that this would mess our lives up because this meditative state is not well suited to the practical matters of everyday life. In other words, when we're this spaced out, we're kind of like useless blobs, who would never get anything done.

This is total hogwash. It's just the opposite. When calm body/quiet mind becomes our lifestyle, we get more done, with more efficiency, and less effort. We become the proverbial turtle, who wins the race with an even pace, over the hare who has burnt himself out. This is because we are in balance, and all of the garbage, which normally slows us down, has been removed. We are able to flow through our work, and all of our life, with little or no resistance. We also have the benefit of an additional source of power – one that was not there before. And this is the strongest power of them all. It is the power we derive from our connection with the divine spirit of a living universe. Remember – ultimately, everything meaningful in life is manifested from our connection with spirit.

Quieting the Mind

We said that relaxing and breathing also helps to quiet the mind. There's a bit more to it than this.

In our crazy culture, quieting the mind is a huge challenge for many (most) people. And those who tell you it isn't are probably kidding themselves. Our minds are filled with self-talk or chatter, which seems to repeat endlessly. Don Juan referred to this as internal dialogue. The one key to becoming a sorcerer, in his system of metaphysics, was learning to stop the internal dialogue.

A sorcerer was basically the same thing as an ascendant being. A sorcerer was able to shift their perception, at will, and they were then able to see the world of energy directly as it moved in the universe. They were also able to act in this world. In this state of altered perception, a sorcerer had powers that defied the rules of linear, cause-and-effect, 3rd dimensional reality, such as the ability to fly and move through matter.

This is precisely the same as moving to higher dimensions by raising our energetic frequency. As ascendant beings, these are the same kinds of powers that will provide us with our protection in a massively shifting world, and our power to create the new world of light and spirit. Learning to stop the internal dialogue is the absolute key to making this happen. As don Juan repeatedly said: "Stop the internal dialogue, and the world collapses."

Internal dialogue is the equivalent of tapes that run in our mind. These tapes are the result of our learning or conditioning or brainwashing in the old paradigm. The message of these tapes is totally contrary to natural and divine law, which tells us that we are spiritually empowered beings. The message of these tapes echoes the refrain from the decadent philosophy of the old paradigm, telling us that the world is a terrible, frightening place, and that we are helpless to do anything about it, due to some kind of a flaw in our nature.

Prior to my current incarnation, I was a psychotherapist in private practice for 15 years in Santa Barbara and Ventura, California. My orientation was cognitive, meaning that I endeavored to help people clear up their emotional problems by changing their thoughts. One of my most valuable lessons, after 15 years, was learning that the internal dialogue, which is the cause of all the emotional problems that are so characteristic of our culture, is exactly the same for all of us, all the time. The internal dialogue of every emotionally imbalanced person I ever worked with always revolved around two basic themes.

The first was self-condemnation. This makes perfect sense, does it not? After all, since it's our fault that the world is so screwed up, does it not also follow that it's our fault that our lives, individually, are so screwed up? That's how our mind picks it up, and that's how our mind runs the tapes. The tapes go round and round. "I'm no good." "It's my fault." "I'm inadequate." And a multitude of variations of this.

The other theme of the internal dialogue is putting pressure on ourselves. And it's the same mode of desperation. Since tape number one tells us we never measure up, tape number two then tells us we must do something about it – constantly. We constantly pressure ourselves to do more, and to be more, than what we are. And since tape number one constantly reminds us of our shortcomings, it's a never-ending cycle. No matter how much we do, it never seems to be enough.

There is one major exception to this. This is those people, and there's lot s of them, who give up all together, and, hence, give in to depressive states. The patterns of thinking are all the same, except they tack on one additional tape – a tape that is the final word, and which is the answer to each of life's issues. "I can't." This is the moniker of every person who is depressed, and the reason why they break down, and feel so terrible.

So yes, negative internal dialogue is hugely destructive. It is the primary cause of virtually every chronic emotional imbalance, including anxiety, anger and depression. Our thoughts do not work independently from our bodies. This is the message of wholistic health, which tells us that our body, mind and spirit are functional units, working together, hopefully in harmony. The message of modern medicine is quite different, telling us we consist of splintered parts, with our thoughts having nothing to do with our bodies. Exactly the opposite is the case. The internal dialogue in our heads, saying things like, "I can't" and "I'm no good," cause us to feel badly. When we feel badly, our emotions are out of whack. And these emotional imbalances are the primary cause of muscular tension in our bodies, and the host of hormonal and biochemical imbalances that are the cause of virtually every physical disease.

When our physical body isn't relaxed, and when our internal dialogue runs amuck, our energetic frequencies also become scrambled. When this happens, we lose touch with ourselves, and with our world. With our frequency scrambled, we lose our ability to resonate with the other positive energies in our world. We lose our resonance with the forces of the natural world, and with the spirit world. And we lose our connection with the vibration of the divine spirit, which is the source of everything good that is manifested in our life. Because we are so shut off, we also stop paying attention.

In addition to paying attention to our body, it's also necessary for us to pay attention to what's going on in our mind. In order to stop the internal dialogue, we must first be aware of it. Again, the tendency in our crazy culture is for people to stop paying attention, and to turn themselves off. When we turn our minds off, the internal dialogue sinks below the level of our conscious awareness, into the deep dark sea of our subconscious mind. Now, we can't see it anymore. It's submerged. And it's here where it does the most damage. Because we are no longer aware of it, we have lost our ability to have any control over it. At this level, it runs us, as opposed to the other way around. And at this level, it usually manifests in the form of some other symptom, either mental or physical. So now, it's even more difficult to see because it's wearing a disguise, in addition to everything else.

In order to stop the internal dialogue, we must work through it. In order to work through it, we must be aware of it. We must be able to see it. My job as a psychotherapist was to help bring the internal dialogue of my clients to the surface, where they could see it. Unfortunately, that was the last thing most of them wanted. Once we see it, we must learn where it came from, and why it's there.

Stopping the internal dialogue simply means letting it go. But it's rarely that simple. It does take some work, for most. These tapes are running for a reason. They have a lot of power, a lot of inertia, behind them. After all, they've been running, unchallenged, for a long time, and playing the primary role in creating our world in the process. They have a job to do, and their job is to keep running. Their job is to keep us right where we are, which means held down in these old paradigm densities. Don Juan referred to this as a "foreign installation," and once we become aware of it, that is how it can feel.

There's only one way to work through the internal dialogue, and that's by becoming familiar with it. This is exactly the opposite of what most people think, and how most healers deal with it. Most people take the ostrich approach, which means sticking your head in the sand, pretending it's not there, and hoping it goes away. This doesn't work.

Actually, just the opposite is the case. Becoming familiar with our internal dialogue means we stop fighting it. And this same principle should apply to everything. We should never fight anything. When we fight with things, we do give them energy.

Here is where another of our sacred laws of a divinely ordered universe enters the picture. This is the Law of Allowance. The Law of Allowance applies for all things in life that we don't like, and that don't fit the picture of a divinely ordered universe. We are confronted with a multitude of these things in 3rd dimensional, old paradigm reality. The Law of Allowance tells us not to resist these things, but to allow for them, with an attitude of non-judgment, and without getting stuck in a lot of negative emotions in relation to them. When we allow for things in this manner, we are capable of disengaging from them energetically. This way, we don't dissipate our energy fighting them, and we don't give them any of our power.

This is the equivalent of saying that the best way we can change something we don't like is to allow for it with the proper energy and spirit, and let the flow of things take care of any changes. We've done our part.

This is precisely how it works with stopping the internal dialogue. We just let the tapes run. And we watch them. We study them. We endeavor to understand their purpose. We get to know them, almost like a friend. At first, when we first become aware of them in this way, they will probably continue to anger or frighten us, but as we evolve, we begin to learn how to detach ourselves emotionally from them. We learn that the internal dialogue can't hurt us unless we let it. We also learn that it really has no power over us other than what we give it. If we allow it to make us crazy, and indulge in these feelings, it will. If we don't, it won't. It's just that simple.

And when we do conscientiously follow our path of spiritual growth and ascension, we do reach the point where we can simply let go of the internal dialogue. We simply dismiss it. We fire it. We don't pay any attention to it anymore. For many of us, it may not ever go away completely, but we're just not listening anymore. The metaphor I use is that it's like the tape recorder is still playing, but it's in another room now, and we can hardly hear it. And most importantly, we no longer allow it to have any power.

When we stop the internal dialogue by disengaging from it, we can then focus our mental energy on getting our mind and our thoughts working properly. This is basically a matter of learning how to reprogram ourselves with the kind of thoughts we want to have in our mind, as opposed to those we don't.

Again, many in the *New Age* movement totally miss the boat on this one too. They are way too careless in how they talk about the mind. They tell us that the mind, or the ego, is the root of all our problems, and they imply that we need to get rid of it. And they tell us that we need to replace it by experiencing life with our heart. That's all fine and dandy, but the critical distinction they fail to make, or ignore, is between a properly functioning mind, conditioned according to the divine laws of nature, and an improperly functioning mind, conditioned by the insanity of the old paradigm. A properly functioning, rational mind is one of our most important tools to navigate the 3rd dimensional world, and one our most sublime virtues as a human being. No, we're not ready to give up the mind just yet. If we did, our world would be in a far bigger mess than it already is.

We need to reprogram our minds with thinking that reflects our newly evolving higher consciousness and spirituality. This is thinking that reflects the metaphysics of a divinely ordered universe, which is guided by an unseen intelligence or spirit – as opposed to the metaphysics of the old paradigm, which reflect a terrible world, filled with terrible people. New paradigm thinking will replace old paradigm thinking. And in new paradigm thinking, we also know the limits of the rational mind, and when to let it go, and trust the powers of our heart, our higher consciousness and our spirituality.

Actually, the simplest and most basic way we can reprogram ourselves is by, simply, feeling good. That's right. That's all there is to it. When we begin to experience the calm body/quiet mind of our spiritual growth and ascension, we will begin to feel true joy, as opposed to the fear and the angsts of our old paradigm conditioning – joy in simply BEING – joy in the connection with our spirit, and with our connection to the divine spirit of a living universe. Joy will become our norm. It will become a habit. It will become who we are. A new tape will be formed. Feeling good breeds more feeling good.

The Healing Power of our Attitude

So, the primary purpose of our spiritual growth and ascension is to create a calm body and a quiet mind. The alternative healing scene today is loaded with wonderful techniques to help people accomplish this, in a lot of different modalities. There are so many – just go down the list. In addition to the more traditional personal growth and coaching methods, there's energy healing, sound healing, yoga, Tai Chi, acupuncture, Reiki, therapeutic massage, shamanism, channeled guidance, sacred ceremonies, sweat lodges, and the list goes on and on. They're all good, and it doesn't really make any difference which technique, or techniques, you choose. Just make sure the primary focus of whatever you choose is calm body/quiet mind.

However, there is one other variable in our spiritual growth and ascension that is hugely significant. Without this, any method we choose will be a struggle. This is our attitude.

The path of our personal growth and evolving our spirituality is serious business. It's not a game. It's not a hobby. It's not something we do to try to be cool. This path does take a 100% commitment. It must be THE most important thing in our life – more important than our partner – more important than our children – more important than our money – more important than who wins the Super Bowl. If we treat it like a game or a hobby, and place it pretty far down our priority list, it won't work. This is precisely the trap most people fall into, and this is why they struggle, and never seem to be able to change.

For it to work, our spiritual growth and ascension must be number one on the list. To many of you, this might seem severe, but all we need to do is remind ourselves that everything important that we manifest in life sprouts from our connection to spirit. If this connection is vital and alive, this is all we really need in life. We can now see those things that were previously at the top of our list – our partner, our children, our money – in a totally different light. We understand that the quality of these things is greatly enhanced by our spiritual growth, both for us, and for others. We become a better spouse, and our relationships become more dynamic and vibrant. We become a better parent, and our children flourish. And we completely change our relationship with money, redefining what it means to be prosperous.

This is also a commitment that doesn't stop. The work is ongoing. There are no time frames. There is no finish line. If somebody says they'll try it for six months or a year, and see what happens, this won't work either. The path may twist and turn along the way, but it never ends. If we try a particular technique, and it doesn't meet our expectations, it's perfectly OK to drop it, and try something else. What's important is we continue the search, continue the commitment.

If we don't find anything that resonates with our heart and spirit, it's also OK to go it alone for as long as we need to. We don't necessarily have to have a teacher or a specific method, at least not all the time. It's OK to be in between teachers, and searching. We can read and meditate and go to workshops on our own – as long as we're doing something to stay on the path.

When we do find the right teacher and technique, this too should not be looked upon as something that goes on forever. Any good teacher should prepare us for the day when we have internalized their lessons, and we don't need them anymore. Graduation day has come, and we become our own teacher. Then too, we can teach others.

Yes, the work goes on forever, but if we're following this path conscientiously, we always reach the point where the work ceases to be work. It becomes a pleasure, and a continuous source of inspiration. It becomes a lifestyle, and one we wouldn't trade for anything. It becomes the most important thing we do, and the primary source of meaning and purpose in our life. It becomes the one thing from which everything else in our life manifests. After all, what better way to spend our time than endeavoring to live life with feelings of peacefulness, joy, reverence, gratitude and trust, and connecting to the divine spirit of a living universe with our vibration?

In addition to 100% commitment, this work also takes sincerity. In other words, when we say we want to change, we must mean it. We must really want to change with every fiber of our being. The reason so many people struggle with this is because they say they want to change, but they really don't. There's no way to sugar-coat the fact that change can be difficult and painful. The conditioning we receive in the old paradigm goes very deep into the fibers of our being, usually tracing its way all the way back to our earliest days as an infant, or even in the womb.

People invariably resist change. They tend to cling to their old, sick, imbalanced self because this is what they know. This is what they are familiar with. It's their comfort zone, and they resist change because they would rather be comfortable than uncomfortable. Change means discarding the old self – getting rid of it. It's very much like dying. No, let me rephrase that. It is dying. The old self dies, paving the way for the birth of the new self. It is the birth of the butterfly from the death of the caterpillar. It is the rebirth of the snake, after the shedding of its old skin. Here again is another instance where our spirituality allows us to let go of all fear. Don Juan said that the sorcerer believes he has already died. Therefore, he has nothing to lose. There is never anything to fear.

Change means taking that vital leap into the unknown of the new person we are creating, and the new life we are creating. After fifteen years as a psychotherapist, I learned that there are few things people fear more than the unknown. It's a black hole where few dare to tread. Many of my clients fired me because they got tired of hearing me bug them about this.

When we begin to loosen up, as in calm body/quiet mind, we begin to take these leaps, and we learn that this too can be pleasurable. We learn that our fear doesn't have the power to destroy us, unless we give it that power. Taking chances, and leaping into the unknown can be fun. Exploring the unexplored areas of ourselves and our life changes from a painful ordeal into an adventure. And this adventure is one of the keys to our spiritual growth and ascension – yet another case of learning how to transform challenges into blessings.

Those who are well advanced on their spiritual path know this well. Taking frequent, dare I say constant, leaps into the unknown is an inherent feature of the spiritual path. Once we learn to give up our need to control everything, the unknown becomes a regular feature of life. And this is totally OK. The unknown is a good thing. After all, in the grand scheme of things, we are really just cosmic pipsqueaks, who really don't know anything anyway. Don Juan repeatedly told Carlos that the world was "magnificent, mysterious and unfathomable." Leaping into the unknown is yet another instance of going with the flow – going with the flow of life – going with the flow of the forces in which we are enveloped – going with the flow of our connection to spirit. And this is an essential feature of our path of spiritual growth and ascension.

Spending Time in Nature

Now that we understand the fundamentals of the ascension process, let's discuss four essential steps to help make this happen: Here they are:

1 – Spend time in nature everyday
2 – Inspirational music and literature - everyday
3 – Food and nourishment
4 – Movement or exercise

Spending time in nature is one of the best ways we have of charging our spiritual batteries. All of the answers to every metaphysical question can always be found by simply looking out our window, and observing nature. Natural or divine law is simply the behavior of the forces of nature and the cosmos, when it is allowed to flow smoothly and in rhythm, unimpeded by factors that are outside this natural flow. We, as human beings, are at our peak, in every possible way, when we think, feel and act in ways that in harmony with this smooth flow of nature – both the nature of our totality as humans, and the nature of the natural world outside our totality.

The shift to the new world of light and spirit is all about reconnecting with the Earth, with her energy, her forces, and her spirit. This is the connection civilized humanity has lost. To do this, we must spend time in nature in its purest forms. In order to have a relationship, it's necessary to spend time together – right? Eventually, it's in the best interest of all of us to live in nature, and in a state of nature, so to speak. The energy in the large industrial cities is far too dense, low and negative. People weren't designed to live cooped up in cities, like chickens. We were designed for the free-range. But until that time, those of you who are stuck in the cities for now need to do everything in your power to get out in nature, as much as possible.

We must spend time in the woods – time around the ceremonial fire - time swimming in the pristine lake – time gazing at the sun, the moon, the stars – time in the sacred garden, – time breathing the crisp mountain air - time walking on the beach, feeling the water with our feet – time feeling the awesome powers of the wind – time listening to the birds, the crickets, the frogs.

Nature is replete with the energy and the forces we need to resonate with. When we have a reverence for nature and for our Mother Earth, and when we go to her with our calm body/quiet mind, we are a sponge for her vital energy and her spirit. In this state of reverent resonance, we become antenna – picking up her sacred frequencies – plugging us into the divine. And that's where we want to be.

Inspirational Music and Literature

Listening to inspirational music and reading inspirational literature are also essential methods of retuning our frequency. And yes, I did say "essential." As in, this is not optional. These are things we must do, if we intend to reprogram our mind, and raise our energetic frequency. I know I'm sounding like a bit of a drill sergeant here, but that's just the way it is – enough said. I'm just the messenger.

I cannot emphasize enough the importance music plays in reprogramming ourselves, and connecting to the divine spirit with our vibration. Music is one of our most essential tools to transform ourselves, and transform our world. In addition to music, we are also talking about all the wonderful things that accompany it, such as singing, chanting, dancing, and sacred ceremonies. Once again here, we take our lead (pardon the pun) from indigenous people around the world, like the Native Americans, for whom sacred ceremonies, including music, drumming, chanting and dancing, were used to reach altered, trance-like states of consciousness, and connect with the spirit world.

This crucial relationship with music and ceremony is something else that civilized humanity has lost. The Baka Tribe, an indigenous tribe in southern Africa, illustrates this relationship beautifully. Their music was recently recorded on CD's by some white folks who went into the jungle, and lived with them. The Baka's entire lifestyle revolves around music, singing, and ceremony. They sing more than they speak, literally. When they hunt, the men sing a yodel-like song, which echoes hypnotically through the jungle, seductively drawing the animals to them. When the women wash clothes in the river, they play the water with the cups of their hands, like a huge, aquatic, splashing drum. And the children, following the lead of the parents, in all the daily activities, burst into heavenly singing on cue, sounding like a band of angels. This is a lifestyle with a very high frequency. You can even hear the cricket-like bugs in the jungle raise their volume, so to be in harmony with the songs and music of the Baka.

We are talking about music here with the power to change the world – music that will help us raise our frequency, so we can shift to the new world of light and spirit. This music will have a particular frequency, a particular vibration. Not any music will do. Most modern music, like rock, country, jazz and rap, totally do not fill the bill. Actually, these modern kinds of music have the opposite effect. They are really not music at all. They are noise – low frequency noise. And their appeal is more to our lower, or base, instincts and feelings, such as animal sexuality, anger, aggression and hyperactivity (movement as a defense against stillness). They appeal to our old paradigm need to be distracted and entertained – not connected to the divine.

Music with the power to change the world is music with a higher frequency, which touches our heart and spirit, and helps us feel uplifted. Church bells or wind chimes illustrate this very nicely. Whenever we hear them, it's as though we are instantly plugged into the divine rhythm of heaven. With this kind of music, we are looking for the same thing as with our calm body/quiet mind. We are looking for music that soothes us, and inspires our higher selves – music that opens us vibrationally to the spirit world. The alternative culture has much to offer in this area today, with a virtual revolution in various forms of sound healing, using crystal bowls, didgeridoo, nature sounds, a wide array of sacred chants, and exotic instruments from spiritual cultures spanning the globe, both indigenous and non.

In addition to this ethereal vibration, this music includes the tribal music and singing used in ceremonies. This kind of music usually centers around the rhythm of the drum. These rhythms are more raw and primitive, like the forest, the desert and the mountains, and the sounds are all louder and faster, but the purpose is the same. It simply uses a different vibration. The purpose is to assist the group in attaining an altered state of consciousness, in which they connect with their own spirits, and with the spirit world. Dancing and physical movement are also essential aspects of these ceremonies, and attaining these trance-like, altered states.

So yes, music is an essential tool to transform ourselves, and to make the shift to the new paradigm. Near the conclusion of my novel, *Infinity's Flower,* the time had finally arrived for my heroes, and the huge group they'd been drawn to, to create the energy needed to begin to move through the portals to ascend to the new world. At this monumental moment in their lives, and in the history of our beloved planet, a moment their entire lives had prepared them for - what did they feel guided to do? Drum, chant and dance. That's right. This is one of the major ways that we have to create a vortex of ascension. Creating the new world has nothing to do with technology, politics, or any other 3rd dimensional structure or process. It's all about energy, frequency and magic.

Reading inspirational literature serves precisely the same purpose – actually two purposes. First, it helps us to feel good (for the right reasons). And second, it helps us to reprogram ourselves, and in this case, to reprogram our mind.

When it comes to reprogramming ourselves, we can do this with both our thoughts and our feelings. When we were talking about the tapes that run in our heads, the internal dialogue, we were talking about thoughts, and in this case, negative thoughts. However, the feelings that spring from these negative thoughts are just as important, and are part of the same overall program. These feelings include fear, anxiety, anger, depression, and a host of others.

Any time we do anything that helps us let go of negative thoughts and feelings, and feel good, we are taking a step to reprogram ourselves. We are replacing our habitual negative feelings with positive feelings, such as peacefulness, relaxation, joy and love. The power of this can never be overestimated. It then simply becomes a question of taking those steps often enough for new patterns to form. We are basically recircuiting ourselves.

Once we begin to learn to quiet our mind, it becomes fertile ground for the sprouting of new seeds, in the form of new and positive thoughts. As strange as it might seem to someone whose mind is locked into the insane thinking of the old paradigm, we do have the capability to place into our minds the kind of thoughts we want to have there. Reading inspirational literature is an invaluable tool for doing this.

As with music, not just any literature will do. The vast majority of people read in much the same way the watch TV. They read junk – with junk here meaning it has no higher purpose. And they read it for the purpose of entertainment and distraction. They don't read for the purpose of getting plugged into the divine spirit with their vibration. They do it to get unplugged. They do it to escape from life, and to numb themselves from the angst of it all. They are filling a void.

Like with music, the reading we're talking about is the kind that wakes us up, and plugs us in, instead of putting us to sleep. It deals with topics that are consistent with our mission and our purpose. And if you've read this far, I'm going to assume we all have a very similar purpose – to wake up to the truth behind the illusion of our world, and to spread the word – to embark on our own ascension process – and to play our part in creating the new world of light and spirit in these monumental times of potential transformation.

Reading this kind of literature excites us, and turns us on, because we are learning, and as human beings, this is one of our most sublime virtues. When we are programmed properly, we inherently enjoy to learn. Even if we're reading the same book over and over, if its message resonates powerfully enough with our spirit, it's still a source of exhilaration and inspiration. These are messages we can't hear often enough. When it comes to reprogramming, repetition is definitely a good thing. And every time we read a highly resonant book, we will see different things, and learn new lessons. As long as we're in 3rd dimensional reality, there are no limits to our learning.

The Ascension Diet

Spiritual ascension means fine tuning our totality – body, mind and spirit. As far as our physical bodies are concerned, it means getting lighter, leaner and more fluid. Proper diet and movement or exercise are also essential aspects of this. And once again, waking up and paying attention are keys to getting this right. And when we begin to get the process of ascension right, one of the wonderful things we learn is that losing weight, and a healthy diet and exercise, are effortless – a natural and inherent part of the process, just like everything else – just part of the flow – a part of ourselves.

As far as diet is concerned, here again people make this way too complicated. Here too we can see how completely people miss the boat, with their susceptibility to quick fixes, miracle cures, fad diets, extreme exercise, etc. So, we're going to keep all this preposterously simple. And it's easy to do this because the fundamentals of healthy diet and exercise haven't changed in...well...forever.

OK – here's preposterously simple statement number one: losing weight is simple and effortless, as long as people have themselves in a state of balance mentally and emotionally. When we have our act together mentally and emotionally, we learn the importance of taking responsibility. We learn that we manifest everything in our life, both positive and negative, with our thoughts and feelings, and through the choices we make. If something is a problem in our life, like being overweight (or excessively underweight), then we need to change the thoughts, feelings and/or choices that created that problem.

Another thing we learn, when we get our act together mentally and emotionally, is the vital importance of paying attention – to everything! If we want to be in balance mentally and emotionally, it is no longer an option to wander through our lives in a trance (at least not that kind – you know what I mean).

OK – how does all this pertain to a proper diet? Let's call it the "ascension diet." Very simple. In order to lighten and trim our physical bodies, and maximize our physical strength, we must take responsibility for the choices we make regarding the food we eat, and we must pay attention to the substances we put into ourselves. The single, most important principle of the ascension diet is to pay attention to the food we eat, and pay attention to our stomach while we are eating or drinking. The instant our stomach is full, we must stop eating – plain and simple. In *Walden*, Thoreau said that it's best to stop eating when we are still a little bit hungry.

And please don't leap to the conclusion that this means some kind of deprivation or abstinence or sacrifice. It doesn't. Healthy, well-balanced, natural food, cooked properly, is delicious, dare I say scrumptious. And eating it is a sublimely joyful experience. We don't have to give up anything. The only thing we have to give up is excess. And eating remains one of the most sensuous, ceremonial and blessed things we do in our lives – definitely in the top five.

And the same principle applies, of course, for eating too little, though this is not as big an issue in places like America, where obesity is so shockingly common. Anorexia only seems to be an issue with movie stars and teenage girls from higher income brackets. Eating too little only becomes an issue when it leads to malnourishment, weakness, or other physical problems. The same basic rule applies here: eat healthy, well-balanced food until our stomachs are full, or maybe a little less.

And enjoy it – every delectable bite! Pay attention to your food. Savor it. Chew every bite slowly, until it's liquid. This greatly enhances the digestive process. Pay attention to the flavors – separate them in your mind's eye. Feel their vitality. Visualize the nutrients entering your body, supplementing your energy, and adding to the personal power you need to be a humble servant of the divine spirit of a living universe.

And make every meal a celebration. Join with your beloved family and friends, and turn eating into a ceremony. Light candles. Join hands, and say a prayer of gratitude for this sacred food and drink that nourishes your totality - body, mind and spirit – and nourishes your soul with the pleasure it gives you.

Of course, I'm saying this so preposterously simply to make a point. There is a bit more to it than this – but not much. Please don't take food to the extremes so many people do, with their obsessions, miracle foods and vitamins, and cure-alls. Food is important – but not that important. It is one essential piece of a much bigger picture, with lots of other pieces. If food was the answer to all that ails us, we would have seen miracle breakthroughs a long time ago. With the advent of the natural food revolution in the '60s, loads of people have had exemplary diets for a long time. Many of them are in great health, but there have been no miracle breakthroughs. Perhaps in an age of epidemic physical and mental sickness, that is the breakthrough.

Keep it simple. The principles of sound nutrition never change. And they never will, not as long as we're in the 3rd dimension. Perhaps when we reconnect with our magical heritage as light beings, we will be able to sustain ourselves on clean water and air, and on the energy that flows freely in the universe. But we don't appear to be there yet.

Yes, there is a little more to it than don't eat too much, or too little. So, let's complete the picture as far as the fundamentals of our ascension diet.

Clean, pure water is a must – lots and lots of pure, clean water – preferably spring water that comes from deep within the Earth. We can't trust our tap water anymore, unless we live in places like Mount Shasta, California, or high in the Rocky Mountains, with a deep well. Much of the commercial, bottled water that passes as clean really isn't. Read the labels carefully, and this applies to all food. Much of this bottled water, particularly from the large corporations, has toxic additives, and most of it has been filtered so extremely that it is basically sterilized or dead. This won't hurt you, but it doesn't have any of the beneficial minerals found in spring water – not to mention the spirit essence of water that is vital and alive, and comes from deep within the Earth.

I live in Wisconsin, and I have bottled spring water delivered to my house every month. It comes from a spring about 20 miles away, outside the little town of Genesee Depot. It is bottled by a company named Century Springs. I am also stock piling this water, in preparation for the infrastructure collapse, which I see coming in conjunction with the shift. If I can do it, you can too.

Another essential principle of our ascension diet is eating food that is as natural or organic as possible. I realize this is inconvenient for many people. But regardless of how far away the nearest health food store is, it is always well worth the time and trouble to get there. We can no longer trust the food in the supermarkets, no matter how natural and healthy it might look. Just remember these food chains are owned by the precisely the same folks at the top of the global corporate ladder, who own everything else in the mainstream, old paradigm system. And remember that their agenda for us is one of control and manipulation, and cutting us off from our multi-dimensional, spiritual potential.

Why would food be any different? As a matter of fact, many of the chemicals in our food and medicine in the old paradigm are a primary means of imposing this agenda upon the sleepwalking masses. The latest scuttlebutt in this area, which I admit I'm not an expert on, is that of genetically modified foods, particularly those that look pure and natural, like vegetables and fruit.

I do have many extremely well informed friends in this area, and they are all telling me the same thing. Genetically modified foods are being used for the purpose of altering our DNA. As shocking as this might sound at first, it really isn't because *the dark side* has been genetically fiddling with human beings for hundreds of thousands of years. We're going to get into this more in Chapter 8. There are many possible reasons for this, and this is a can of worms I don't want to go more deeply into at this point, as it would get us too far off track. For now, all we really need to know is they do this for the same reason they do everything else – to weaken us, so to make us easier prey. Plus, it's a game they play, and they enjoy the sport – like a cat playing with a mouse.

So take the extra time, and spend the extra money, and get as much of your food as possible from trustworthy, natural sources. Eating naturally means eating as much raw, whole food as possible, especially vegetables and fruit. With vegetables, green leafy vegetables are a must, as they are far and away the most efficient means to build fresh, new blood. I have several large Cobb Salads every week, and plenty of sandwiches with a thick stack of leafy greens.

Make sure your diet is balanced. Cover all the major food groups. Didn't we hear that in fourth grade, or something? Grains, such as brown rice, are one of the most fundamentally balanced foods there are. Nuts and beans (the pinto variety) are an excellent source of protein. Meat, fish, fowl, eggs and other dairy products are not essential, but if they are in your diet, make sure they too are in balance. I, personally, eat all of the above, and derive tremendous nourishment, energy and pleasure from them. Everything in moderation is another good basic rule of the ascension diet.

When you do cook your food, don't overcook it. With vegetables, steam them ever so lightly. They should still be crunchy. With any processed food, including canned and frozen, read your labels very closely. Avoid all chemical preservatives and additives. With canned food, there are many commercial products available that appear to be of good quality. I am stockpiling canned vegetables for the impending infrastructure collapse, and with corn, for example, the ingredients are corn, water, and salt, and it's distributed by a small company in Illinois that touts itself as natural. I feel OK about that.

So, there it is – the ascension diet. Drink lots of pure clean water. Eat good, healthy food, and don't eat too much of it, or too little. That's it – plain and simple. Don't make it more complicated than necessary. And don't look to food as a cure-all, which is the equivalent of not taking full responsibility for what ails us, and what we don't like about ourselves. It is one important piece in a much larger whole, and none of them are necessarily more important than the others. And very importantly – enjoy your food. Feeling positive feelings is always healing, and always feeds upon itself (pardon the pun again). This is how we reprogram or recondition our totality – mind, body and spirit.

This is where our metabolism in relation to our weight enters the picture. Metabolism is defined here as the rate at which energy flows through all the parts and systems of our body, and through our body as a whole. Metabolism is a key variable with our weight, and the rate at which the substances we ingest, including air and sunlight, are converted into energy is only one factor in determining this. Our metabolism is a function of our totality, body, mind and spirit, and we play the primary role in determining this as a function of our thoughts, feelings, and the choices we make. When we choose the path of ascension, and when we begin to feel the peacefulness, joy, reverence, gratitude and trust that are an inherent part of that path, this raises our energetic frequency. This, in turn, raises our metabolism. As we raise our metabolism, it becomes easier and easier to lose weight. It just falls off, without any real effort. We just become lighter. It becomes our lifestyle – just the way we are, which is always the key to any diet that works. We have formed a new, happy tape – one that is of our making.

Movement and Exercise

The same applies for movement or exercise, which is another essential aspect of raising our metabolism, and fine tuning our physical bodies. Movement or exercise works best when it is simply part of an active lifestyle – when it is simply what we do, and who we are, on our path of spiritual ascension. In the ascension lifestyle, our frequency and our metabolism are high because we are always moving, at least energetically – as opposed to being lumps of stagnant flesh. It is a lifestyle that is highly charged, even when we are resting – highly charged by our connection with Grandmother Earth, and highly charged by our connection with the divine spirit of a living universe.

With movement or exercise, people also fall into the trap of making this more complex and complicated than necessary. Just like with eating, this means seeing exercise as overly important, or a cure-all, as opposed to one piece of a bigger whole. The end-result is things like extreme exercise, which can actually be harmful, due to the excessive stress placed on the body. Like with eating, or any addiction, people indulge in it in order to cover things up, run away from them. The closer things come to the surface, the faster they have to run. Plus, our time and our energy are the most precious things we have in 3rd dimensional world, and it is such a shame to waste them.

As far as specific exercise, the basics of what we really need are as simple and self-evident as the ones we just covered with eating. It's all really very natural – like breathing, healthy sexuality, or anything else natural. All our physical body requires is moderate, non-stressful exercise, on a daily basis, with a focus on two things. One is stretching and relaxing all of our muscles. And the other is getting our heart rate up moderately, for about 20 minutes a day.

Stretching and relaxing all of the muscles of our body, from the tops of our heads to the tips of our toes, is important for so many reasons. Remember the importance of paying attention. It gets us in touch with ourselves. It also relaxes us, which frees up the pathways along which the energy flows through our bodies. With energy flowing more smoothly, we get charged up. As opposed to the more extreme exercise, which tire us out. Practices like meditation, yoga and Tai Chi are perfect for this, or any practice that stretches and relaxes our muscles. This does come naturally, so we can actually learn our own exercise/movement programs at home without too much difficultly, and change it as we go along.

Getting our heart rate up moderately for 20 minutes a day also doesn't have to be that big a deal. This can be done with a brisk walk, or a hike, or dancing. Getting our heart rate up in this manner is like flipping a switch, where our metabolism kicks in, and then stays up for awhile. When you complete the exercise, your metabolism is higher, not lower, and so is your energy, and it lasts. You feel charged, not drained.

I am blessed to live in the country of Wisconsin, in an area where there are several large parks, which are nature preserves. I take about 3-4 hikes per week (perhaps more in good weather) in the woods and in the fields of these parks, straight through the winter. This also allows me to spend time in nature, with my calm body/quiet mind, which plugs me into the energy of the natural world, and charges my spiritual batteries. For the stretching and relaxation part, I have two sets of exercises, which I have devised myself – one standing up, and one on the ground. Much of it I have stolen from various schools of yoga, martial arts and aerobics over the years, and much of it I've improvised. It's just the way my body likes to move. I do these on the days I don't hike. And yes, I do take days off to just rest, from time to time.
I also meditate almost every morning for 20-30 minutes, as part of my sunrise ceremonies. In addition to quieting my mind, my purpose here is to learn to sit com-

fortably on the Earth/floor, with my tailbone on ground. This is due to an important lesson I learned recently, when I attended my first authentic (and I stress this word) indigenous gathering/ceremony.

My biggest challenge over the four days was sitting comfortably on the Earth for long periods of time during ceremony, like in the sweat lodge, or in the circle around the fire. So, I am endeavoring to teach my 61 year old body how to do this. After two weeks, I am noticeably looser, more comfortable, and better aligned, while sitting on the Earth, and also, much to my pleasant surprise, throughout the rest of my life. I have learned something that I've missed all these years, and that's the importance of our physical bodies in meditation. In recent years, as I've gotten older, I've just done it sitting in a chair, without making my body move or stretch in any way. The over-all effect is nowhere near the same. Perhaps this is why I stiffened up.

The ascension lifestyle embodies the way of the warrior, as elucidated by don Juan. A warrior's defining characteristic was what don Juan referred to as impeccability. For a warrior, every act counted. There was no such thing as an inconsequential or meaningless action. A warrior lived fully in each and every moment because they knew that in the grand scheme things their death was never too far away. There was never any guarantee that the next moment would not be their last. A warrior approached every act as though it was their last battle on Earth.

The life of a warrior was all about energy. This meant maximizing their energy, storing it, and making sure they directed it, or moved it, properly. Every act they performed, and every moment they lived, was a full and efficient expression of their energy. When life is lived in this way, it is literally impossible to be anything but lean and fluid. It's as though everything is life, even resting, is exercise.

A warrior doesn't need the perfect parking place. They enjoy parking far away, and walking, briskly. There are no mundane, boring tasks. A warrior does menial errands with energy and enthusiasm, and with the proper mental attitude. When a warrior prepares food, or does housework or yard work, they do it with reverence, and with an appreciation of how these acts fit into the blessing of the whole. Even when a warrior takes a nap, this is done with purpose, and with the proper energy. It's like the age-old mantra says: *Before enlightenment – chop wood and carry water. After enlightenment – chop wood and carry water.* This is why a warrior always sparkles.

Once launched on our spiritual ascension, we will be lighter and livelier. Our bodies will be calmer, and our minds quieter, but our energy and our metabolism will be higher. And there is one other thing we will begin to experience. We will begin to experience genuine joyfulness – joyfulness at having assumed complete responsibility for our own life – joyfulness at the wonders we learn to manifest in the physical world – and joyfulness at our connection with Grandmother Earth – and joyful at our connection with the divine spirit of a living universe.

Addendum to this Chapter – the Ceremony of Life

We'll it has happened again. Things are changing so fast that it's difficult to keep up with the pace of it. I am learning so many new things about the shift, and I personally am changing so dramatically and quickly, as I travel on my path of ascension, that as soon as I finish a segment or chapter, it quite often needs to be updated or revised - which, of course, is thoroughly resonant with the shifting energies of this monumental time.

Perhaps you've noticed that in the last several pages I've changed. This is due to a significant event that does need to be reported, which had a profound impact on my spiritual evolution, and also adds something essential to the list of items for our ascension lifestyle. This is the critical importance of ceremony.

As I write this, it is August 2009. I already mentioned that I recently attended my first authentic, indigenous gathering/ceremony. This was a little over two weeks ago. It was led by Mayan Elder, Erick Gonzalez, of Earth Peoples United (EPU). Erick and EPU are doing amazing work, both at Deer Mountain in California and Patziapa in Guatemala, to bring about the kinds of changes we're talking about here, and create the new world of light and spirit. I don't want to toot this horn too much right now, as that would get us too far off track. But I do want to encourage you to go to the EPU website, and take a look for yourself - www.earthpeoplesunited.org.

The gathering lasted four days, and was attended by about 30 people. We camped out in pretty rugged conditions in the mountains of northern California. One of the most important lessons I learned, or relearned, was the vital importance of ceremony in the indigenous lifestyle. I already knew this in my head, but never have I practiced it in such depth, over a sustained period of time. For four days, everything we did was ceremony. We celebrated the rising of Grandfather Sun every day. There was a sunrise sweat lodge. There was a sunrise pipe ceremony. And there was an all-night prayer, song and sharing vigil, in which we maintained our circle around the sacred fire for 12 hours, beneath the moon and the stars. Some of us slept, or perhaps I should say lay down, for a couple hours, but it was up again with the rising of Grandfather Sun, with the blessing and passing of the bowls of corn, meat and berries. On one afternoon, there was the ceremony of the entire community working together on the building of the new counsel house. On another, there was the putting up of a teepee. On another, there was a hike up the hill to the natural spring, where pure, clean water gushes from Mother Earth, which we bottled, and took back to camp. And every meal was a sacred ceremony.

Ceremony, then, becomes an essential feature of the ascension lifestyle. Ceremony is so vital for such obvious reasons. Ceremony is one of our most important ways of forming our link with the spirit world – with our words, our prayers, our music and song, our actions, and with the purification of our bodies. Ceremony is ways that we have of opening the door to the spirit world, and doing it very explicitly. In order to make this connection, the door must be open on both ends. It is always open on the other end, the end of the spirit. This is how spirit works. It is always open, and it's simply a question of us connecting with it, on our end, with our vibration. This is the purpose of ceremony.

Like everything else, ceremony too need not be overly complicated. After my experience at Deer Mountain, I brought the importance of ceremony home with me. In spite of the fact that I was unfamiliar with most of the particulars of the

Mayan ceremonies that Erick led, I added ceremonies to my life, and I took some of my usual activities, like hiking in the woods and meals, and transformed them into sacred ceremonies.

A fundamental ingredient of ceremony is prayer. Prayer is nothing more than talking with the divine spirit or any other spirit. Prayer consists of two basic parts: expressing gratitude and asking for help or guidance. Another thing we should know about prayer is that the spirit world likes it when we talk to it. This is just like any other relationship. In any relationship, we can't just assume that the other party knows what we are thinking and feeling. We must make it explicit. We must say it. This shows that we are serious, and that we care. It also can serve the purpose of helping to clear things up in our own minds, like what we want, and what's important.

When we speak to spirit, it is impossible to say, "thank you," often enough. And we must be specific about all the things we are thankful for. And we don't express our gratitude because it is an obligation. We do it because that's how we genuinely feel, which puts our relationship with the divine spirit, and our place in the cosmic scheme of things, in the proper perspective. We see ourselves as immersed in an infinite sea of blessings, and as humble servants of the divine. All of the blessings in this world spring not from us, but from our connection to spirit. Yes, we are co-creators of this magnificence, but only as a function of this connection. It's the same when we ask for help or guidance. We really are cosmic pipsqueaks in relation to the immensity of the spiritual forces that are outside of us. Without guidance and connection with these forces, we are nothing.

The ascension lifestyle is a series of ceremonies. As soon as one is closed, another is opened. Life becomes a ceremony – a ceremony in which we give thanks – a ceremony in which we feel reverence – a ceremony in which we ask for guidance. When life becomes a ceremony, we embody these things. We are living the life of peacefulness, joy, reverence, gratitude and trust, the vibration of which connects us to the divine. When life becomes a ceremony, our opening to the spirit world is always there. And our communication with it is an ongoing dialogue. And the spirit world loves this, and loves us when we do it. We are never wasting its time, or talking too much. Remember – the divine spirit can be in more than one place at a time, so it's no biggie.

Best of all, when life becomes a ceremony, with our door to the spirit world always open, this is when the spirit world will talk to us. This is when we will receive its lessons, messages and guidance. This is when what we are asking for, in our prayer, will be manifested.

Chapter Seven

The New World of Light and Spirit

Visions of the new paradigm
A totally different world
We are going to have to change

It's Up to Us

Let's begin by reviewing several of the important features of the new paradigm, or the new world of light and spirit, that we have already touched upon. Then, we will dive into this more deeply, and get as clear a vision of this world as we are capable of – which, by the way, leads us directly into one of the crucial things we need to know about this. In spite of what many in the *2012 and the shift* genre are saying, we don't know for certain what this new world will look like. We don't even know whether or not we will create it. The outcome of all this has not yet been determined.

As far as outcome is concerned, this is not something that is going to happen all by itself. It's up to us, the human beings of Planet Earth, to make it happen. And there are limitless possibilities, ranging all the way from doomsday for the human species on one end, to the creation of the new world of light and spirit in the 5th dimension on the other. We know for certain that something huge will happen. We just don't know what.

Another way of saying this is that what we have here is not a predetermined outcome, but rather an opportunity or possibility. This is an area where virtually all the ancient indigenous prophesies agreed. The shift is a rare and blessed opportunity to create the new world of light and spirit with the power of our vibration. None of this is a done deal.

In the exceedingly unlikely event this time passes, and nothing happens - we just keep going along as usual - it will be because we have failed – a possibility I am careful not to energize, but one of the multitude of possibilities none the less. I hesitate to even say this because I'm afraid people will read all kinds of meaning into it that isn't there. But let's just suppose that we're wrong about all this. There is no shift, and there are no Earth changes (even though this is already happening). Still, there is one aspect of all this that we definitely know, for 100% certainty, and where there will definitely be a shift. Unless the human race changes its course, it will render its environment uninhabitable in the very near future. I suppose humanity could limp along for a few more decades, and if so, it is also a virtual certainty that the *New World Order* agenda will be completed, driving the world even more out of energetic balance. But we know that humanity cannot sustain itself much longer. If nothing else, we know that the shift means the end of the human race in its current form.

When (or if) we do create the new paradigm, another thing we do know for certain is this will be a completely different world. It will bear practically no resemblance to the old paradigm. It will be a different dimension of reality.

This is a major source of misunderstanding and confusion about all this. There are those who believe that the shift to the new paradigm will come about by old paradigm methods – in other words, by fixing the old paradigm. This is very much like rearranging the deck chairs on *The Titanic*. There is only one way to create the new paradigm, and that is with new paradigm methods, which means one, and only one, thing – with our higher consciousness and spirituality.

This fundamental misunderstanding about the relationship between the new paradigm and old paradigm was vividly demonstrated by the election of Barack Obama as President of the US in November 2008. Most of the political liberals and progressives and the *New Agers* saw this as a grass roots revolution, and believed it was a critical step in what they loosely referred to as the shift. I guess it's good news that the term the shift has become so popularized, but this doesn't hide the fact that these well-meaning folks completely missed the boat on this one.

Nothing is more old paradigm than traditional, mainstream politics. It's a game that totally fixed, behind the scenes, by *the dark side*. It's all part of the hoax, part of the illusion of the old paradigm. Obama was selected, and placed on the throne the same as Bush, Clinton, the other Bush, and all the others before them. His election was business as usual in the old paradigm. It had nothing to do with the shift, and hopefully, almost a year later (September 2009, as I write), many of our progressive and *New Age* friends are able to see through all this.

New Paradigm Methods Versus Old

So, the new paradigm will be a completely different world, and one that we can only create with completely different methods - new paradigm methods. We've already discussed how this rare and blessed opportunity exists because the Earth's vital energy fields are shifting as a function of its position at the end of the 26,000 year cycle, which is the beginning of the new cycle. These energy fields are holographic, which means they consist of the two basic elements of the universe – consciousness and energy.

Amidst these shifting fields of energy and consciousness, we, the human beings of Planet Earth, have this rare and blessed opportunity to shift our energy and consciousness. This is the essence of the shift. And this is the only way we can create the new world of light and spirit. These are our new paradigm methods.

But it is also necessary to know how to use our new paradigm methods. Here too, we use these methods in a new paradigm, not an old paradigm, way. The way of the old paradigm was to reach a conclusion, through our rational thought process, and then take an action based on that. It's all about us thinking something, and then doing something.

The new paradigm way is very different. The new paradigm way isn't about thinking and doing, and it's not about achieving an outcome. It's about being. In the new paradigm, we don't necessarily have to do anything, with our thoughts or actions. The new paradigm is all about connection, or reconnection. It's all about connecting with the forces of the natural world, and with the rhythm and flow of the world around us.

We make this connection with our vibration, and our receptivity to these forces and to the spirit world is optimized when we experience our lives with feelings of peacefulness, joy, reverence, gratitude and trust. Doing this is not about doing. It's about emanating. It is also about acquiescence, which means letting go, and allowing our totality, body, mind and spirit, to merge with the forces of energy and consciousness in the field around us, which are increasing in intensity at an accelerating rate. Being, emanating and acquiescing are the heart and soul of our new paradigm ways.

They are also the essence of the new world of light and spirit. But as long as we're at it, let's clarify one other aspect of this. And this is a matter of terminology or semantics. I often refer to "creating" the new world of light and spirit. Technically, this is inaccurate. We don't create anything in this regard. In fact, when it comes to manifestation, we never do. When we manifest something, we actually attract something that's already there, and we do this with our energy and our consciousness.

The 5th dimension, or the new world of light and spirit, is already there. What we do when we manifest this world is implicit in the term "ascension." We don't create it, but we move to it by raising our energetic frequency. When we raise our energetic frequency to the point where it matches that of the 5th dimensional energies, we simply merge with this dimension and with these energies. This world is already right there, overlapping ours. We simply become it. And we don't do this with our physical body in the 3rd dimension. We do it with our energy body or with our totality, mind, body and spirit, in the 5th dimension.

Here again, this leads us to one of the crucial features of *2012 and the shift* and this rare and blessed time we are living in. What distinguishes this time of potentially monumental transformation is not the existence of the 5th dimension, but rather the opportunity we have to ascend or to move to the 5th dimension. What distinguishes this age are the portals that are opening to the 5th dimension, which will continue to open further. Yes, it's true the veils between the dimensions are thinning, and at no point during this 26,000 year span is it easier to take the leap across the gaps that separate them than it is now, and in the time immediately ahead.

One of the reasons why I spend so much time on these basic, underlying spiritual principles is because this helps to give us a sense of what the new world of light and spirit will be like. Remember – we don't know for certain what this world will be like.

One of the best ways we have of visualizing this new world is the glimpse we have when we attain our own transcendental states of consciousness. Many of us have experienced altered states of consciousness, such as dream journeying or astral traveling, in which we actually enter other dimensions – or, altered perceptual states, in which we move outside our physical bodies, and into dimensions of pure light, or some other dimension. When all of channels are quiet and clear, many of us have received messages from the spirit world, either through spoken words or through powerful emotional experiences. And many of you have experienced other altered, transcendental and perceptual states, in which your energy body has departed the 3rd dimension, and moved to other realms.

These kinds of states are what the new paradigm will be like. And as long as we're in the 3rd dimension, talking about it, it is often difficult to come up with words to describe it.

The Quantum World

One of my favorite ways of conveying a picture of the new world of light and spirit is with the model of quantum physics. After Einstein made his revolutionary discoveries, the quantum physicists of the first part of the 20th Century delved more deeply into this world of energy and light, and discovered a completely new world. It was a world that didn't obey many of the customary rules of classical, Newtonian Physics, which was the prevailing science of the day. This new world also placed in doubt many of our most commonly accepted beliefs about how the "real world" worked. They discovered a world, in which there were such bizarre things as the law of cause and effect no longer holding up, and particles/waves of light that could exist in more than one place at the same time.

It is fair to say that the world they discovered was another dimension. It was a completely different world, and this is what a dimension is. It is also interesting to note that this world was identical to the world shamans, sorcerers, indigenous peoples, and esoteric spiritual traditions have been telling us about for thousands of years.

The new world the quantum physicists discovered was a world in which everything in the universe, at its base, was pure energy. This energy was in a state of lightning-fast movement or vibration. Energy configurations, or forms, were distinguished from others by the frequency of their vibration. As this energy, or light, lowers in its frequency, it reaches a point where it congeals into various forms of what we call physical matter. The process of ascension, which we've talked so much about, is simply a reversal of this process.

Everything is this new world was not only in a state of constant motion, but it was also connected to everything else in this world. This connection was energetic. It was a vast, dynamic spider web of luminosity, like a giant, pulsating amoeba. If one part of it moved, large or small, the whole thing moved.

They also learned that there was a relationship between the behavior of this energy, and these energy forms, and the manner in which they observed it, as in how they thought about it, which was reflected in how they set their experiments up. Different experimental approaches to the same particle/wave of energy yielded different outcomes. In other words, they, the experimenters, played a vital role in the outcomes of their experiments.

Taking this one step farther, this is the same as saying that the consciousness of the observer has a direct bearing on whatever is observed. Factoring out the variable of their own consciousness was one of the primary mistakes made by the old paradigm scientists, which rendered the world they observed lifeless and meaningless. We can never factor out consciousness – either the cosmic consciousness of the divine spirit, or our consciousness as a human being. Remember – everything in the universe consists of two basic things: consciousness and energy. We do play a part in the world we create. And I emphasize "play a part." We don't create it in total, as *the Secret* tells us.

On a more subjective level, much to their astonishment, the first generation of quantum physicists (Bohr, Heisenberg, Oppenheimer, et. al.) all agreed, to a man, that this new world was so dazzling that it had to be guided by an unseen intelligence of some kind. For a terrific rendering of the story of the early quantum physicists, I refer you to Fritjof Capra's wonderful book, *the Tao of Physics*.

The early quantum physicists came away from the experience with an enhanced spiritual perspective of how the universe worked. There was no way this new world could be random. Though it seemed like the more they knew the less they knew, they could intuitively see a hand at work in this. This was a world that yielded no final answers. It only yielded paradoxes, echoing once again what spiritual traditions, from cultures spanning the globe, past and present, have been saying for tens of thousands of years, and longer. Though they could never pin this energy down, in its precise details, they could see, and they knew without a shade of doubt, with their higher selves, that it all fit perfectly into a divinely ordered whole. And they felt blessed to be, and to play, a part in this whole – with their consciousness, and with their energy.

The Sorcerers' World

It is easy to see how this quantum world mirrors the worlds from ancient spiritual traditions, particularly the indigenous. Don Juan was a sorcerer from the lineage of what he called the Sorcerers of Ancient Mexico, which went back 10,000 years. Unfortunately, Castaneda was never more specific about the origins of these teachings, such as a specific tribe or tradition. There are those who believe that don Juan's system was Toltec, but, unless I'm wrong, Castaneda himself never made this reference in any of the 11 books. It is reasonable to say that these teachings were indigenous, in some way. We know this because, like all indigenous teachings, they were derived primary from the natural world, and the intimate connection the early sorcerers had with the natural world. From there, it was passed down from generation to generation, from teachers to their apprentices.

Like every spiritual leader from every indigenous culture, from every era, don Juan spoke the language of quantum physics to a tee. In altered states of consciousness, don Juan and the sorcerers of his lineage were able to perceive that everything in the universe consisted of energy. Peyote and other types of medicinal plants were often used to facilitate reaching these altered states, but when a sorcerer became fully proficient in this art, they were able to reach these states volitionally. This process was referred to as *seeing*. When these sorcerers *saw*, they were also able to perceive that everything in the universe was connected to everything else by luminous, pulsating fibers.

In this state, they *saw* human beings as luminous balls, shaped like an egg.

There were two points on this configuration, where the outside luminous fibers entered the human form. One was about the size of a tennis ball, located behind the luminous egg, at the height of the shoulders, and about one foot away. This was known as the assemblage point. It was here where the luminous fibers from the outside converged, and human perception was formed. The art of sorcery was all about learning to move the assemblage point, so that altered states of perception could be reached. The other point was in the umbilical region, at the belly button. This point was called will. Fibers also converged at this point, and this was where human emotions were assembled.

When sorcerers *saw*, they were not only able to *see* this energy directly as it moved in the universe, they were also able to act in this world of energy. Just like with our process of spiritual ascension, they were able to do this by acquiescing or merging with this energy. In other words, they entered this world, and became one with it. And just like we discussed earlier, they did this by relaxing their physical bodies, shutting off the internal dialogue, and opening themselves with their energetic vibration to this world.

This was not done with the physical body. It was done with the energy body. It was a journey, on the wings of perception, which was performed purely with consciousness and energy - the two fundamental components of the quantum world, and the sorcerer's world. Don Juan often referred to this process as dreaming, and in the early stages, the apprentice usually practiced it while their physical body was in a state of sleep. However, again, when the sorcerer became proficient, they learned how to shift their assemblage point at will, and they could achieve this altered state any time they chose.

The sorcerer's ability to *see* the world of energy, and to act in this world, is what gave them the power to perform stupendous feats, which, from the perspective of ordinary 3rd dimensional reality, appeared like magic. Just like in the quantum world, this world of energy worked according to a completely different set of rules – rules that defied the logical, rational, linear, cause-and-effect rules of 3rd dimensional reality. Like quantum particles, when sorcerers acted in this world, they were no longer bound by many of the physical limitations of a dense, material world, such as gravity. They could do things like fly, and move through physical matter. They could travel dimensionally, and encounter beings and spirits in other worlds.

When they acquiesced to the world of energy, these sorcerers were basically abandoning themselves to forces of the natural world that were external to them. Trust was an essential feature of this. Without 100% trust in this process and in these forces, none of this could be done. Without 100% trust, the sorcerer would probably die trying. With this trust, when the sorcerer successfully merged with the forces of this new world, they would then achieve a certain amount of control over what was happening. It was always a perfect blend of abandonment and control, which leads us to yet another divine paradox of the world of energy and spirit.

It's most intriguing to read Castaneda's first-hand accounts of these experiences. Don Juan is never actually doing anything. He is always being pulled and pushed, assisted if you will, by the vital forces in which he is enveloped – by the forces of the trees, the rocks, the flow of the water in the stream, the desert wind, the crows and coyotes, the mountains, the sunrise, the twilight. And Castaneda's state of consciousness is always part of the deal. He too is always in an altered state when he makes these observations, and his state is always mysteriously blended with don Juan's. He often *sees* the energy configurations. He often strongly feels in his own body what don Juan is doing. He can feel the same pushes and pulls of the forces acting upon don Juan. And Carlos gets to the point where he is quite adept at shifting his assemblage point, leaving his physical body, and journeying through the same realms of altered perception as don Juan.

The Source of Our Power

Are you beginning to get a picture of the new paradigm – of the new world of light and spirit? That's why I go through all this – to give you the inkling of a picture. Remember – I'm not able to tell you exactly what this new world will be like because nobody really knows. But on the basis of what we do know, we can paint pictures. I can send you images, loaded with feelings, which your energy fields will pick up, and transform into an impression that will resonate, or not, with you.

That's what we're doing right now. I am using these primitive words as a vehicle for my soul to talk to your soul. That's what art does. Art is the use of a 3rd dimensional medium (books, paintings, sculptures, etc.) for the purpose of communicating something on a higher level. And when my soul talks to your soul, we are no longer in the 3rd dimension. Mission accomplished.

The dreaming or journeying of the sorcerer is also one of the best ways we can depict how the energy body separates from the physical body, and moves to other dimensions. That's exactly how it will be to make our ascension to the 5th dimension. It also answers one of the most common questions, and a very troubling one, about how we, as human beings, can possibly survive such colossal Earth changes and massive paradigm shifts. It does indeed appear to be a formidable challenge, when you consider such things as a possible magnetic pole shift, or floods and earthquakes of such proportions that entire land masses would sink, with others rising to replace them – or, when you consider the David-and-Goliath nature of the challenge we face with the *New World Order* tyranny perpetrated by *the dark side*.

We will have the capability to persevere in this great challenge, and transform it into the blessing the divine spirit intended it to be, because we will be different. As we progress on the path of our ascension, and as we raise our energetic frequencies, we become more like the sorcerers and shamans from indigenous cultures. As ascendant beings, we have powers and capabilities far beyond those of 3rd dimensional beings. And perhaps the greatest source of our power as ascendant beings is our ability to wage this battle, or engage in this challenge/blessing, in higher dimensions.

If we were to wage this battle on the turf of *the dark side* in the old paradigm, we would be squashed like bugs. In that world, they have all the power. They have all the money. They have all the soldiers, all the guns, and all the bombs.

The new paradigm is our battleground. It is the battleground of the dimension of energy and spirit. And one of the greatest sources of our power in this paradigm is to not to battle at all. That's their game.

Our most powerful weapons are our energy and our spirit. We generate these powers in lots of ways, but certainly the most important is our connection, or reconnection, with our most important power source of all – the divine spirit of a living universe. And we're talking about doing this both individually and collectively. We haven't talked much about this yet, but the collective aspect of creating the new paradigm is an essential piece of all this. We can't create the new world of light and spirit as separate individuals. We must do it as a group. We must be connected, and by this we mean energetically connected.

As we've discussed, the primary way we form our connection with the divine spirit is with the power of our vibration of peacefulness, joy, reverence, gratitude and trust. So, we don't need to do anything, and we don't need to fight anybody. We simply must emanate.

Participating in the Great Awakening

But there are a few other essential ways we generate the power to create the new world. One is by sharing what we are learning, and participating in the great awakening that is currently rocking our world. People by the thousands, by the millions, are waking up to the truth about how our world really works, and the illusion perpetrated by *the dark side*, which is designed to trick us into giving up our freedom and our spirit.

For most of us, after we have awakened personally, we feel divinely compelled to spread the word, and share this awakening as far and as wide as we can. Part of this awakening is learning that there's only one thing that allows *the dark side* to spin its web of illusion, and get away with it, and that's ignorance. When looked at in this way, this web, which can seem so invincible, becomes quite fragile indeed. When enough of us wake up to the game, and stop playing it, then the illusion will fall apart, and there will be no more game. It's all really terribly simple. We have the power to defeat *the dark side* quite easily, without firing a single shot. And our most powerful weapon is our awareness.

When we awaken to the horrors of *the dark side's* game, the sequence of emotions is usually pretty much the same for all of us. First, we are shocked, outraged and frightened at the dire scenario that we have been unknowingly been placed into. This information can be quite overwhelming for most folks. But, if we have an awareness of how to manage our emotions, we will work through these negative emotions, and disengage from them, so we can focus our energy on what matters most, and that's doing something about this horrendous situation, and embarking on our spiritual ascension.

After working through these emotions, we are able to feel the tremendous burst of liberation and excitement that comes next – excitement because the missing pieces to the metaphysical jigsaw puzzle have been put into place – excitement because now our world makes sense to us. Everything in a divinely ordered universe must make sense, and when it does, when all the pieces pop into place, it feels good. It feels good to know with certainty that you are correct about something this huge. It feels exhilarating. It is the Biblical adage come to life: Ye shall know the truth, and the truth can set you free.

Once we awaken, the part each of us plays in this epic drama is pretty much the same for all of us. There aren't a lot of choices. After we awaken, the next step is to detach ourselves from the illusion of the old paradigm, and embark on our own ascension process. An inherent part of this is assuming, or reassuming, complete responsibility for our own lives. This means getting ourselves out of the mainstream system as much as we possibly can. We must learn to take care of ourselves again, rather than be dependent on others to exploit us. And this means taking care of ourselves totally.

Taking Complete Responsibility for Our Own Lives

We create the new world of light and spirit both individually and collectively. As a collective, the first step is to form sustainable communities. This not only gives us a base from which we are able to survive, but once we have that base, this provides us with the safety and security so we can focus on what really matters, and that is our ascension, again, both individually and collectively. This is what Earth Peoples United (www.earthpeoplesunited.org) is doing in two places – forming sustainable communities at Deer Mountain in Northern California, and at Patziapa in Guatemala, on the shore of Lake Atitlan, at the base of the San Pedro Volcano, in the heart of the Mayan world.

We must learn to grow our own food again, and generate the seeds for the coming generations. We must reestablish our harmonious relationship with Grandmother Earth in every possible way. Our sustainable communities must have access to pure, non-contaminated water that comes from the Earth. We must learn to provide our own shelter, and our own fire and heat, and other sources of energy should we decide we need them.

And our sustainable communities must return to true self-rule. In the natural world, this means the power of the community starts with the individual, and builds upward from there to the family, then to the extended family, then to the community or tribe. It also usually means that the leaders of the tribe are the ones who are the most fit for the job, and earn that position based on that. In a community that is truly divinely connected, this is something everybody will agree upon pretty easily. When survival is at stake, and we truly need to take care of ourselves, that's usually the way it goes.

I realize this is a stretch for many of you now – particularly those of you who are living in cities, and still in the system. But everybody, regardless of where we are living, and how, can begin to work on these things in their own way. And it all starts with taking complete responsibility for our own lives. Taking responsibility is an essential step in the process of ascension. It is an essential step in creating the new world of light and spirit. Allowing ourselves to be tricked into relinquishing this responsibility is where everything started to go haywire to begin with.

At this point, to many of you, creating the new world of light and spirit may seem like a lot of work. In order to jump on board this very fast-moving train, you may need to get to work on yourself spiritually, and you may need to start thinking about making some serious changes in how you live your life. You may need to start thinking about breaking the cycle of dependency of the system, and you may need to start thinking about taking the leap into the unknown of taking complete responsibility for your own life.

Well – I'm here to say: that's true. That's what this is going to take. This is simply the way it is. This is something all the prophesies agree upon. But I don't deliver this message for the purpose of discouraging people, or making the task sound too daunting. If you just shift things around a little bit, as far as how you look at it, this is the most positive news imaginable.

If this message has you feeling discouraged or overwhelmed, then you're on the wrong track. This message is all about getting back on the right track – individually and collectively. If you're feeling discouraged and overwhelmed, then you're probably clinging to old paradigm energy, which is non-sustainable. And again, all the prophesies agreed that those who cling to old paradigm energy will be in for a very rough ride in the shifting times ahead. You don't have to be one of them.

And besides, what better thing do you have to do with your life than get back on track? The formula is really quite simple, and it's all been laid out for you here. This exceedingly rare and blessed opportunity looms before you, like a dream – the opportunity to embark upon your own personal ascension – the opportunity to play your part in creating the new world of light and spirit. And besides, regardless of your situation in life, working on your personal growth and getting yourself properly aligned spiritually is always the best possible thing you can do with your life. That is the source from which everything meaningful in life manifests.

The choice is yours. Which paradigm do you choose to live in – old or new? The time will come, very soon, when all of us will be forced to make this choice. As I am writing (September 2009), that time has not yet come – but it will. There is no sitting on the fence here. We must go one way or the other. And if this is starting to sound like a big deal, it is.

It always comes back to the same thing. The most important source of our power to create the new world of light and spirit is our energy – both individually and collectively.

Critical Mass

The collective aspect of this is often referred to as *critical mass*. Our power to change the world as a group is exponentially greater than our power as separate individuals – even ascendant beings. In order to change the world, we must be connected, and this means connected energetically. Stated crudely, we are like a giant battery, and every time a new person awakens to the truth about our world, reassumes complete responsibility for their lives, and embarks upon the path of ascension, the power of the battery increases, and does so at an exponential rate, if enough people are doing this.

Critical mass is the energetic level we need to reach in order to tip the balance of power in the world in our favor. *Critical mass* is reached quantitatively, as the term mass would imply. This means our numbers, literally, need to reach a certain point, and when they do, things will simply start to change, automatically.

Without an awareness of this concept, this might look like magic, and indeed, it is. It works very much the concept of *the 100th monkey*. I don't know if *the 100th monkey* is fable or fact, but for those of you who don't know, it goes something like this. One monkey learns something, like how to suck up ants through the stem of a plant. This monkey shows another monkey how to do this, and passes this knowledge along. The second monkey then passes it on to another, who passes it on to another, on down the line. As soon as *the 100th monkey* has this knowledge, then instantly, every monkey in the world (or region) has this knowledge, through some mysterious process of the collective unconscious of monkeys.

This is precisely how *critical mass* works. Once we hit that magic number, energetically, *the dark side's* house of cards will begin to topple, and we will be freer to acquiesce to higher dimensions. Much of this may happen in ways that are impossible to foresee or imagine. They will not occur in the accustomed ways, as in the side with the most money, the most guns and the biggest army wins. This is because they are happening energetically, following a different set of rules – new paradigm rules, like the rules of the quantum world or the sorcerer's world. And like the mysterious powers of shamans and sorcerers, these things will happen in ways that seem otherworldly, but which are still very much of this world. And as the veils between the dimensions continue to thin, the spirit world will be able to move closer, and provide help and guidance, giving yet another touch of magic to all this.

Critical mass is all about magic. It's all about enough of us doing as much as we can reasonably do, and more, to set the table, so to speak, for the shift to the new world of light and spirit. Then, when the time comes, and the forces are right, we will simply be swept away to the new world on the wings of our acquiescence to these forces.

When we hit *critical mass*, the odds shift significantly in our favor. What may seem like magic really isn't magic at all. When enough of us wake up to the truth, and refuse to play *the dark side's* game by taking responsibility for our lives, it creates energy. When that energy hits *critical mass*, it will exceed *the dark side's* ability to contain it anymore. It will burst forth, and illuminate the world. We are far more powerful than we know.

We will have the power to create the new world of light and spirit because we will be different. We will be ascendant beings, with powers like shamans and sorcerers from indigenous traditions. This is another reason why we cannot possibly lose. Just imagine, if this *critical mass* of us banded together in various parts of the world, forming sustainable communities, and reassuming complete responsibility for our lives. It would be a force that could not be stopped.

The World of Dolphins

Let's paint another picture of the new world. We've already discussed how we must be different if we are to create the new world. Perhaps, when we become ascendant beings, we will be more like dolphins.

Let's just take a look at dolphins for a minute. Dolphins appear to be infinitely joyous creatures. You can see it in their smiling faces. You can see it in the playful way they move their bodies, and in the way they are always playing with each other. And you can hear it in the high-pitched, laughter-like sounds they make. These are definitely happy creatures. And they also appear to be loving creatures. After all, they are one of the few remaining animals that continue to have an attraction and a fondness for humans.

What do dolphins do? Well, not much, really. Like so many of the indigenous people we've been talking about, they appear to have a very simple life, a life reduced to its basic essentials. In addition to laughing and playing, dolphins take care of what they need to in order to survive, as in eating, mating and taking care of their children. And yes, dolphins do take complete responsibility for their own survival. They are not dependent on anything outside of themselves to do it for them. Dolphins take care of themselves by being totally in the rhythm and flow of the natural forces in their environment. They don't have to work at this. It's all part of the flow. Dolphins live in harmony with their world, and everything they do springs from this. I think it's fair to say that dolphins are continuously in a state of *BEING* in the moment.

As we've already made clear, as spiritual people, all of this is precisely what we endeavor to do on our path of ascension. We endeavor to *BE* totally in the moment, each and every moment, and to *BE* in the rhythm and flow of nature and the forces of the natural world of which we are a part. We endeavor to be like dolphins. And dolphins do this naturally and effortlessly. They don't have to think about it. As ascendant beings, this too is what we must aspire to. The more we work at it, and practice it, *BEING* ascendant will simply become the way we are – like dolphins.

When we look at dolphins with our 3rd dimensional, old paradigm eyes, they look quite similar to any other large animal or fish (mammal), with the exception that they are friendlier and less threatening. There is considerable evidence that dolphins are far more advanced than this. There are many credible folks who believe that dolphins have their origins in extraterrestrial worlds, like many other beings on this planet, and that they traveled here, or were planted here, long, long ago.

Their system of sonar communication and their social organization do appear to be highly advanced. Because we don't understand their language, there really isn't any way for us to know. We do know that as ascendant beings, there are forms of communication that are far more advanced than the various forms of spoken languages human beings currently use. These human languages appear to be as dense, clumsy and primitive as everything else in our 3rd dimensional, old paradigm reality. Communication in words is imprecise indeed, as words have different meanings for different people. Think about it for a minute – as human beings, we are incapable of communicating through our language with the vast majority of the rest of the people of the planet because we all speak different languages. Same species, and we can't communicate, not if we rely upon language. I don't know this for a fact, but I'll just bet that all the dolphins of the planet, regardless of type and region, are able to communicate through the universal language of their sonar, or something else.

Communication in the New Paradigm

In the new paradigm, we will learn to use different forms of communication. We will learn to move past words, with all their imprecision, and into forms of universal communication, with little or no ambiguity. Pure sound, as in tones, like the dolphins, is one example. Many of us who are living a new paradigm lifestyle are already doing this, with our ceremonies, which use drumming, music, chanting and dancing to reach higher states of consciousness, and tap into the spirit world. These are truly universal forms of communication, as they are all designed to do precisely the same thing – connect with the divine spirit, and with the spirit world. The divine spirit doesn't need words. Communication at this level is all about vibration. Those of us who are plugged into spirit can participate in any sacred ceremony, in any language, from any culture, and totally "get it" because of the sound, the vibration, the movements, and the feelings, as well as the heart to heart and spirit to spirit aspect of this type of communication. Feelings like peacefulness, joy, reverence, gratitude and trust don't need words. A gentle touch or a smile speaks volumes.

As ascendant beings, in the new paradigm, our communication will also move beyond the limits of our physical bodies. It will be beyond sound, and it will move into the higher frequencies of energy that cannot be heard with our ears, or detected with any of our other four physical senses. We have some words to describe a few of these forms of communication. One is extrasensory, which simply means communication you just pick up, in the energy and forces around you. ESP is perception of the "I just knew it" variety. Another is telepathy, which is communication between minds, in the form of thought waves or energy. Like everything else in the 5th dimension, this kind of non-verbal, high frequency communication is between our energy bodies and higher consciousness, not our physical bodies. And those are the pathways along which it travels. In its highest form, it is communication between our hearts, between our spirits. And we really don't have words to describe it. It just is.

In Chapter One of my novel, *Infinity's Flower – A Tale of 2012 & the Great Shift of the Ages*, I demonstrate several possibilities about how this kind of communication can work. My two primary heroes, David and Kelly, are hiding out in a small cabin in the wilderness on an Indian Reservation in South Dakota, something we all might be soon be forced to do, when *the dark side's New World Order* agenda either becomes too oppressive, or forces us to make a choice with one of its policies, like mandatory vaccines or microchip implants.

David and Kelly are visited late one night by a shaman, a light traveler, named Hibutu, from an indigenous tribe that has never been touched by modern civilization, deep within the jungles of South America. Hibutu's physical image materializes before them in a cocoon of luminescence, and he takes them, or their energy bodies, on a light journey, or dream journey, to his village, where they meet his wife, also a shaman, named Mahnya, and several members of their tribe, named the Togi, obviously a play on the Kogi of real life.

The only verbal communication the Togi use with David and Kelly are primitive sounds, such as ahh, mmm, and hah. When they make these sounds, together with facial expressions that convey joy, love and yearning, David and Kelly feel that something is taking a hold of them, and possessing them. Then, in a mutual, trance-like state, the Togi plant pictures in their minds, which communicate with perfect clarity, far exceeding what words ever could. And David and Kelly don't even need to concern themselves with responding because they know that the Togi, in this state of possession or union, are able to read their thoughts, their feelings, and their essence with perfect clarity.

Perhaps this is something similar to what dolphins do, with their sonar communication. We don't know because we don't speak this language. It is a possibility, particularly if they are more highly advanced beings. I do know, personally, that whenever I hear dolphin sounds, it strikes a chord very deep within my soul. These tones and high frequencies draw me, hypnotically, and I feel the way I do when I am in my own heightened spiritual state. And I know with certainty that there is a lot more to it than just high-pitched mammal sounds.

Government in the New Paradigm

There is one more thing about dolphins we could emulate, and take with us to the 5th dimension. We've already hinted at this when talking about how dolphins take complete responsibility for taking care of themselves, and don't depend on anything external to them to do it for them. In other words, dolphins don't need government. They can take care of themselves, and they do this naturally, just by being in the flow. And, as ascendant beings, dolphins don't have any problems. Government is all about fixing all the problems that we, as such a flawed species, have created. It's all about protecting good people from bad people. But if there are no problems and no bad dolphins, there's no need for government – an extremely valuable lesson here.

So, how does all this apply for human beings? What part does government play in this discussion? What kind of government would we have in the new paradigm? And if our current forms of government are swept away by the shift and the collapse of the old paradigm, what forms of government should we replace them with here on Earth, in the interlude before the shift?

This is definitely another possible scenario of the shift, and one we must consider. We must always remind ourselves of the extraordinarily volatile nature of these times, and when things really start to happen, they are going to happen very rapidly. All the prophesies agreed on this. Perhaps, by the time you read this, they already have. I sometimes have doubts that there is even enough time to publish this book.

Our current governments could be swept away in the blink of an eye, and there are many different ways this could occur. One thing that could trigger this is a collapse of our energy grid and technological infrastructure. Even in normal times, this is always a distinct possibility due to the extreme fragility and interdependence of this system. If one part goes, the whole thing could go. This could happen any time, and in any number of ways. In the modern world, this infrastructure depends upon an intricate network of satellites surrounding the Earth, which is vulnerable to space accidents or other tinkering, or which could be knocked out by an unanticipated shower of large meteors – not to mention the other colossal Earth changes that might accompany the shift, such as a pole shift. One ingenious hacker could take down the whole thing.

We could be without infrastructure, and without government, in the blink of an eye – sort of a state of nature, if you will. And I say: what a blessing! This is just what we need. It is the perfect opportunity to begin building the new world of light and spirit, and the perfect foundation to start from. And if we're properly prepared, and if we've begun to form our sustainable communities, then we will be in a position to handle this challenge. And if it does come to this, then it would definitely be a good idea to get out of the cities. They will be places of unmanageable chaos, and whatever remains of our current government will be there, in full military authority.

There is also the distinct possibility that this will occur before any kind of dimensional shift or transformation. In other words, we'll still be here, in the 3rd dimension, in our present physical form. This would be a situation in which we would be forced to take responsibility for our own survival, and begin to build the new world, or perish. How wonderful!

Without giving the story away, this is what happens at the end of *Infinity's Flower*. After an epic roller coaster ride of events, our band of heroes, greatly expanded in numbers, and other bands of spirit warriors around the country and the world, are left with no infrastructure – no money, no electricity, no nothing. They must start from scratch to build the new world. But they are not afraid because they know they have the only two things that they need: their connection with Grandmother Earth, and their connection with the divine spirit. Yes, the door is wide open for a sequel. I wonder if I'll have the time, or whether I'll simply be living all this – perhaps at Deer Mountain or Patziapa, Guatemala.

Under this kind of circumstance, we would need to figure out what kind of government to have. What would government in the new paradigm look like?

There are a couple of possible scenarios to look at here. Let's answer the easiest question first. What kind of government will we have when we ascend to the 5th dimension? The snappy answer – none. And just like dolphins, we won't need it. It doesn't fit this world. As ascendant beings, we will have reconnected with the rhythm and flow of nature and the forces of the natural world. We will have made this connection with our vibration of peacefulness, joy, reverence, gratitude and trust. We will be in a state of harmony and balance both within ourselves and external to us. As such, there will be no problems and no bad people, so there is no need for government.

This may sound kind of silly, but in this way, the 5th dimension is a lot like the traditional idea of heaven. Bad people don't get in. Only ascendant beings will be able to move to the 5th dimension. In this case, St. Peter's Gate is a frequency fence, and the bad guys get blocked with their low vibration. If there aren't any bad people, what do you need government for? Besides, we will have transcended the material world. Doesn't this eliminate just about every problem or issue that government deals with anyway?

But let's take a look at the other scenario, mentioned above. What if our current governments in the 3rd dimension are swept away before a dimensional shift, and we are in the position of replacing them with something else. I'm only going to discuss one possible scenario here because this is the only one I see that will allow us, as ascended beings, to take advantage of this opportunity to create the new world.

If our current governments were swept away, we can make a few assumptions. Even if our systems of money or energy don't collapse, which is highly unlikely, we can still assume that things in general would be in a severe state of disarray. The most extreme chaos would be in the cities, and that's where whatever remains of martial law would be found. It's pretty fair to assume that out in the country people could do whatever they pleased – the farther away the better. And people in remote places, far away from the cities, with fertile land and fresh, clean water, would have an opportunity to start over, and build a world of their choosing.

This is where our sustainable, new paradigm communities need to be. These will be places where we will be able to survive, and we will be safe to do what we need to do spiritually to complete the ascension to the 5th dimension. So, as far as government is concerned, we are back to the model of the tribe. If this sounds like we're getting back to the basics, we are. By tribe, I mean a small community, population in the hundreds at the most, which is self-sustaining, and which lives in harmony with nature.

Before we talk about the government of our tribe, there are a few other things we need to make sure we understand about it. This tribe is a new paradigm tribe. It is a tribe of ascended beings who have taken complete responsibility for their own lives and that of the tribe. It is a tribe of spiritual warriors who are united in their mission to transform the challenges in our world into a blessing, and create the new world of light and spirit. It is group who are together because they want to be. These are not helpless victims, who are forced anywhere by circumstances. They are united. They united by their purpose. They are united by their common path of spiritual ascension.

These are ascended beings, who are united by their vibration of peacefulness, joy, reverence, gratitude and trust, and by their link to spirit. These are all very powerful bonds. This group will be strong, and it will be powerful. It will also be unified by the feelings of love that everybody has for everybody else (even people they don't particularly like). Because they are ascended beings, connected to the Earth and connected to spirit, there won't be too many problems, at least not as far as the community is concerned. The main reason for all the problems in the old paradigm world of today, and hence the need for big government, is the fact that people have allowed themselves to become so hideously unplugged from the rhythm and flow of nature and life. Once that reconnection is made, the problems start going away, as does the need for government. In this kind of a community, people can just live their lives freely.

In a community of ascended beings, united in purpose, the affairs of everyday life tend to just take care of themselves, just like everything else in life. That's how things work when people, or groups of people, live in harmony with the forces of the natural world. It sounds so simple, but it's totally true. Things just flow, like dolphins.

Of course, there's work to be done, lots of work to be done. Taking responsibility for one's survival takes work – always. But it always gets done. And it always gets done well, and on time. And everybody participates, from the spiritual leaders and elders on down to small children. And people participate according to their abilities. Those who are the most learned and skilled in any task would become the leaders of that task, and this would happen naturally, in the flow. They don't need anybody or anything external to them to decide this for them. They know. The farmers would do the farming. The builders would do the building. Mothers would do the mothering. And parents would educate their own children.

And everybody, the entire community, is always in perfect agreement about what needs to be done. They don't need government to figure this out for them. Nature is their guide. When people are properly attuned to nature's signals, nature is always very clear in her communication about what needs to be done. In an ascended community, people would just do it.

As far as actual government is concerned, all this type of community would need is a council of elders, made up of both men and women (grandfathers and grandmothers). Again, a member of the community would become an elder based upon their ability. It would be no secret who the leaders were in all the various areas – spirituality, healing, farming, art, music, technology, etc. These leaders would simply rise to the top, and be recognized by the community as their leaders. Would they be elected by a vote of the tribe? Possibly, but even that doesn't make that much difference.

As ascendant beings, these leaders would lead simply by being themselves, and doing what they do naturally. Once established, the council of elders would select its own members, but again, this simply means recognizing those members of the tribe who had earned to be chosen. And the council of elders would select a chief, or a leader who would lead them, and be a final arbiter on most matters.

If we're in a state of nature, or close to it, that's really about all the government we need. And one of the beauties of all this is it happens automatically, all by itself, as part of the flow of nature. None of it even needs to be written down.

Some of you may think this is far-fetched, or excessively idealistic. We must continue to remind ourselves that this community is a group of ascended beings. As such, everything will be totally different. We have never lived in such a world. So, we become very cynical about human nature, and we believe that such a world could never exist because human beings are such scum bags. This is exactly the way our controllers, *the dark side*, want us to think. We can't imagine a world populated entirely by people who are wise, healthy, balanced and ethical, or a world that is governed by the cream of this crop, instead of parasitic, bureaucratic flunkies.

This is why we must look to our sisters and brothers, the dolphins, for a model for this. This is how it is done, and it is within our nature to do it too. We are capable of this, and on the path of our spiritual ascension, this is what we must aspire to.

The Right of Every Individual to be Free

We won't need many laws in our sustainable community. The laws of nature will be our laws. Spiritual laws will be important guides for us, such as the law of living in harmony with the Earth, and the law of not interfering with the natural flow of energy in the universe.

Whatever secular laws we have in this community would rest upon the foundation of one fundamental law. This is the right of every individual person to be free, which is our birthright as a child of the universe. Anything that interfered with this right would be considered contrary to the laws of nature, and therefore illegal. It would be up to the council of elders and the community to decide what to do with anybody who consistently disobeyed this law. Banishment from the community makes the most sense. But in a community such as this, this is unlikely. Once we learn to get back into the rhythm and flow, we don't want to go back. Why be in disharmony when you can be in harmony? It just doesn't make sense, and deviations from this would be rare – just like the dolphins.

Like the original Constitution of the US, which, in theory, was a wonderful document (with some notable flaws), the power or authority of our community would start at the bottom, with the free and empowered individual, and work its way up from there. That is its cornerstone, and if it is taken away, the entire edifice crumbles. We are at our best, as a species, when people are free and empowered to be themselves. This is the source of everything that distinguishes us, and everything important that we do, such as our intelligence, our creativity, our ingenuity, and our ability to transform the challenges of the 3rd dimension into the blessings of the 5th. The council of elders would have the wisdom to know this, and act accordingly.

The next step on the ladder of power or authority would be the family. In our ascended community, the sanctity and autonomy of the family would not only be honored, it would be protected. The traditional nuclear family, consisting of mother, father, children, grandchildren, great grandchildren, etc, would be looked upon as mini-governments in and of themselves. The disintegration of the family in our modern world is one of the surest signs of the decay and the collapse of the old paradigm. In the natural world, the family is the soil from which the empowered individual sprouts, grows and develops. So again, without the family, the entire system collapses.

The breakup of the family, and parents surrendering their right and their responsibility to raise and educate their own children, is totally contrary to the laws of nature, and a clear sign of the disconnection from life's rhythm and flow. We can see this so clearly in the animal world, where even our pet dogs and cats remember how to nurture and teach their children according to the laws of nature that are encoded in their genes. Our dogs and cats learn the essence of being dogs and cats from their parents. Without this connection, nature and natural development is thwarted, and these dogs and cats will be cut off their true nature, and their power. I live on a small lake, in the countryside in Wisconsin, and I can see this in the ducks, which have fallen into the trap of depending on handouts from humans for their food. As a result, they have become unplugged from their true nature. They have forgotten how to take care of themselves, including migrating, which is essential to their survival. They swim around aimlessly all day long, totally bored, and end up fighting amongst themselves because they have nothing else to do. Sound like any other species we can think of?

The government of our small, self-sustaining community of ascended beings doesn't need to be a whole lot more complicated than this. And if we are to create the new world of light and spirit, it looks to me, and my guidance tells me, that communities like these will have to be the nuclei from which the new world will manifest. There's no other way it can happen. Remember - we cannot use the old paradigm as our instrument to build the new world. The existing system is just way too messed up, and it is totally the wrong energy. We must start over. We must return to a state of nature, or to say this differently, we must get more primitive. In a state of nature, the easiest and most natural social unit to form is the small, self-sustaining tribe. It's just enough people to make things work, and not too many to make things too complicated.

Then the question becomes whether it's within the natural scheme of things, or whether it's necessary for any other reason, for these tribes to join together into bigger tribes, and hence, the possible need for bigger, or at least different, forms of government. And ultimately, in this state of nature, is it necessary for all the people of planet Earth to join together into some form of world government? Certainly, the prevailing thinking in the old paradigm is that this is imperative because the problems of the world are way too vast for any single nation to tackle on its own.

In answering these questions, we must remind ourselves, once again, who we are, and what our mission is. As ascendant beings, whose mission is to create the new world of light and spirit, we are seeking a world in which there will be no need for government. And while we're here in the 3rd dimension, preparing for the shift, the less government we have the better. That's nature's way, which makes it the way of the new paradigm. So, any discussion of forms of government bigger than a tribal council of elders, in a state of nature, is going in the wrong direction. It simply doesn't fit because it plunges us right back right where we don't want to be - in the old paradigm.

Is global government necessary? And I'm not referring here to a malevolent, totalitarian global government, like the *New World Order*. Of course, we don't want that.

But what about a benevolent world government, administered by ascendant beings? The prevailing belief among liberals, progressives and *New Agers* is that this is what we need. But again, let's not forget our premise for why we need global government to begin with. We need it because the problems that are ripping apart the modern world are global in nature, such as pollution, climate change and killer viruses. When we become ascendant beings, who are living in harmony with nature, the problems will all start to go away. Remember – the problems exist to begin with because we are not ascended beings, who are living in harmony with nature.

So, the question morphs into a different one. As ascendant beings, who are living in harmony with nature, do we need global government? And the answer clearly is no. Why? What do we need it for? Everything's perfectly OK the way it is, just like the dolphins. That doesn't mean we can't all get together and love each other. That doesn't mean we can't transact business with each other, and trade goods and services. But we don't need global government for that.

Technology in the New Paradigm

Obviously, an important part of the message here is that we need to become more primitive in many ways to create the new world. Now, I know a lot of you techno-geeks are probably gnashing your teeth at hearing this. But no need to because this is not an anti-technology message. Besides, there's nothing inherently wrong with technology. It's all in how it's used.

The problem with technology in the old paradigm is that we have allowed ourselves to become dependent on it. And just like everything else in the material world of the old paradigm, this is at the expense of the source of our greatest power - our higher consciousness and spirituality. The old paradigm looks primarily to technology to solve the problems of the world, and we in the new paradigm know that this is folly. The key to changing the world is not in any plan, program or policy. The only way to change the world is by changing the collective human heart.

There will be technology in the new paradigm, but like everything else, it will be different. And we will look at it differently, just as we will look at this entire world differently. We are no longer dealing with a world strictly of matter. New paradigm technology will include the human element and the spiritual element, both of which were completely extracted from old paradigm technology. The variables of this new technology include our consciousness, our energy, and yes, our spirit, as well as the consciousness, energy and spirit of everything else in the universe, both macroscopically and microscopically. When old paradigm science factored out the consciousness of the scientist and factored out God, it was measuring a world that was essentially dead. They cut their world off from spirit, which is essentially what is killing the old paradigm. It is a world cut off from its life source.

New paradigm technology will rely far more upon natural materials, taken directly from Grandmother Earth with gratitude and reverence, such as plants, stones and crystals, rather than synthetic materials, such as plastic. And at its most evolved levels, new paradigm technology won't use material substances at all. In the 5th dimension, the primary components of technology will simply be our higher consciousness and higher frequency energy. In the new paradigm, we will have the capability to move from one dimension to another on the wings of our energy body and consciousness. We won't need a massive material ship for this. This is a form of the highest technology. In my novel *Masters of Destiny*, a scientist invents a diagnostic device, which uses the leaves of living plants to detect and measure energetic imbalances in the human body.

When looked at in this way, old paradigm technology can begin to look quite primitive and crude, with all of its wires, plugs, gadgets and hardware, all of which require a source of tangible, low frequency electricity. Old paradigm science and technology are geared to the higher densities and lower frequencies of energy in the 3rd dimensional material world. In contrast, in the new paradigm, a crystal pyramid, placed on a vortex of the Earth's energy, and in alignment with a key energetic point in the heavens, has the capacity to attract and store higher frequency and holographic forms of energy. This is a high-tech gadget of the highest order.

When we return to the flow, nature is our technology. For example, when we learn to communicate telepathically, our brain, which is the transmitter of these signals, is a magnificent computer. Will we have even fancier computers in the new paradigm? Probably not. What do dolphins need computers for? The Maya, the

Hopi and the Egyptians didn't use computers to make their observations of the stars and of nature, to do their calculating, or to build their amazing structures. A plant photosynthesizing light into green leaves and flowers is a miracle of high technology.

An Intergalactic Sisterhood and Brotherhood

Are you beginning to get a feel for what the new world of light and spirit might be like? Again, all I can do is paint pictures. So far, we've had the picture of the quantum world, the picture of the indigenous sorcerer's world, and the picture of the dolphins' world. And hopefully, our discussion of government and technology in the new paradigm adds a few more strokes to this picture.

So now, let's add a few final strokes by addressing a few other questions about ascension and the new world. Since ascension is moving with our energy body to a world of pure consciousness and spirit, what happens to the 3rd dimensional material world? And what about Grandmother Earth? Do we just leave her behind when we move to the 5th dimension? And the time is coming very soon when all of us, the people of planet Earth, will be forced to make the choice which world we want to live in – old paradigm or new. What's going to happen to those people who choose to stay in the old paradigm?

Let me start by saying that I don't have all of the answers regarding the shift. There are also aspects of this that I choose not to pursue. Sometimes too much is too much, and we definitely can overanalyze this to the point where it becomes more of a head-trip than a spiritual experience. For me, the spiritual aspect always comes first, and all the various particulars, as far as possible scenarios, predictions, and those sorts of things, are secondary in importance. And sometimes they can be a downright distraction.

So, question number one: when we ascend to the 5th dimension, what will happen to the 3rd dimension, and what will happen to planet Earth?

Our analysis of the shift so far has focused primarily on us, human beings, and our situation on planet Earth. However, we are not alone in this. This monumental opportunity to transform from an old and dying world to a completely new one exists for everything in the 3rd dimension, and this means everything in our entire solar system. This includes all of the divine spirit's creatures here on Earth, both plant and animal, as well as the spirit essences of these creatures. It includes Grandmother Earth, who, after all, is a living, breathing, sentient organism, with a soul. It includes all the other elements of Grandmother Earth, including the air and the water, and all of her other minerals and crystals, and other mysteries unknown.

Our solar system is traveling through the photon belt as a unit, and every particle of it will be included. The solar system too is a living organism, with consciousness and spirit, and it too feels the shifting energy. In *Last Cry*, Ghost Wolf discusses many of the transformations of the solar system during the shift, such the appearance of a second sun, and the Earth changing its orbit to revolve around it. Whenever we begin to feel like the shift isn't that big a deal, all we need to hear is something like this. Yes indeed, this is huge!

Even outside of our solar system, the events that are transpiring on planet Earth are attracting a lot of attention, and are seen as exceedingly important. We are told this through numerous, credible human channels, who receive transmissions from other worlds, such as extraterrestrial beings, other-dimensional beings, and/or spirit beings.

Since everything in the universe is connected to everything else, it appears as though the energetic imbalances on planet Earth are of such a magnitude that they could send ripple effects throughout the universe. The planet Earth is apparently a very special place in the cosmos, and what is happening here is part of an intergalactic battle between the forces of good and evil that has been going on for eons, practically since the beginning.

Remember the Lucifer Rebellion, and the attempt by these fallen angels to control the forces of nature to suit their purpose of getting out. This amounts to a rebellion against the divine spirit, and an effort to rewrite the laws of nature and creation. If they were to succeed, this would be a giant step toward turning the cosmic scheme of things on its ear. If *the dark side* succeeds in their *New World Order* scheme, making micro-chipped slaves of all the Earth's people, for the purpose of feeding off their energy and spirit, this would be a major coup. It is the equivalent of hijacking the entire planet, and redirecting its natural forces in a different direction, one that they control.

And as we can see, this is perilously close to happening. However, this coup would be short-lived, and this is where it's flabbergasting how such intelligent beings in some ways can apparently be so shortsighted, with such major blind spots, in others. *The dark side's* lack of a spiritual perspective does have its consequences. This coup will be short-lived because if *the dark side* continues on its current course, this will render the Earth uninhabitable in the very near future for human life, as well as virtually all other animal and plant life. Since they are at least part human, living off the same environment as humans, we can only assume this would create major problems for them too.

Do they understand any of this, or have they become such cosmic megalomaniacs, blinded by their own power, that they believe they can discover some way to change these natural laws too? We often hear that the illuminati, or *the dark side*, have built, and are building, massive underground structures, where they can survive the colossal Earth changes that are coming with the shift.

Besides, and this is something that's never made sense to me. When they come to the surface, and the human species has perished, this means two extremely important things, both of which are serious problems for *the dark side*. First, they wouldn't be able to play their game with us anymore, and judging by their behavior over the last 6000 years, they really enjoy this game, where they get to play the great trickster.

And second, we have already discussed the very real possibility that they feed off the energy of human beings. Like the pact with the devil, they feed upon the energy of our soul, which they trick us into giving to them. And they also feed, energetically, off the negative emotions they stir up in the world – fear, hatred, anger, violence. No, it looks to me like they would want to keep human beings around.

Without us, they lose a major source of their power. Besides, they could have gotten rid of us a long time ago, if they wanted.

Back to the point - when we ascend to the 5th dimension, to the new world of light and spirit, we do not do it alone. We are joined in this by all the other entities and beings of the 3rd dimensional world. The 5th dimension is not limited to humans. As I understand it, neither is it limited in its location, as in the Earth or this solar system. Basically it is open to anything in the universe that vibrates at the proper 5th dimensional energy. It will be a true intergalactic sisterhood and brotherhood. And just to make sure we're clear - when we talk about humans and other entities and beings in the 5th dimension, we are not talking about physical bodies. We are talking about the consciousness, the energy bodies, and the spirit essence of these humans, entities and beings. And yes, it is very similar to the concept of angels. The fifth dimension will be a band of angels.

All of this begins to address the question of what happens to the Earth? The consciousness, the energy body, and the spirit essence of the organism that is the Earth, as well as all of her creatures, and every other aspect of her, will join us in the ascension to the 5th dimension. And the same is true for the sun, the moon, all the other planets, the asteroids in between Mars and Jupiter, and any life forms we may not know about, and every other particle of the solar system, as well as the universe. The main distinction between our solar system and the rest of the universe is our location at this time on the 26,000 year cycle, where the portals to the 5th dimension are more wide open. This gives us an advantage, just as it would any other world that moved through this energy field at some other time.

And all of these entities and beings will have the same opportunity to experience the transformation from an aspect of themselves that is old and dying to one that is being reborn. This is the true essence of the shift. We have already discussed our ascension process as humans, and the personal transformation that is involved. The Earth and these other entities and beings are experiencing precisely the same process of transformation. It is both like a cleansing and a purification through fire. To become ascendant beings, we must cleanse ourselves from the poison of our old paradigm conditioning, and recreate ourselves in harmony with higher frequency consciousness and energy. Like a phoenix, we must be reborn from the ashes not only of the old paradigm world, but of our old paradigm selves. In order to become ascendant beings, we must first die.

What's going to happen to the Earth? Grandmother Earth is experiencing precisely the same need for a cleansing. And she needs it. She has been abused now for a very, very long time – 6000 years by our civilization, and far longer when you take into account the ancient civilizations that were primarily extraterrestrial in origin. Back in those days, things were not always enlightened either, as far as living in harmony with the environment.

And Grandmother Earth has already begun her cleansing process. The Earth's vital energy fields are shifting as a result of her entry into the photon belt, and she has begun her transformation. She is a world out of balance, and the only way to regain her balance is to transmute into something else. We can see and feel this in global warming, the full impact of which is not yet upon us. We can see and feel this in radically changing weather patterns, everywhere on the planet, and in extremes of weather, of all possible kinds, the magnitude of which we haven't seen in a long time. We can see and feel it in dramatically increasing earthquake and volcano activity, again everywhere, triggering tsunamis, which, are of a magnitude, again, not seen in a long time.

Mother Earth is feeling it. The fires of purification are burning deep within her belly. The time for her cleansing has come. Perhaps the time has come for her to reverse the polarity of her electromagnetic fields, totally changing her face, and that of the life on it. Perhaps it is time for her to get back in balance by correcting the tilt of her axis. Or, maybe she'd feel better if she changed the direction of her rotation. It is definitely time for her to fight back. Like all of the universe's organisms, it is time for her self-healing system to kick in, and for her to purify herself of the toxins and pests which have disturbed her sacred balance. And we all know what this means. If the human race doesn't get itself back on the course of nature's design, quickly, the Earth will swallow the human race up.

All of this points us in the direction of answering the question: what's going to happen to the Earth. The Earth, as an organism with a physical form, in the 3rd dimension, is going to be just fine, though with a considerable likelihood it will be without humans. I haven't heard or read anywhere, in any of my research on *2012 and the shift*, that this meant the end or the death of the Earth in the 3rd dimension. People often say this, but they've got it wrong. They say that we, human beings, are destroying and killing the planet. We're not. We're killing ourselves. We would be gone way before the planet ever died. Once again, George Carlin said it so perfectly. "The Earth has been through far worse than us. The Earth will shake us off, like a bad case of fleas."

In *Return of the Bird Tribes* by Ken Carey, the indigenous spirit entity that channeled the information in this book agrees, when it tells us that there is nothing that has been done to planet Earth that cannot be repaired.

And I think everybody can probably figure out the answer to the question: what's going to happen to those people who choose to remain in the old paradigm? The more I know about this topic the more difficult it is to tip toe around the severity of this. Those who choose the old paradigm are clinging to the destructive energy of a dying world. The old paradigm cannot possibly sustain itself because it is fundamentally in violation of natural and divine law. One way or another, it must end, and the time is near. It doesn't please me to say this, but it's only reasonable to take the next step, and to say that those who cling to this dying world will be in for a very rough ride, and there won't be anybody or anything to take care of them anymore. Trust me – I hate saying these things, and I know I'm going to tick off a lot of people here. But the laws of nature are the laws of nature. And perhaps the best thing Grandmother Earth could do to return herself to a state of balance is to thin out the vast majority of those humans who live in disharmony with her. Remember – this is a choice that each and every one of us makes. Ignorance is not an excuse. Hopi prophesy tells us this has already happened three times, with the Creator sparing those who remained true to the ancient ways. And for those who don't like the spiritual perspective, we can always substitute the terms "nature" or "the Earth" for "the Creator." The result is the same. The forces of nature and Mother Earth, in ways we will never understand with our rational mind, spared those who continued to live in harmony with them.

And I don't think I need to elaborate upon that any further. There is only one thing that those of us who are committed to creating the new world can do for these lost souls, and that's to do our utmost to help them to awaken, and join us in this great mission. But we cannot help them, if they're not willing to help themselves.

When people talk about the shift, they often talk about "the end." One thing we know is ending for certain is humanity in its current form. If humanity doesn't change, the Earth will no longer support it. But if humanity does change, then humanity has this exceedingly rare and blessed opportunity, along with the spirit of the Earth, and all of her creatures, to get out – to ascend to a higher world – a world of angels from other worlds and dimensions – a world of union with our intergalactic sisters and brothers from the stars. As ascendant beings, we have no choice but to take advantage of this opportunity.

Chapter Eight

The Last Time

The last time there was a shift
Real versus fake history
It's time to get to work!

Who was Around 26,000 Years Ago?

As we examine *2012 and the shift*, a reasonable question to ask is: if this is part of a 26,000 year cycle, what happened 26,000 years ago? What happened the last time the Earth experienced something similar to what we're on the verge of experiencing now? What happened the last time the Earth had a facelift or a cleansing? Our history in the old paradigm tells us there weren't any people around then, at least none that weren't more like apes than people. So, the question of how they handled this 26,000 year opportunity to create a new world appears to not apply.

In looking at this question, the first thing I do is check with my most important source. This is the prophesies and the histories of our ancient indigenous peoples, from everywhere on the planet, including the Hopi and virtually every other Native American tribe. This information was passed down primarily through their oral lore, which, contrary to what many people believe, was meticulously guarded and preserved.

When we do this, one of the first things we learn is these indigenous versions of history are totally different from the traditional version we are spoon fed in Western culture. Somebody's got to be wrong here. And since everything else in the old paradigm is part of a monumental hoax, it's pretty safe to assume its history is too. Plus, these ancient indigenous histories, even from completely different parts of the globe, give very similar pictures of what was happening on the Earth. Obviously, this gives them considerable credibility.

We all know the traditional, old paradigm version of history, as we have all been hearing it since grade school. Humanity and civilization, in their present forms, emerged around 6000 years ago. This was known as Sumer or Babylon, and was located at the confluence of the Tigris and Euphrates Rivers in what is now Iraq. Isn't it interesting that this part of the world is again such a focus of world attention, with the creation of the state of Israel in this sacred Muslim land at the end of World War II, and the recent invasion and conquest of Iraq by the US government and military? I, for one, definitely smell a rat here.

This history also implies that this new civilization kind of popped up out of nowhere, in a relatively advanced state. All of a sudden, there it was. There is no discussion of where they came from, or how they evolved to the point they were at. Sounds to me like we've got another missing link here. What gives?

And then, the story goes on, these people expanded outward from there to other parts of the globe, where all the other cultures we see in the world today developed.

Sound familiar? Well, let's not get all bent out of shape over it because there's a lot more to it than that. It's not so much that this part of the story is inaccurate, as it is the volumes that have been left out.

One of the first things we learn from our ancient indigenous histories is that many of these indigenous people inhabited the planet for far longer than this, and we're talking about tens of thousands, possibly even hundreds of thousands, of years. These histories tell us that many of these people were here 26,000 years ago, making first-hand observations of what was happening, and passing it down in their lore. And it appears that some of these people may have been here 52,000 and 78,000 years ago, providing a vast perspective of Grandmother Earth's major eras.

Somebody was here, watching these things, and making these reports. How do we know? We haven't covered this yet, but the last time the Earth experienced a shift there was a great flood. We know about this from innumerable accounts of it in myths, histories, scriptures, and sacred texts from ancient cultures spanning the globe, indigenous and non-indigenous alike, including the Christian Bible.

So, this may seem kind of stupidly self-evident, but we can deduce a couple of things from this. First, this was a huge flood, of global proportions, because it was felt everywhere. And second, there were lots of folks, in lots of places, watching it, or who at least knew about it. After all, Noah and his whole gang were here, though with the Bible we never have any idea of the time frames we're dealing with. Besides, so much of the history of the Old Testament is so totally at odds with mainstream history, but that's another can of worms all together.

On the surface, many of these ancient indigenous people may appear to be quite primitive. They lived off the land, in harmony with nature, in small tribes or communities, and with very primitive technology, at least in the context of how we understand modern technology. They had no gun powder or electricity, among other things. And yet, as far as their higher consciousness and spirituality were concerned, they were highly advanced, never having lost their connection to the divine spirit of the living world they called home. In previous chapters, we discussed how sorcerers and high priests from ancient indigenous traditions were capable of performing acts that defied logical, linear, cause-and-effect reality. We call this magic or the supernatural. Since most of these things exceeded what humans can do with machines, isn't it reasonable to think of these things as acts of high technology – just without the machines.

It's all in how you look at technology. These indigenous folks were keen observers of astronomy and the forces of nature, and they understood the laws of nature and the universe. They were technically competent enough to sustain themselves, and to live in harmony with their world, with little or no waste. They were apparently happy and healthy, at least relative to the neurotic and diseased state of the modern world, with stable families, and with a stable social order, and with children who actually revered their elders, and looked to them for guidance.

They were impeccable in their use of natural materials in the things they built, which were of exceedingly high quality, such as their tools, dwellings, boats, clothing and musical instruments. Many of them also used natural forms of technology, like the ones discussed in the last chapter, such as crystals, pyramids, and the use of sacred geometry in the altars and other structures they built. The fact that they never invented things like gun powder and electricity, which were the foundation of our modern forms of technology, is totally consistent with how they saw their world and their spirituality. They didn't need these things. And if they had invented them, it probably would have knocked their relationship with nature out of balance.

Plus, their world sustained itself. They even left the world a better place when they were done than when they found it. So, which is more high-tech? Or perhaps the question should be restated. Which world is more advanced? Our modern world, with all of its so-called high technology, which has plundered the very environment that supports it? Or a world that meets the needs of our everyday life with perfect efficiency, including our higher needs, plus sustains itself, and the environment that supports it, indefinitely? Who is more advanced – civilized humans or dolphins? To me, this is a no brainer.

Ancient Civilizations and ET's

As far as real versus fake history is concerned, we also know a few other things, both from our ancient indigenous sources, as well as several other sources.

We know that ancient, highly advanced civilizations existed here during these same time frames – tens of thousands, hundreds of thousands, perhaps even millions of years prior to what passes as the beginning of our "official" history. Proof for this is fairly obvious, once we wake up and open our eyes, and again, once we know these things, it's difficult to imagine how we ever could have believed anything else.

We need look no farther than the thousands of ancient structures, literally everywhere on the planet, for which our official history has no reasonable explanation, and prefers that we just look in the other direction. Just a few of the more well known are the Great Pyramid at Giza in Egypt, Stonehenge in Great Britain, the ruins at Machu Picchu in Peru, the Mayan pyramids throughout Guatemala and Central America, and the list goes on and on. Even in such non-sexy places like Wisconsin, my home, and Indiana, there are massive mounds that appear man-made and pyramids of unknown origin.

The technology (there's that word again) required to build these structures far exceeds that of the primitive civilization we are told was newly emerging 6000 years ago, or that of the primitive savages we are told inhabited these other regions. Most of them were built according to the principles of sacred geometry. This means they were made of substances, and shaped in such a way as to optimally attract holographic energy. They were also built precisely at the intersection of the Earth's meridian lines. These meridian lines are an energy grid, which surrounds the Earth in the form of horizontal and vertical lines, similar to the Earth's longitudes and latitudes. The intersections of these lines are vortexes, where the energy is at its peak.

These structures were also invariably aligned with stars, constellations and astrological points of reference, which were of major importance to the builders. This was both for energetic reasons, as well as the possibility, in some cases, that these stars may have been where the builders, or at least their genetic relatives, originally came from – more about that in a moment. Some of these structures were built of stones so massive, cut so intricately, and fit together and placed so high up, that this could only have been done with some form of laser and anti-gravity technology. The ancient Nazca Lines, in Peru, are carvings in the Earth of various animals that are so large they can only be seen in their entirety from so high up in the air it would require a flying craft of some kind.

We also know that extraterrestrials arrived here during these same ancient time frames – tens of thousands, hundreds of thousands, perhaps millions of years prior to the alleged beginning of our civilization. We know too that they were primarily responsible for the development of these ancient civilizations. And we know that they've been tinkering in human affairs ever since.

There's so much evidence for the existence of ET's, past and present, I hardly know where to begin. Since most people, at least in my world, believe this, I don't think I need to spend much time on it. If you've come this far with me, I'm probably either preaching to the choir, or you're totally freaking out. But just to make sure we cover all our bases, let's just brush upon some of this evidence.

Here again, let's start with the records of our ancient indigenous people. And once again, we have an abundance of evidence of a wide variety of star people from the verbal lore and visual artifacts of indigenous people from virtually everywhere on Earth. In the verbal lore, I suppose this can be interpreted in different ways, as all words are abstract, and mean different things to different people. But when we see the artistic depictions of these beings in cave drawings and carvings on other artifacts, such as pottery and jewelry, there can be no doubt. These beings were not human, at least not entirely, and they came from the stars.

And in many cases too, these indigenous people were the star beings. There are those who believe that the high priests of Atlantis, who were probably extraterrestrials (at least partly), knew of the coming Earth changes, and fled to other lands before it happened. There are those who believe these Atlanteans became the Maya, and others believe they became the Hopi. Both make sense to me.

Hopi history tells us that they survived the Earth changes, on three previous occasions, by moving underground, and living for thousands of years with a race of beings known as the *Ant People*, who also guided them. This is also a possibility for other inhabitants of the planet during these times, which is one possible explanation for how the original Sumerians seemingly popped up out of nowhere, at an advanced stage of evolution.

In the contemporary world, proof for the existence of ET's, and the fact that they have been tinkering in human affairs for a long time, comes from organizations like *The Disclosure Project* and *Project Camelot,* and other whistleblowers, in which ex-military and government agency personnel are coming forward, and blowing the whistle on what the government has been covering up regarding ET's and UFO's for over 50 years, at least.

It is common knowledge in UFO circles that contact was made in the 1950s, and that certain contracts were agreed upon between the ET's and the US Government, in which the ET's agreed to share certain advanced high-tech gadgets, such as Velcro, computers and cell phones, and the government agreed to keep this a secret. Doesn't it often seem like the pace of the development of our technology is way ahead of itself? This is one reason why. The movie *Men in Black* depicted this quite nicely, and should be mandatory viewing for anybody who wants to learn how these behind-the-scenes games are played. It is also commonly believed that these contracts are soon to expire, if they haven't already, heralding a new era of ET contact, as well as yet one more major event in our world that converges around this unprecedented time we are now in, and the shift.

It is also safe to assume that any ET's who would conspire with our government would have to be malevolent in nature, or at least did not have the welfare of humans and Mother Earth as a high priority, or any priority. There are a couple of reasons for this. We already know how malevolent this government is. Any ET with an ounce of awareness would know this, and would not enter into this alliance unless they shared this agenda. Plus, we also know that benevolent ET's would never do this because they are bound by the divine law that forbids interference in the autonomous affairs of other planets or worlds – just like on *Star Trek*. So, they would have to figure out other ways – also just like on *Star Trek*. Beam me down, Scottie.

Plus, once again, as we discussed previously, the most important source of our knowledge of ET's and UFO's is our own personal experience. So many of us have had encounters, sightings, and abductions, both positive and negative, and both in normal and altered states of consciousness. Again, in my world, those who have not had such an experience are definitely a minority. Some of us are crazy, but not all – not by a long shot.

We know that the ET's came here, during these ancient time frames, for the purpose of colonization. Throughout the universe the Earth was seen, and is seen, as quite a jewel, a sentient organism, with such an abundance of organic life and natural resources, not to mention esthetic beauties galore – which is also an important reason why the Earth has become the stage for this epic intergalactic contest between the forces of good and evil. Yes indeed, it's true – this is a very special place, and this is a very special time.

ET's – *Our Relatives From the Stars*

We also know that the ET's interbred with the indigenous people they found here during these ancient times. This created a new kind of being, a genetic hybrid – part ET, part human. And once we know this, well, our world's never quite the same again. Once we concede the possibility of an extraterrestrial genetic component to humanity, which is a totally reasonable possibility, a multitude of intriguing possibilities instantly springs into the picture. I'm only going to go over a few of them here, but enough to give the basic idea of the forces that are at work.

A very compelling case can be made that the Caucasian, or white, Race is just such a genetic hybrid. This would explain why they have endeavored to dominate the rest of the world for the last 6000 years, plundering it in the process. This also explains the unfair advantage they have had in this, with their advanced (different) forms of technology, such as gun powder and electricity.

It's very intriguing, and instructive, to pose the question how exactly the white race acquired this knowledge? There are a couple of possibilities. One is pretty obvious. They received it directly from their extraterrestrial brothers and sisters, at certain points along the path of this long history, like in the 1950s, as we already mentioned. These would be contacts that were, or are, very close, as in face to face. Or, they received this knowledge indirectly from the ET's, as it was passed down through the ancient secret societies, some of which trace their way all the way back to Atlantis and other ancient civilizations.

There is another possibility, and this is the one that's intriguing. It is also one that completely rearranges our view of the world – one more time gang. There is the possibility that the white race developed these forms of technology, which gave them the physical power to conquer the world, whereas the indigenous peoples didn't, as a function of genetic predisposition. And please, this does not mean that one is smart, and the other is stupid, or one is advanced, and the other is primitive, or any such thing.

But let's take a look at this for a second. If the white race is genetically part ET, this means that their genetics are wired, or programmed, to fit another world, not this one. There is also the distinct possibility that some of these ET's are very different from people, as in not even humanoid, and the worlds they are from very different from planet Earth. Take this one step farther, and we can safely say that their genetics are not a good fit for this world. This could explain why the white race has been so out of balance with this world throughout history, leading to the brink of destroying the very environment they need to survive. Since they are not indigenous to this world, at least in part, they do not have the same inherent sensitivity to it, as somebody who is.

Compare this to the genetic make-up of the Native American, or any other indigenous person, who is indigenous to this world. For these people, the Earth is their sacred mother, who they revere, and would never do anything to harm. They have a genetic connection to this world. It is a loving relative. And their lifestyle is built on their understanding that not only does their life originate with the Earth, but also depends upon it for its sustenance and life-force. The Earth and all of its elements are the source of everything.

This genetic factor could be one of the many reasons why so many totally well-intended white folks, like myself, struggle as much as they do with their spirituality. An essential component of spirituality is our connection with the forces of the natural world and with the rhythm and flow of life's vital energies. If part of us is genetically set up for another world, instead of this one, then making this connection would present more of a challenge. That doesn't mean we can't do it – just that it would take more work, and more time. It doesn't come as naturally to us as the Native Americans because we don't have as much of an affinity for this world. I'm sixty-one years old, and I worked on this stuff for over 40 years, in a variety of areas, through booms and busts in my life, before I started truly "getting it." That's a long time, and this is possibly one of the many reasons.

Another very compelling case can be made that *the dark side,* or the Illuminati, who we spoke of earlier, is also a genetic hybrid – part ET, part human. Certainly there is a correlation here between the Illuminati, at least the ones we know of, and the white race. We don't know exactly who the Illuminati are. The people, or beings, who own and control the world are a shadowy group indeed, and that's how they like it. When we trace them as far as we are able, we find the foremost moguls of banking and industry, with names like Rothschild and Rockefeller, and we find the amazingly wealthy royal families of the world, mostly European.

The vast majority of these people are white. And when we talk about the white race plundering the planet, this tiny group of white people, at the top of the pyramid of power, are the ones making the decisions to do it, and how. The vast majority of the white race are mere pawns in this game, along with all the other people of the planet.

So, what's the difference between the Illuminati at the top of the pyramid and the rest of the human race? Once again, when we trace it back as far as we can, another thing that we learn about these people (or beings) is that they are all relatives. They are all cousins, distant and not so distant. It's all one big, happy family. When the genealogy of these people/beings is traced, we discover that they all come from the same interlocking bloodlines. Most of these bloodlines can be traced back two or three thousand years, or so, into our "known" history, before things start to get murky, which makes sense because at this point all of this history became murky. And when we trace them back, we always end up in the same place, with the emperors, the kings and the queens, the high priests and priestesses, and, in general, with the highest levels of the aristocracy in the ancient world.

As I understand it, and I admit I'm no expert here, the traditional view of history says that the folks of Sumer and Babylon migrated to form the ancient civilization in Egypt, and also became the seafaring Phoenicians, who formed the ancient civilizations in Greece and Rome. From there, these bloodlines continued their expansion, both by land and by sea, up into England and the rest of Western and Eastern Europe, and subsequently to the rest of the world.

As we try to make sense out of this, we continue to bump into the problems of real versus fake history. We already know that the traditional version of history is full of holes, and must be taken with a grain of salt. We already know there were other indigenous people at many other places on the planet, who survived the flood, possibly the Maya in Central America and Mexico and the Hopi in the Southwest US. So, this civilization in the Middle East wasn't the only show in town.

Book of the Hopi, by Frank Waters, which is straight from the mouths of the Hopi Elders, gives a different version of the birth of humanity, and its migration to the other parts of the globe. This Hopi history is far more ancient than 6000 years. It says that we are currently in the Fourth World, with the world already having experienced three cycles of purification. At the end of the previous three cycles, those humans who had kept their connection with the divine spirit and with divine law, a miniscule minority, were guided by spirit entities to safety underground, where they lived with *the Ant People*, until it was safe to emerge upon the surface of the Earth again. The Third World was destroyed by water, and when the waters receded, they emerged on an island of high ground, built boats out of reeds, and sailed to the east, until they arrived at the west coast of America. From here they traveled to the Grand Canyon area where they settled, and the migration to the other parts of the globe started from there.

And we can find other versions of the flood, the emergence and the migration in the sacred texts and the ancient histories of other indigenous peoples from all over the Earth.

But to get back to our traditional version of history, it's also a pretty safe guess that these precursors of Western Civilization, like the Phoenicians, due to the knowledge they brought with them from earlier civilizations, were not as primitive as history would like us to think, and actually sailed extensively to other parts of the planet. Phoenician artifacts and artifacts from the earliest civilization in England have been discovered as far away as North America. And real history abounds with these kinds of anomalies.

But let's get back to our main point – way too many threads to all this. In spite of all the historical anomalies, the genetic connection between the Illuminati of today and the kings and queens and the aristocracy of the ancient world rests on a very credible foundation. I'm not going to go into the details of all this here. That would get us too far off track. For an outstanding rendition of all the specific names and families and dates, I refer you to two books by David Icke, *The Biggest Secret* and *Children of the Matrix*, which researches all this in exhaustive detail.

When we watch these bloodlines throughout history, something else we learn is how fanatic they are about retaining the purity of these bloodlines. These people/beings give new meaning to keeping it in the family, making sure they only breed and have offspring with those of common genetic lineage. This too can be interpreted in a wide variety of ways. Remember – these folks saw themselves as divinely ordained. It makes sense that a small group of chosen ones, with a direct link to God, would want to keep that link intact. They see this as the base of their power.

And when we consider the possibility of an ET genetic component, other possibilities leap into the mix. If there is such a component for the white race, then its genetic influence is probably very minimal for the vast majority of them. So, if you are an "average" white person, and feel absolutely no affinity for any of this, this is why. However, when you get to the top of the pyramid of power, it makes sense that the ET genetic factor would be much more substantial, allowing these people/beings to know who they were, and where they came from, and what they were on Earth to do – another reason to keep the bloodlines pure.

There are those who believe that these genetic hybrids, at the highest levels, are able to shapeshift, which means they have the ability to appear in both forms – human and ET. Even in the alternative culture, many people struggle with the concept of shapeshifting, and have a difficult time understanding and accepting it. However, this concept is quite common in most indigenous cultures, past and present, with their well developed powers of the supernatural, and their awareness that all physical matter is energy and spirit. It is also not too far a stretch for the new paradigm perspective of the spirituality in this book, which is derived from the forces of nature and the cosmos. Nature transmutes things into other things all the time. Just look at the growth of any organic form, like the human body, where all the elements of the form are created from practically nothing. This act of creation is profoundly supernatural, and yet we learn to take it totally for granted. So, the changing of a human form into another form is not that far-fetched at all.

And maybe, just to make sure we cover all the possibilities, this is one of the reasons why the people/beings, who are truly in charge, at the pinnacle of the pyramid of power, prefer that we not know who they are. We wouldn't like what we see.

There are lots of people who think what I'm about to say is totally nuts, even to the point of an anathema (what's new?). But I am fascinated by David Icke's theory that the ET genetic component of the Illuminati is actually reptilian in nature, and that they come from a reptilian ET genetic strain. David traces these bloodlines with painstaking detail, and uncovers the recurrent theme in their ancient histories of the involvement, or intervention, of reptilian beings. We can see this in their sacred texts, scriptures and mythology. In the Christian Bible, it is a serpent that tempts the first humans to break their sacred vow with the creator by eating from the tree of knowledge. We see it in the crests of so many of these aristocratic families, which are adorned with dragons and a wide variety of reptilian creatures, both winged and non-winged. We see it in the ancient architecture of Europe, such as castles and cathedrals, which were built by the Illuminati, and in which gargoyles and other reptilian creatures are so predominantly displayed. The crest of the city of London, probably the foremost Illuminati center in the world, has two flying reptilian creatures on it, and at the entrance to the city there is a statue of a similar creature. The symbol of the modern medical profession, controlled by the Illuminati, is the caduceus, which is two intertwined serpents. And it goes on and on and on.

As long as we're on the topic of our genetic history, there is one other aspect of this we must cover. It does appear that at some point in our long history, human beings have been genetically tampered with. In every one of our cells, over half the strands of DNA have been turned off or deactivated. Mainstream science and medicine do not make a big deal out of this. They call it junk DNA, and that's the end of it. And this is not believed to have any adverse effect upon us.

Well, once again they've got it all wrong. And once again, they demonstrate their brain-boggling lack of understanding of how the human body works, and how the world works. Plus, the entire premise of junk DNA makes no sense metaphysically. As you hear me say over and over, in a divinely ordered universe, everything makes sense, and everything happens for a reason. The divine spirit doesn't create junk. If we don't know why something's there, we just haven't learned it yet.

Old paradigm science and medicine have a glaring misunderstanding of the function, or functions, or our DNA. As the core of the gene in each cell, DNA is seen as playing a part in our heredity, and how our traits and physical structures get passed down to us, and match our genetic blueprint. In the modern world, our genetics is seen as the primary factor in determining who and what we are. With the age-old nature versus nurture argument, the scales have definitely tipped in favor of nature.

And our 24 strands of DNA are seen as the primary chemical agent of this. And with this model, once again, we have human beings as robots – genetically predetermined, with little or no say in who or what we are.

Well, if you've read this far, you probably see what a hideous misunderstanding this is of human beings, and our totality, body, mind and spirit, and of our full potential as multi-dimensional beings. As far as understanding the purpose of our DNA, new science is way ahead of old science. New science has opened its experimental parameters not only to include the critical influence of our environment and learning, but also our consciousness and spirituality. Therefore, the world it looks at is whole – not just a tiny part of the whole. New paradigm scientists, like Bruce Lipton and Leonard Horowitz, are making revolutionary discoveries and hypotheses about our cells, genes and DNA, and a far wider range of their functions. And it begins to appear that our DNA plays an important role in how we experience our higher consciousness and spirituality. And once again, new science is telling us the same things ancient spiritual traditions have been telling us for thousands of years.

I'm no expert on this, and it's way too huge a topic to cover here. But there is one part of this we must look at, as it is very pertinent to our theme. Many of the new scientists believe that one of the primary functions of our DNA is as a receiver of electronic and higher energy signals. As we already know, the universe is a sea of pulsating energy, which is all interconnected. The primary thing that distinguishes these various types of energy is the frequency of their vibrations. As we move away from the material world, and into higher dimensions, the energy rises in frequency, and becomes more rarified or ethereal. These higher frequency realms are realms of the spirit or the spirit world.

Human beings live in this sea of energy, with its different dimensions. The universe is continually sending out these cosmic signals. Our ability to tune into the ones with the highest frequencies is the equivalent of picking up signals from the source of creation, the divine spirit of a living universe. This is what it means to communicate with the divine. New science is telling us that the strands of our DNA are our primary mechanisms for doing this. They are microscopic antenna, which then transmit these signals to the rest of our totality – body, mind and spirit.

So, our DNA plays a vital role in our higher consciousness and spirituality. Since half the strands of our DNA are switched off or deactivated, this can greatly interfere with our capability to pick up these signals, and our capability to fulfill our multi-dimensional potential as spiritual beings. Could this be yet one more instance of *the dark side* tinkering with us to make sure we don't pose too big a threat to them? Like so many of the other things we've talked about, it fits the overall picture, and it is one of very many possibilities.

And once again, if this is true, it does not mean we are incapable of reaching our spiritual potential. It does mean we have one more obstacle to overcome, and it might take more work. This may be another reason why so many of us struggle with our spirituality, at least more than we would in a world that hasn't been so hideously tampered with.

One of the more fascinating theories about the development of the human race comes from Zechariah Sitchin. Sitchin was the translator the ancient Sumerian

Tablets, which were stone tablets from early Sumer, written in the original Sumerian language. According to Sitchen, the tablets tell a wild story, which goes far back into history, and involves a race of beings from another world. These beings came to Earth for the purpose of colonization and natural resources. Sitchin maintains that the Tablets say that these ET's genetically created human beings in laboratories, over 200,000 years ago. Their purpose was to create a work force or slave race. This fits in rather nicely too, doesn't it? Another of the multitude of possibilities. And whether our DNA was tinkered with then, or some other time, is open to question.

The Flood of 13,000 Years Ago

OK – that wraps up our review of real versus fake history. Now, lets' get back to the original question. What happened the last time the Earth experienced something similar to what we are on the verge of experiencing now? What happened the last time the Earth experienced a purification? What happened the last time there was a paradigm shift?

I don't understand what I'm about to tell you, other than there is a solid consensus among those who bother to research this that it's true. But as far as I can tell, on the basis of all of my sources, in many different areas of exploration, the last time the Earth experienced a major facelift or paradigm shift was approximately 13,000 years ago. As we already mentioned, this was the time of a great flood, so great that entire continents were submerged, with others rising to replace them.

Before we talk about the details of this shift, let's talk about the discrepancy with the numbers. Obviously, 13,000 is not 26,000. Obviously too, it is exactly half of 26,000. So, there is a correlation here, at least as far as the proportionality of the numbers, but not one that fits our theory.

I don't have an explanation for this. Nor have I ever heard one from any of the 2012 scholars, at least the credible ones. From a purely statistical point of view, there are a couple of obvious possibilities. One is that the flood and facelift of 13,000 years ago was an independent event, which was not a feature of the 26,000 year cycle, and which was caused by other, unrelated factors. Somehow I doubt this, and the 13/26 proportionality does seem to be telling us something - that there is some kind of correlation here.

Perhaps there is a mini-cycle (or cycles) within the bigger cycle, at which powerful energies are released at certain points of proportionality along the cycle - like the cycle of the seasons (or the phases of the moon), where the energies have a particular power at the solstices and equinoxes, which are at 90-degree intervals on the cycle.

Maybe this is just something I haven't learned yet. If anybody has an answer, I'm open to hearing it.

There seems little doubt that 26,000 is our number. That is the length of time of the cycle we are dealing with here. This comes from virtually all of our sources. It is also totally consistent with the astrological alignment of 12/21/12. If there are other cycles within this grand cycle, they certainly will not be of the transformational amplitude of 12/21/12 because this does mark the end of the old world, and the opportunity to create the new one. This only happens once on this cycle.

Some of our sources on this are very accurate, like the Mayans, with their incredible calendar, and their pyramids and other artifacts, which were made with such mathematical and astronomical precision. And there can be no doubting the accuracy of Winter Solstice, regardless of what calendar you're using. The sky doesn't lie.

Many of our sources on this, like the Hopi and the other American Indians, are very murky, pointing more to these times in general. Often, these prophecies have to do not with dates, but with occurrences. In other words, we'll know when the time arrives by what's happening. And when we look at our sick and dying world today, nothing could be clearer than the time has arrived. As we've already discussed, *Book of the Hopi* tells us that we are currently at the end of the fourth world. However, as far as specific dates are concerned, just like the Bible, it's completely up in the air, and open to our interpretation.

And we must always keep reminding ourselves that there is so much about all this that we just don't know – at least not yet. When we take on the challenge of topics like *the great shift of the ages*, ascending to higher dimensions, *The New World Order* and *the dark side*, we are definitely leaping into the new frontier. This is going down the proverbial rabbit hole of truth, which just keeps going and going, and where few have gone before. If you've come with me to this point for the first time, I congratulate you. It's an act of courage. This is not the safe world of the knowns. It is the far more challenging world of the unknowns, where miracles happen. It's a world where we don't necessarily have all the answers, other than knowing that answers do exist.

But this is precisely how leaping into the unknown of a new frontier of information works. Taking such a leap begins with forming our hypothesis, based both upon what we do know, and, very importantly, based upon using the intuitive or creative part of our mind to sketch out the details of things we don't know – in other words, to come up with ideas that are completely new, and for which we don't have any proof, yet. This is how the creative process works. We come up with ideas that are completely outside the traditional box, based on what we feel in our gut, or on our intuition, or on what our spirit tells us. Then, we can move backwards from there to find the proof.

This is why imaginative thinkers are always flying by the seat of their pants, and open to attack by inside-the-box thinkers (or skeptics), who demand proof first. This is what Einstein did, when in meditative or dream-like states, he came up with his theories about energy, matter, light and relativity. Then, he went back to the lab to prove it all. But think about it for a minute. If we always required proof for everything we know, we'd never learn anything new. We would be eternally stuck in the mud of old ideas. The sorcerer don Juan called everything we don't know the *nagual*, and he believed there were many things human beings could never prove. These were things that were inherently beyond the scope of the rational mind. They were things we simply knew because we could see them through the eyes of our higher consciousness and spirituality. And once you reach the status of sorcerer, or ascended being, that's good enough.

The Last Time

We do have it on very solid evidence, from the majority of our sources, both scientific and non-scientific, that approximately 13,000 years ago the Earth experienced a flood, the size of which was so massive that entire continents were submerged, with others rising to replace them. The current geography of the Earth is the result of this last shift – approximately.

It is also widely believed that it was at this time that the ancient civilization of Atlantis sunk into what is now the Atlantic Ocean. Like Western Civilization today, Atlantis had probably been in a state of decline for a long time, but it was the great flood that did it in. More about this shortly.

We don't know for certain what caused this flood, and rearrangement of the Earth's land masses. There are many different theories and possibilities. It could have been the result of widespread earthquake and volcano activity. There are those who believe that this may have been the last time the Earth's north and south electromagnetic poles shifted, and that the intensity of such a shift in electromagnetic energy can cause these kinds of Earth changes. Again, this is something we don't know because it is completely outside our scope of experience, and our science. When we remind ourselves that the Earth is an organic being that is held together by the forces of this complex electromagnetic energy field, it makes sense that a radical shifting of this field would result in a radical shifting of this organic being.

Immanuel Velikovsky, a Russian scientist, came up with a very compelling theory on all this in the 1950s, involving an astronomical event of colossal proportions. The timing of Velikovsky's event predates our 13,000 year estimate significantly, but it is relevant to the flood and Mother Earth's facelift. And like so many who leap into the frontier of the unknown, his ideas were radically at odds with the traditional scientific models of his day, so it was branded insane. But as modern science takes a closer look, much of this theory is looking quite feasible.

Velikovsky postulated that the flood and other massive Earth changes were caused by a comet-like body that passed perilously close to the Earth. Subsequently, this body settled into the orbit and became what is now Venus, which does have many of the characteristics of a comet. Velikovsky goes on to postulate that this body had a similar effect upon Mars, destroying the civilization and the life that existed there at that time.

According to *Book of the Hopi*, the Hopi believed the flood was the direct intervention of the Creator, who intended to destroy the third world with water. This was because the humans had made such a mess of this world by improperly using their freewill to stray from divine law, and chose instead the temptations of the material world. But a precious few of these people did remain true to the ancient wisdom. The Creator spared these, and allowed them to live underground, until the waters receded, and they emerged to begin to build the fourth world. It's not too big a leap to interpret this less figuratively, and we end up in precisely the same situation we're in today. Like we said previously, "nature" is synonymous with "Creator," and performs the same work. And this is precisely the most important message of this book. Our salvation in these changing times depends upon remaining true to divine law, and living in harmony with the Earth.

A very good case can be made that the flood and the cataclysms of 13,000 years ago were caused, at least in part, by the beings who controlled the ancient civilizations of these times. And here again we have the theme of the Earth's inhabitants abusing and living in disharmony with the Earth, and the Earth needing to protect herself and fight back, with a cleansing or purification.

When we follow the threads of all this down the rabbit hole of truth, it is also more than likely that the same forces of *the dark side*, discussed earlier, were also in power in these ancient civilizations, with the same agenda as in today's world. It is a certainty that the indigenous people of the planet of those times were not the driving force behind these high-tech civilizations – not unless they completely changed the way they thought and lived, which they didn't. Just like today, these civilizations were not friendly to the Earth, and their primary motivation appeared to be colonization, and exploitation of the Earth's resources, without regard for consequences.

In *Last Cry*, Ghost Wolf tells us that during the Atlantean era, the entire Earth was enveloped in a cloud of water vapor, similar to Venus today. This insulated the Earth, creating a climate that was uniformly tropical, and forming the basis of the myth of the Earth as a tropical paradise, like the Garden of Eden. But the Atlantean's use of laser technology, as well as highly destructive nuclear technology, burnt a hole in this cloud cover, and caused the falling of all this water down to the Earth in the form of the great flood.

Other Things the Prophesies Tell Us

As far as the last time the Earth had a facelift, the prophesies from indigenous cultures spanning the globe have many other things in common they are telling us about the last time things shifted, and are likely to again. And remember – these prophesies were derived directly from their history because they were here. In the vast majority of cases, we don't have the luxury of chronological precision, due to the tendency in most indigenous histories to focus on events, not dates. All that we know for certain was that there was a shift, and certain things did happen.

One thing that comes up again and again in all these histories and prophesies is the shifting of the Earth's electromagnetic field and the reversing of its north-south electromagnetic poles. Electromagnetism is one of the most powerful forces in 3rd dimensional reality. It is the glue that binds the world together. The prophesies tell us that in times of paradigm shift, this is one of the forces that shifts. And when it does, the entire nature of reality changes. This is why this is such an extraordinary opportunity.

I also find it noteworthy that such allegedly primitive folks, like the Maya and the Hopi, had the knowledge of such a sophisticated scientific concept, as well as so many others. Could it be they were not as primitive as we are led to believe? At the beginning of the third world, the various Hopi clans did their famous migrations, in which they traveled the width and breadth of the Americas, from pole to pole, and coast to coast. There are maps to prove it, as well as Hopi artifacts in all these places. In Hopi mythology, or history, depending on how you look at it, the north and south poles are guarded by two deities, called the twins, who control the electromagnetic axis, as well as the rotation of the Earth.

The changing of the rotation of the Earth is another of the common themes of the prophesies. The Earth's rotation is currently clockwise, and there are those who believe its natural rotation is counterclockwise. There are also those who believe the Earth's rotation has changed more than once in its long geological history. On page 79 in *Last Cry*, Ghost Wolf says that the Hopi prophesies tell us that "the rotation of the Earth has been manipulated by some not so benevolent star beings," and that in the final days the twins will return, and be joined by the Blue Star Kachina, and "they will return the Earth to its natural rotation, which is counter-clockwise."

From everything I've read, I don't know if there is a direct correlation between the changing of the Earth's rotation and the switching of its north-south electromagnetic poles. These two phenomena are mentioned simultaneously so often that it leads me to believe there is. We know that the strength of the Earth's electromagnetic field is diminishing, and heading toward zero. Does this mean that when it reaches zero, this is when the poles will shift, as well as when the Earth's rotation will switch? That seems to be the implication. If anybody can edify me further on this, I would appreciate hearing from you.

All of these colossal phenomena are substantiated in the prophesies by accounts of such things as the Sun changing its direction in the sky, or rising and setting at the same point on the horizon on the same day. Many of these ancient accounts also mention torrential winds being triggered by these events, with velocities far exceeding the worst of our storms in the modern world. Many of them also mention the correction of the tilt of the Earth's axis, as a part of this purification process. We've already discussed how the Earth is currently in a state of energetic imbalance, and the tilt of its axis is a possible manifestation of this. There is also the possibility that this tilt is the result of the high-tech transgressions and meddling of the ET's from earlier civilizations. Eliminating this tilt might be a feature of the Earth getting itself back into the proper energetic alignment.

Many of the prophesies also have the common theme of several days of total darkness, followed by several days of total light, or perhaps this could be the other way around, with the light preceding the darkness. Ghost Wolf believes that this depends upon whether the Sun enters the photon belt first, or the Earth. If it is the Sun, then the days of light will precede the darkness – and vice versa if the Earth enters first. Then, many of the prophesies say, when the Sun rises after several days of darkness, it will be the new Sun, or the Second Sun.

As we discussed in the last chapter, it's extremely important for us to remember that we, the human beings of the planet Earth, are not going through this shift, or this time of monumental transformation, alone. It's not just about us. Our entire solar system is traveling through the photon belt as a unit. And it is a living organism, with consciousness and a soul. Every particle or wave, both macroscopic and microscopic, of this living system is feeling the effects of this shifting energy. And these effects are also felt in higher dimensions, which means in realms of higher frequency energy, pure consciousness, and spirit.

Many of the prophesies tell us about these possible changes to our solar system. We've already mentioned the emergence of the new or the second Sun. There are those who believe Sirius will transmute into the new Sun, and others believe it will be Jupiter. Others believe there will then be two suns. Hopi prophesy is loaded with celestial events that herald the coming of the new age. Major among these are the appearance of the Blue Star Kachina, which means the end of time is near, and then the Red Star Kachina, or the Purifier, which means the time has come.

When we hear these kinds of things, it's very important, once again, to remind ourselves that the world our indigenous sources saw and experienced was quite different from the one we see and experience in old paradigm reality. If we look at their world through our old paradigm eyes, it won't make any sense at all. This is because their world overlapped with the spirit world. Everything in their world was a representation of the spirit force of that thing. When the Hopi talk about Blue Star Kachina and Red Star Kachina, they are also talking about the spirit essences of these celestial bodies. In Hopi tradition, the Kachinas were very important and powerful spirit guides. They could appear as many things, including human beings. And now, they were returning as stars in the heavens, as signs of the end of the old world, and the opportunity to birth the new world.

In this way, the appearance of the Blue Star Kachina and the Red Star Kachina very beautifully illustrate the essence of the shift. And we really can't see this unless we look at it through our new paradigm eyes. And again, we mean this literally, not metaphorically. Like our indigenous sisters and brothers, we will only be able to see this when our world truly overlaps with the world of the spirit. The prophesies are telling us that this time of monumental transformation is primarily spiritual in nature. Only with our spirituality do we have capability to create the new world. And the appearance of bodies/beings like the Blue and Red Star Kachinas is telling us that the veils between us and higher dimensions and the spirit world are thinning. This is a time when the spirit world is moving closer to us, and when we have this incredibly rare and blessed opportunity to merge and become one with it. This is the essence of the shift. As Ghost Wolf says on page 82, "Our relatives from the stars are coming home to see how well we have fared on our journey."

An Amazing Convergence of Forces and Events

In this section, our emphasis has been on the last time, or times, something like this has happened, and our focus has been on Earth changes. In relation to this, there are a few other things we should keep in mind. This is not the first time this has happened, and on each of the previous occasions, humanity did not get it right. There was no ascension to a higher dimension, at least collectively. A select few, who retained their connection to spirit, may have popped out to a higher dimension, but that's it. And there was no creation of a new world. Humanity was basically wiped out, again with the possible exception of a select few who were spared by the Creator, or by the mysterious forces of nature, to begin to rebuild the world, and hopefully get it right this time. But apparently, humanity keeps making the same mistake of falling into the trap of allowing itself to be seduced by the comforts of the material world, at the expense of the spiritual.

But as I've knocked myself out trying to explain, this too is too simplistic a way of looking at it. We, the humans of planet Earth, have not been alone in all this. We must always factor in the outside interference of beings from other worlds, who had no vested interest in living in harmony with the Earth, or in our welfare as the rightful inhabitants of this world. These beings not only engaged in acts of horrid abuse against Mother Earth, but they also endeavored to trick or brainwash us into accepting our role as slaves of their dark agenda.

So, it's not all our fault. We have been up against some very powerful forces. And those indigenous humans, who saw through the trick, and who remained true to the ancient wisdom, had to be destroyed because this wisdom was the greatest threat to their power.

Seemingly, the plan has worked exceedingly well. However, *the dark side* could not kill off all of them. And now, indigenous elders from tribes spanning the globe, who fully recognize the critical importance of these times, are coming out from behind their shrouds of secrecy, and reaching out to all the people of the world with the ancient wisdom. This is a revolution of incalculable proportions and power. And the people of the world would be fools not to take advantage of this monumental and blessed opportunity. Like I said, they found me, and if you choose, they will find you too.

And in focusing on these Earth changes, we may have ignored the other crucial aspect of the shift, which is the paradigm shift. This is the paradigm shift, as in the death of the old, materialist paradigm, and the birth of the new paradigm of light and spirit – at least the opportunity to do so. And I am talking here about the human aspect of this, as far as our ability to make it through these times, and survive as a species.

There isn't necessary a direct connection between these Earth changes and the collapse of the old paradigm. There probably is, but not necessarily. The old paradigm, as in our materialist civilization, is going to collapse – regardless. It doesn't need floods or earthquakes to spur this on. It is going to collapse because of a way of life that is fundamentally in disharmony with nature and divine law. We can already see this happening in our world, independent of any Earth changes, with the collapse of virtually all of our economic, health and social structures.

And when the old paradigm finally goes completely, the question then becomes whether there is a *critical mass* of us, who have the capability to begin to build the new world here on Earth. Whether this happens before, during, or after the coming Earth changes is something there's no way we can know for certain.

And in addition to sustaining ourselves here on Earth, we then have the matter of this incredibly rare opportunity to transcend this dimension, and build a new world in a higher dimension. Where does this chronologically fit into this series of events, Earth changes and paradigm shifts? There's no way to know that for certain either. All we know for certain is there is an amazing convergence of happenings, forces and changes at this momentous time, and there is good reason to believe there is a correlation between these and the window of time around Winter Solstice, 2012.

And if the Earth changes come first, then there is the matter of surviving them, at least if they are that severe. And here is where we must always remember that our ability to survive in the face of apparently devastating Earth changes, like those prophesized for this time of ours, always depends on the higher powers of our spirituality. This is why it is so important for us to get to work on ourselves – like NOW!

About the Author

Jack Allis is an author and spiritual teacher. His message is simple, yet profound, echoing the ancient indigenous prophesies from cultures spanning the globe, including the Hopi and the Maya. These are times of monumental transformation, known as the shift, in which the old world is coming to its inevitable end, so a new world may be born. The ancient wisdom all agrees that there is only one way to do this. We, the human beings of planet Earth, must reconnect with our heritage as spiritual beings, and begin to live again in harmony with the forces of nature and with our one true mother, Mother Earth.

A huge topic? A formidable challenge? Yes, indeed. But Jack tackles it in eloquent and inspiring fashion in his latest book, *Prophesy, Challenge & Blessing – Visions of 2012 & the Shift*. What most people see as doomsday is actually the most unimaginable blessing, as we have all been blessed with this opportunity to not only spiritually transform ourselves, but to also to play our part in creating the new world.

This topic is not purely academic. It is deeply personal. And Jack is a foremost leader in showing how to make this happen. He is the personal embodiment of his message. He lives minimally and close to nature in a tiny cottage on Little Okauchee Lake in Wisconsin. And he again takes his lead from our indigenous brothers and sisters by demonstrating how to practice our spirituality through the use of ceremony, which means connecting with spirit through prayer, sacred chants, fire ceremonies, and much more.

He is also actively involved with Earth Peoples United (EPU), which is led by Mayan Elder Erick Gonzalez. In order to survive these times, we must build sustainable communities, and EPU is doing this in two places. One is at Deer Mountain, in the mountains of northern California, and the other is at Patziapa on Lake Atitlan in Guatemala.

In conjunction with *Prophesy, Challenge & Blessing*, Jack has also released a feature-length DVD with the same title. He has also written two other books, *Infinity's Flower – A Tale of 2012 & the Great Shift of the Ages* and *Infinity's Children*, in addition to his popular monthly newsletter.

Jack also works with individuals and groups, teaching how to overcome the obstacles we face in life, and how to transform ourselves with our higher consciousness and spirituality. If you're too far away to meet in person, he does this by telephone or email.

Jack's formal education consists of earning a California Marriage and Family Therapy License in 1989 and a Masters Degree in Clinical Psychology from Antioch University in Santa Barbara, California in 1987. He was in private practice in cognitive psychotherapy (mind/body) in Santa Barbara and Ventura from 1989 until 2001, when he moved to Wisconsin.

A true Renaissance man, Jack has dedicated the last forty years of his life to seeking out diverse and non-traditional knowledge, which touch virtually every area of life, including holistic health, philosophy and spirituality. On his journey, Jack has acquired in-depth knowledge of Taoism and the philosophies and spiritual teachings of the Far East, meditation and martial arts techniques from a variety of cultures, the philosophical and spiritual teachings of shamans and indigenous spiritual cultures spanning the globe, both past and present, the revolutionary discoveries of quantum physics, organic gardening and farming, astrology, the philosophy of Objectivism, sovereignty and our vanishing freedoms, alternative theories of money, economics and history, and a variety of esoteric teachings.

For more information, please visit his website at www.jackallis.com.

PROPHESY, CHALLENGE & BLESSING
Visions of 2012 & the Shift
By Jack Allis

NOW AVAILABLE ON DVD

90 Minutes

Plus two bonus segments

- The Process of Ascension
- Understanding the Dark Side

Includes excerpts from Jack's live talks.
Complete with dazzling images and captions.

AVAILABLE AT WWW.JACKALLIS.COM
Or call 1 (800) 995-0796 Ext. 9486

Along with Jack's other books:

- *Infinity's Flower – A Tale of 2012 & the Great Shift of the Ages*
- *Infinity's Children*

www.ingramcontent.com/pod-product-compliance
Lightning Source LLC
LaVergne TN
LVHW051837080426
835512LV00018B/2921